The Devil Makes Work

Leisure in Capitalist Britain

John Clarke
and
Chas Critcher

MACMILLAN

First published 1985

Published by
Higher and Further Education Division
MACMILLAN PUBLISHERS LTD
Houndmills, Basingstoke, Hampshire RG21 2XS
and London
Companies and representatives
throughout the world

Printed in Hong Kong

British Library Cataloguing in Publication Data
Clarke, John, *1950–*
The devil makes work: leisure in capitalist Britain
1. Recreation——Great Britain
I. Title   II. Critcher, Chas
306'.48'0941   GV75
ISBN   0–333–23395–6
ISBN   0–333–23396–4 Pbk

'Popular culture is one of the sites where this struggle for and against a culture of the powerful is engaged: it is also the stake to be won or lost in that struggle. It is the area of consent and resistance. It is partly where hegemony arises, and where it is secured. It is not a sphere where socialism, a socialist culture – already fully formed – might be simply "expressed". But it is one of the places where socialism might be constituted. That is why popular culture matters. Otherwise, to tell you the truth, I don't give a damn about it.' (Stuart Hall, 'Notes on deconstructing the popular', in Ralph Samuel (ed.), *People's History and Socialist Theory*, Routledge & Kegan Paul, 1981, p. 239.)

'And what I'd say is simply this. I don't believe that theories about socio-cultural reproduction and social class can in fact be reconciled with the evidence about the diversity of leisure behaviour. Now if you think it can achieve the reconciliation, then do it. And I don't believe you can.' (Kenneth Roberts, in Alan Tomlinson (ed.), *Leisure and Social Control*, Brighton Polytechnic, 1981, p. 66.)

Contents

Preface   xi

1 Idle hands   **1**
Trouble in paradise?   4
Preparing for leisure   5
Leisure as work   7
The price of pleasure   9
Further reading   12

**2 Breaking the mould: a brief encounter with the
    sociology of leisure**   **13**
Stanley Parker   16
    Occupational hazards   16
    A worked-out theme   19
Michael Young and Peter Willmott   22
    Keeping it in the family   22
    Homing in on leisure   25
    The onward march of history   28
Robert and Rhona Rapoport   30
    Peddling the life cycle   30
    The generation game   32
Kenneth Roberts   36
    A singular case of pluralism   36
    Missing links   40
Where do we go from here?   44
Further reading   46

3   Passing the time away: the historical development of
     leisure   **48**
     A brief case for history   48
     The 1800s: 'Merrie England'   51
     The 1840s: 'hard times'   56
     The 1880s: 'Coronation Streets'   60
       The shape of things to come   66
       Separate spheres   69
     The 1920s: 'love on the dole'   71
       Something old, something new   71
       Keeping spirits high   74
       It's still the same old story   75
     The 1960s: 'You've never had it so good'   79
       Fings ain't wot they used to be   80
       Private lives   81
       Talking 'bout my generation   82
       Young, gifted and black   85
       Profit and loss   86
       The good old days?   88
     Further reading   90

End of Part I: a pause for reflection   **93**

4   We sell everything – the mixed economy of leisure   **100**

     Market well   101
       'Last orders please'   103
       'A fine and private place?'   106
       Subsidising pleasure   112
       Making a mass of things   115
       'Going too far'   120
     The state of play   122
       Licensed leisure   123
       Disorderly conduct   125
       Home and away   126
       Learning to enjoy ourselves   128
       'Healthy minds'   130
       'Healthy bodies'   132

The new 'people's palace'?   134
The nation at play   137
Rolling back the state   140
Further reading   143

5   Divided we play: leisure and social divisions   **145**
In a class of its own   147
    'Will the real working class please stand up for
    itself?'   150
    Knowing your place   151
Leisure through the ages   153
    Growing pains   155
    Boys will be boys   157
Engendered leisure   159
    May the best man win   161
Coming home to roost   164
    Getting away from it all   170
    High days and holidays   172
    'You don't know what you're missing'   173
The social division of leisure   175
Further reading   179

6   Future imperfect: leisure and the post-industrial
    society   **181**
Are we being served?   185
An endangered species?   187
A terminal case?   190
A sense of direction?   196
Further reading   198

End of Part II   **199**

7   **Conclusion**   **211**
The sociological imagination   212
The long revolution   216
Women's oppression today   220
Leisure, culture and hegemony   225
Further reading   230

x   *Contents*

Epilogue   **231**
   It's a free country   232
   'Entertaining programmes'   234
   'Let's have a party'   237
   'Time gentlemen, please'   239
   Further reading   240

Author Index   241
Subject Index   243

Preface

It has taken us a long time to write this book about leisure, not least because it has had to be written in our spare time – of which we have too little. We begin with this point not to gain sympathy, for there are too many people experiencing a lack of work to justify complaints from those who feel they do too much. We begin here because, at a personal level, this point illustrates some of the paradoxes of leisure. Writing this book was voluntarily undertaken, and to make room for it, other pleasures were foregone. If the writing of it appeared to be leisurely, not least to our long-suffering publishers, it certainly felt like hard work to us.

The psychological meaning of the work–leisure couplet for the individual has become one focus of the academic study of leisure, although it has often been formulated in ways which make our experiences of leisure unrecognisable. The fact that leisure is a common, everyday experience for most people makes it more, rather than less difficult to analyse. This has not, however, prevented its rapid growth as an area of academic study.

It is not possible to write about leisure without being aware of the ways in which 'leisure' already means something. Everyone has some experience of using free time. Leisure is the subject of political discussion, and has a place in the political culture of Britain. Leisure is a source of work for a growing number of leisure administrators and managers who have developed 'professional' analyses of what leisure means and how it can best be organised. Leisure is also the focus of academic analysis – it forms one of the subject areas of the different social sciences. Sociologists, psychologists, economists, geographers and historians have addressed the problems of what people do in leisure and what those activities mean.

Because leisure is already colonised by these different approaches, because it is already made to 'mean something', we have had to address our book to a consideration of those meanings. Our relationship to these existing definitions is a critical one. Consequently, part of the task of this book is to examine the political, professional and academic definitions of leisure – to interrogate their assumptions about leisure, to question the conclusions which they offer in order to present our own. We make no apologies for this approach, which organises the first two chapters of this book. We do not believe that meanings are all equal, that all views are equally valid, and we have spent some time trying to argue that the consequences of errors, distortions and misunderstandings need to be highlighted.

In trying to shift the analysis of leisure we have insisted that leisure is not, and cannot be analysed as, a self-contained sphere of life, cut off from other aspects of British social organisation. We have drawn on historical studies which illuminate how the current status and organisation of leisure has come about, and have stressed the conflicts and competing interests that are at stake in the creation of leisure. In part, this is because we fear that social sciences, and leisure studies in particular, have played little attention to the historical development of the object with which they deal. The professional segregation of history and social sciences (you study the past, we'll study the present) involves an attempt to divide the subject-matter – society and its processes – which is profoundly unsatisfactory.

These, then, are the concerns of the first part (Chapters 1, 2 and 3) of this book. By engaging with already existing definitions of leisure, and by considering how leisure as an aspect of social organisation has developed in Britain, we hope to establish the foundations for a different way of examining leisure in contemporary Britain.

In the second part (Chapters 4, 5, and 6) we have tried to put this different approach to work. One central point of this difference is our commitment to moving the main focus of attention from the study of what people do in leisure to the conditions under which leisure is experienced. There is an expanding 'leisure industry', alongside the provisions of the state, which provide an institutional framework within which leisure choices take place. We have tried to offer an account of leisure which considers the way in which social groups – differently positioned in the social structure of British capitalism – encounter these institutions of leisure, and create leisure activities. To garble a famous quotation from Marx – people make leisure, but not under circumstances of their own choosing. This book is an attempt to understand that process – the interaction of constraint and creation – and to examine its social and political consequences for British society.

It is worth adding a few words about what this book *is not*. It is not a synthesis of all that is known about leisure in modern Britain. We are not specialists in the leisure studies field, nor even 'accredited' historians or sociologists. Our intellectual biographies were shaped in the development of cultural studies, which is more concerned with making connections across academic specialisms than with the pursuit of particular disciplinary interests. Leisure is an important topic in its own right, but we have less interest in what is 'known' about leisure than in what the study of leisure can tell us about the nature of contemporary society.

However, this book is not a new 'theory of leisure'. It does not attempt to finally lay to rest all those complex definitional questions about what is or is not leisure. We do not believe that these questions can be solved by ever more elaborate analytical juggling. Rather they have to be seen as part of the complex patterns within which leisure is organised and lived in British society. Nor, finally, is this book an original study of leisure, it does not contain new factual evidence about how particular individuals or groups spend their leisure time. We have attempted to draw leisure out of its artificial social and academic segregation – to argue against its status as a separate sphere, and to connect it to the social and political processes and structures of British capitalism. Our interest, then, is not really in 'leisure' itself, it is in what leisure can tell us about the development, structure and organisation of the whole society. It is our view that the study of leisure for its own sake (like any other aspect of the society) is an irrelevancy. The purpose of studying any particular element of the social order is to *connect* – to understand the ways in which one particular element is shaped by other structures and ways in which that one area affects and contributes to the development of the rest.

We hope that the intellectual debt which we owe to our friends and colleagues from the Centre for Contemporary Cultural Studies is obvious in what follows. Beyond that, we are also grateful to Susan Boyd-Bowman, Alan Clarke, Elaine Wade and Garry Whannel for their critical reading of drafts of this book, without which it would have been much worse than it is. Like most men, our work depends heavily upon the labour of women. Our thanks are due to Margaret Parker and Susan Boyd-Bowman for both tolerating our obsession and encouraging us to see it through to a conclusion, and to the many secretaries at the Open University and Sheffield City Polytechnic whose efforts are condensed in the final product.

A note on further reading

We have resisted the conventional practice of including lengthy footnotes and constant indications of our sources in writing this book. We hope, by this means, to have made the structure of our argument clearer and more immediately readable. Instead, each chapter is followed by suggestions for further reading in which we have identified studies on which we have drawn, and books in which particular points of our argument can be usefully followed up or taken further.

Acknowledgement

We are grateful to the Controller of Her Majesty's Stationery Office for permission to reproduce the material on pages 108–9.

1
Idle hands

*Such brutality and insolence, such debauchery and extravagance, such
idleness, irreligion, cursing and swearing, and contempt of all rule and
authority. ... Our people are drunk with the cup of liberty.* (Josiah Tucker,
1745, quoted by Edward Thompson in 'Time, Work-discipline and
Industrial Capitalism', in M.W. Flinn and T. C. Smout (eds), *Essays in
Social History*, Oxford University Press, 1974, p. 56.)

Britain in the 1980s, it seems, stands trembling on the brink of
becoming a 'leisure society'. Our future could be more relaxed,
more creative, more enjoyable ... if only. If only ... we could shed
our obsession with work; if only we could take advantage of the
possibilities of new technologies and new methods of production;
if only we could break our three hundred year love/hate affair with
'Protestant work ethic'; if only we knew how to use our free time
constructively, there are enormous pleasures to be gained.

The 'leisure society' offers an emancipatory vision of the future.
It presents the possibility of going beyond the present stage of
social development to the discovery and satisfaction of 'higher'
needs than the present materialistic obsession with work allows.
One statement of these prospects will suffice:

> There is a trend away from the materialistic orientation of the
> past and a greater concern with the humanistic aspects of life,
> with the perception of things rather than things themselves,
> with subjective rather than objective measures. Indeed, the
> measurement of quality rather than quantity becomes the
> ultimate goal.

1

To put it a different way, the GNP, the gross national product, is no longer viewed as an adequate measure of the well being of society. I do not wish to underestimate the importance of that index, but it must be viewed in the context of other variables. Once a society has reached a certain minimum of material, that is, economic, well being, other domains of life begin to take on increasing importance. There is little doubt that many of the so-called post industrial societies have entered this stage. A large proportion of the population of these countries can, at last, lift their heads from the ground, from the burden of toil, and strive for loftier goals. (J. Neulinger, 'Leisure lack and the quality of life: the broadening scope of the leisure professional', *Leisure Studies*, 1982, vol. 1, p. 66.)

These images of the 'leisure society' are at one and the same time opportunistic, and deeply rooted in the way our society thinks about the organisation of work and leisure. The opportunism can be detected in the way the rediscovery of leisure coincides with the reappearance of mass unemployment. Leisure has an uncanny habit of becoming a matter of public debate when large numbers are suddenly left with a lot of 'time on their hands'. But this transformation of unemployment into leisure is only possible because of a much more profound set of ideas about the relationship between work and leisure.

The prospect of the leisure society relies on a very sharp contrast being drawn between the realms of work and leisure. Work is represented as drudgery, approached with a grudging acceptance of that which must be done. It contains little *intrinsic* satisfaction, and is undertaken to obtain the money which allows needs to be satisfied outside work. The mechanisation, fragmentation and routinisation of work have received extensive analysis from generations of industrial psychologists – concerned at the effects of such work experience in creating bored, alienated and dissatisfied workers and their associated problems of low output, poor quality, high absenteeism and high labour turnover. As a consequence, the organisation of work has been subjected to successive waves of 'humanisation' – better personnel relations, better communications, job rotation and the like. Extensive though such efforts have been, it seems that they have failed to remove the essential experience of work as a painful necessity for the majority of workers. Modern systems of production appear to have moved us well beyond the 'dignity of labour' prized in the Protestant ethic.

By contrast, leisure seems to offer the prospect of being all those things that work is not: the source of satisfactions, gratifications and pleasures. Where work is the realm of dull compulsion, leisure represents freedom, choice and creativity. Where work is that which must be done, leisure is the pursuit of freely chosen self-interest. Historically, ideas about the necessity of work have led to an identification of leisure as *compensation*: life as a daily circuit of misery and pleasure. Leisure was prized as the 'escape' from the dull routines of labour. In this duality of work and leisure, the individual was seen as undertaking work instrumentally as the price which must be paid for pleasures to be enjoyed outside work.

Leisure, then, became the site of desirable experiences. It offered freedom (no bosses or supervisors); choice (your own time); the fulfilment of needs (rest and recreation); and the potential for 'self-actualisation', and self-expression. It matches the ideals of a humanistic psychology – the freely choosing and creative individual who has transcended the 'lower order' needs of mere survival (food, clothing, shelter) and moved into the realm of expressive self-development. But outside of science fiction, the desirable goal of leisure has always been hedged around by the confines of employment – the compensation has had to be *earned* through work.

At particular historical moments, though, the possibilities of transcending this circuit of misery and pleasure – a movement beyond leisure as mere compensation – have been spotted by optimistic future watchers. These moments have coincided with changes in work, or, more accurately, with changes in the technologies of production. The discovery and subsequent disappearance of the leisure society has recurred in a stable cycle of events. Technical innovation in production has the effect of supplanting human labour (from the first textile machinery through automation to computer-controlled robotics and microtechnology). Innovations applied on a wide enough scale produce widespread unemployment. Commentators argue that the expansion of such 'labour saving devices' will free the majority from the compulsion of labour. Images of the leisure society are propounded. New sources of demand for labour appear, unemployment declines and the 'Leisure Society' and its visions of emancipation from labour are quietly shelved until the next period of innovation.

But this time, so the story goes, is different. The new technologies of production imply a qualitative change in the need for labour. Full employment is no longer a feasible social objective, and nor (with the Leisure Society waiting to be ushered on stage) *should* it be so. Emancipation is just around the corner if only ... .

Trouble in paradise?

This image of 'emancipation' which the Leisure Society offers is slightly clouded by signs that all may not be well with leisure. The gaps between the future potential and the present practice of leisure suggest that 'something needs to be done'. Contemporary leisure practice persists in being troublesome. It is the site of as many problems as pleasures. Free time, it seems, is alarmingly open to abuse, and the list of abuses is both long and familiar. Free time seems to be inconveniently associated with the 'devil's work' rather than emancipation: drunkenness, illicit sexuality, crime, violence, vandalism, physical and psychological demoralisation and urban riots. Lord Scarman surveying the causes of the 'Brixton disorders' of 1981, provided the following familiar commentary on the interconnection of free time and undesirable consequences:

> It is clear that the exuberance of youth requires in Brixton (and in similar inner city areas) imaginative and socially acceptable opportunities for release if it is not to be diverted to criminal ends. It is clear that such opportunities do not at present exist in Brixton to the extent that they ought, particularly given the enforced idleness of many youths through unemployment. The amusement arcades, the unlawful drinking clubs, and, I believe, the criminal classes gain as a result. (*The Scarman Report*, Penguin, 1982, p. 22.)

The dream of the leisure society is constantly undercut by the nightmare of 'idleness'. Folk wisdom is not often shared by official commentators in our society. But on this occasion, both are united in the belief that 'the devil makes work for idle hands', and authoritative voices have long expressed their fears about the consequences of leisure. This unstable mixture of 'free time' and 'anti-social' behaviour has been a persistent theme of nineteenth and twentieth century British capitalism. In the 1920s, Cyril Burt's study of *The Young Delinquent* was highlighting the same associations:

So long as there is neither school nor work, mischief fills the empty hours. Many of the transgressions, it is true, are trifling such as playing games at prohibited times or in prohibited areas. But, on occasions, the loafing, the roistering, and the aimless wandering lead the idler into depradations more serious than a mere infraction of police regulations; and some of the most serious assaults and sex delinquencies disturb the Sabbath calm. (*The Young Delinquent*, University of London Press, 1925, p. 160.)

It is possible to discern a schizophrenia about leisure here. Viewed from one side it is emancipation, a society peopled by freely choosing and creative individuals. From the other, it is the dark entanglement of idleness and vice. The Protestant Ethnic may be most visibly associated with 'work', but that by no means exhausts its grip on the British imagination, for there is a Protestant *Leisure* Ethic too. Free time – to avoid the descent into the murky waters of idleness and the devil's work – has to be 'constructive'. It has to be spent wisely. The embrace of leisure's potential is always something less than whole-hearted. It lives with the constraint imposed by the fear of freedom and its *illicit* pleasures.

Preparing for leisure

The threat of dangerous leisure has created considerable enthusiasm for the idea of preparing individuals to use their leisure 'properly', to inculcate the habits of *self-discipline*, which will ensure that free time is spent wisely. A recent letter to the

Observer, stresses the educative groundwork that needs to be done to smooth the entry of the leisure society:

> Periodic spells of retraining throughout a working life, sabbaticals, work sharing, financial encouragement for one parent to remain at home – all these can help; they are also expensive.
> Cheaper, more difficult, but just as vital is to change attitudes. This must come from sensitive government, constructive journalism, good management, parents and, above all, from the schools.
> Five is not too young to begin to learn that education should be as much for living, as for a working life. Excellence in academic and technolgical skills, yes, but to learn to use talents, to develop interests and occupations, skills and hobbies, beyond the usual curricula should be equally central to the school life rather than remain on the periphery.
> The Protestant work ethic lies deep in our souls but is no longer enough on its own.
> If we are to retain a cohesive and happy society, we must create a climate in which a fulfilled life means the ability to find dignity and satisfaction in both work and in alternative pursuits.

(Jane Prior, *The Observer* 24 July 1983)

It was, in fact, with the greater institutional and professional acceptance of 'progressive' and 'child centred' educational philosophies in the 1960s that education for leisure began to establish itself as a reality. The development of community and social education programmes, with their concerns for 'relevance', entailed a commitment to educate the young for leisure. Such curricula, however, tended not to be 'offered' across the secondary education sector, but were predominantly aimed at the 'non-academic' streams. Even though the revival of 'vocationalism' and training – sponsored by the Manpower Services Commission – appears to place the emphasis back on work, the social skills which the young unemployed (or about to be unemployed) are taught include the skills of constructive leisure.

In this sense, the 'vocational' orientation is not the opposite of a leisure orientation. Both have been directed at the (working class) 'non-academic' stratum in education. Both offer pragmatically 'relevant' tuition to those not able to cope with more abstract and academic pursuits. By contrast, without needing to be either narrowly vocational or broadly social, academic achievement is deemed to fit the individual for 'life' in all its aspects. Social education, in its various forms, has been institutionally reserved for the non-achievers. Leisure as compensation makes yet another reappearance, here calculated against future work prospects, rather than the reality of labour.

Leisure as work – the rise of the leisure professions

This segregation within education highlights a major point about the concern for the 'constructive' use of leisure. The concern about idleness is not general – it is *socially* focused. The 'academic stream', with their cultural capital, can be relied upon to put *their* leisure time to good use. As always, it is 'the others' in whom the mix of idleness and vice represents a danger. They are the 'culturally deprived'. Compensation for this deprivation has not been the sole preserve of education. The state has expanded its activities in leisure provision and organisation in the post war period to try to meet the 'needs' of the deprived. Play centres, sports centres, leisure centres, community centres have flourished since the 1960s to improve the quality of leisure and foster social integration. Their rise has been accompanied by an expanded role for central government bodies and 'quangos' in the funding and organisation of leisure provision (e.g. the Central Council for Physical Recreation, The Sports Council, the Tourist Boards, etc.).

With the expansion of intervention has developed a new 'professional' – the 'recreation manager'. Responsible for organising provision to meet leisure 'need', backed by professional training and qualifying courses, and with their own professional body (the Association of Recreation Managers) they are apparently burdened by a sense of duty:

> since the average citizen is unable to invent new uses for his leisure, a professional élite shares a heavy responsibility for discovering criteria for ways of employing leisure and creating enthusiasm for common ends within the moral aims of the

community. (W. Sutherland, 'A Philosophy of Leisure', *Annals of the American Academy*, Sept. 1957, p. 134.)

Cultural deprivation as manifested in leisure follows a pattern characteristic of 'social problems'. Concerned observers establish the existence of the 'problem' (be it behavioural disorders, a lack or unmet need). Intervention is constructed through skilled professionals who can analyse and assess the problem and devise ways of solving it. These solutions also have the merit of integrating the sufferers of the problem back into the 'moral aims of the community'. The 'corporatist' strategy rests on the definition of leisure as a 'problem', requiring specific techniques of management through professionally acquired skills. Like other social problems before it (drug use, delinquency, truancy, the problem family), it is expected to succumb through the cultural reintegration of the 'victim'.

Although it has come late into the ranks of social problems professions, leisure management is already showing the familiar signs of professional mastery. One of these is to translate the *social* process that it deals with into *professional* definitions:

What is leisure? Let me merely state that a more meaningful question is: What are the issues or concerns that leisure professionals deal with?

From here, the profession can move on to an assessment of its mission, beginning from a sobering realisation of how enormous the challenge is:

Leisure lack is widespread in our society as well as the rest of the world. It besets the young and old and the middle aged, the poor and the rich, and members of the majority and all the different minorities. It invades homes, schools, hospitals, prisons, industry, playgrounds and even outer space. What is most threatening is that it is on the increase: the more progress we make at a technological level, the more this phenomenon seems to undermine the gains we otherwise would expect in the quality of our lives. (J. Neulinger, 'Leisure lack and the quality of life: the broadening scope of the leisure professional', *Leisure Studies*, 1982, vol. 1, p. 57.)

A widespread disorder, alarmingly on the increase, threatening all sections of the population alike – but fortunately, the profession is on the move. Investigations are being made, concepts refined, techniques developed. We may yet be enabled (by our professional enablers) to lead a full and constructive leisure life. It is heartening to know that our needs are being looked after not only by the expansion of state intervention, but also by the lavish attentions of the commercial sector.

The price of pleasure

A relatively neglected matter in discussions of the leisure society is the extent to which the provision of leisure goods and services has become an expanding arena for capital investment. New needs and new sources of satisfaction are continually being constructed by the 'entertainment business' which is now one of the major economic sectors. It is not the least ironic aspect of the leisure revolution that those same new technologies which at the point of production are reducing the demand for labour, reappear in leisure in the form of new consumer entertainments to occupy our time. Workers displaced by computer controlled technology can now visit their local shopping centre and be invited to contemplate the purchase of a home computer, complete with a programme to manage their household finances.

Otto Newman has recently considered some of the paradoxes engendered by this intensified 'capitalisation' of leisure, arguing that far from leisure being a 'separate sphere' characterised by freedom and spontaneity, it has instead come to take on many of the characteristics associated with the realm of work:

> Leisure may become routinised in the same way that work and consumption has ... On the one hand, leisure appears as a form of free time, holding out the promises of spontaneity and periodic liberalisation. On the other, leisure is seen as assimilated into the values prevailing elsewhere, and hence is equally marked by the materialist imperative dominating work and consumption, ... Time counts as money, value must be obtained, the more of everything there is to be got, the more hectic becomes the pursuit. Add to that the more recent

development of leisure goods capitalisation, the immense impact of the tourist industry, the powerful 'holiday' emphasis
throughout the mass media, plus the closing off of 'the wide
open spaces' and the process is almost complete. Leisure life
becomes structurally closely aligned to values of work and
consumption, leaving the ideology of spontaneous autonomy,
itself a compelling force in the interest of stabilisation, as the
symbol of liberalisation.

Leisure, we are told, needs learning like all other social
pursuits. Self instruction alone is neither desirable, nor, given
the scope, can it even hope to become fully effective ... The
mounting range of institutional leisure courses, and even more,
the massive growth in the USA of leisure counselling as a
profession, attest to do this. Time wasting offends the sense of
social propriety, boredom presents a source of destabilisation,
and unused resources are regarded almost as a sin. (O. Newman, *Corporatism, Leisure and Collective Consumption*. Centre
for Leisure Studies, University of Salford, 1983, pp. 100–1.)

Newman offers a view of the leisure society which is a considerable
distance from that with which we began, based on a very different
assessment of the sets of institutional structures and social arrangements which characterise contemporary capitalism. In the following chapters of this book, we shall be examining some of these
developments and the peculiar status of 'leisure' in British capitalism. We have focused in this introduction on the contradictory
public images of leisure, and the tension between optimism and
fear which characterises them.

But it is important to recognise that these 'debates' about leisure
are grounded in complex social forces. The career of 'education
for leisure' and its selective audience highlights one of those social
bases. Leisure as compensation, leisure as idleness, and leisure as
substitute for employment are not ideas which address all sections
of society equally. Behind the rhetoric stands a familiar social
distribution of *who* does the labour of drudgery, *who* is suspected
of idleness and vice, and *who* is likely to be the victim of
'involuntary leisure'. The class structure of British capitalism is not
one which is confined to the sphere of production, but organises
the field of leisure too. The working class do not merely (!) work –
they also consume, take pleasure and re-create themselves. Equal-

ly condensed in the 'leisure problem' are the structures of gender divisions of British society. Patterns of employment, domestic work (and all the accompanying consumer techology), and free time intersect with the 'normal' roles attributed to men and women.

But these structures are strangely absent from most discussions of the Leisure Society. Somehow, as Newman suggests, the ideology of spontaneity, and freedom remove such distasteful thoughts when we talk of leisure. There, our divisions magically abolished, we can at least play together as 'equals': This, too, is a recurrent theme in the history of British leisure; from Arthur Hope's reflections that:

> Class divisions are difficult to maintain amid the healthy rivalries of the open air, and 'footer shorts' and naked bodies make for equality. ('Breaking down of Caste', in J. H. Whitehouse (ed.), *Problems of Boylife*, Macmillan, 1912, p. 302.)

to a regional director of the Sports Council contemplating the place of sport in a new recession:

> In spite of considerable effort and improvement we now seem to be getting close to where we were in the 1920s. Except for one thing – and that is the impact made on recreational provision and awareness in the last decade or so, on a community with an already long tradition of sporting involvement. I hope that this interest and development will be fully utilised to help the deep problems we have. Without getting it all out of proportion – if we have to wait for 'Work for All', let us at least try to help by providing 'Sports for All'. (In Sports Council, *Sport And Leisure*, 1981, vol. 22, p. 13).

In this chapter, we have tried to sketch some of the complexity of meanings and definitions that have a stake in leisure. These meanings pull in different directions, providing different approaches to the 'problem of leisure'. It is this contradictory and ambiguous status of leisure in British society that interests us. In what follows, our task is not to supply a more simple definition of leisure which will remove these ambiguities, but to understand *how* leisure comes to be the subject of these competing definitions:

to grasp leisure as the site of social conflict. Our search for this understanding begins in the academic analysis of leisure in Britain.

Further reading

Edward Thompson's essay 'Time, work-discipline and industrial capitalism' remains the classic statement on the development of work and leisure in British capitalism, and highlights the emergence of the 'leisure problem'. Originally published in *Past and Present* (1967), vol. 38, it has been much reprinted, including in M. W. Flinn and T. C. Smout (eds), *Essays In Social History* (Oxford University Press, 1974). In *Hooligan: a History of Respectable Fears* (Macmillan, 1983), Geoffrey Pearson provides a compelling account of the recurrent moral panics about 'dangerous youth' and their abuses of free time.

Tony Watts, *Education, Unemployment and the Future of Work* (Open University Press, 1983), surveys a number of different 'scenarios' of the future development of work and leisure. The journal of the Leisure Studies Association – *Leisure Studies* – is a regular source of articles by academic commentators and professionals working in the leisure field.

Finally, some of the arguments which helped to shape this book can be found in a more theoretical form in J. Clarke, C. Critcher and R. Johnson (eds), *Working Class Culture: Studies in History and Theory* (Hutchinson, 1979), and in the discussions collected in A. Tomlinson (ed.), *Leisure and Social Control* (mimeo, Brighton Polytechnic, 1981).

2

Breaking the mould: a brief encounter with the sociology of leisure

For though abstract discussions about theoretical premises have a limited value, it matters very much, in history as in other social sciences, what starting points are chosen. (Richard Johnson, 'Culture and the Historians', in J. Clarke, C. Critcher and R. Johnson (eds), *Working Class Culture*, Hutchinson, 1979, p. 41.)

In this chapter, we shall be considering the major academic approaches to the study of leisure focusing in particular on the way in which the sociology of leisure has developed in Britain through the 1970s. We must emphasise that we have chosen to concentrate on those contributions to leisure studies which provide the most advanced analyses of leisure, and which approach the subject with a degree of theoretical awareness and sophistication. This means that we have left out of our account the bulk of leisure studies – the massive explosion of recreation research which has taken place under the aegis of growth in leisure provision by both commerce and the state. We have ignored this body of research because, although highly sophisticated in its deployment of statistical techniques, it has been bound to very narrow functions of policy making and leisure planning. Its main ambition has been to forecast changing patterns of recreation demand, and has little to contribute to the *analysis* of leisure as a social practice.

Within sociology, the topic of leisure is still a relatively marginal one – textbooks, for example, frequently ignore it altogether, or include it as a subsection of a chapter on work. Before the publication of Kenneth Roberts' textbook *Leisure* (1970) and Stanley Parker's *The Future of Work and Leisure* (1971), there could not be said to be a British sociology of leisure. The few books available which dealt with leisure emerged from either the American traditions of functionalist analysis or mass society theory, or from the more European tradition of philosophical speculation about human nature and play. Further, such evidence as is presented relates to American and Continental patterns of leisure which cannot be easily generalised to the British context.

One significant exception to this was the implicit focus on leisure inherent in the tradition of British 'community studies'. Studies like these focused predominantly on 'traditional' working class communities, and were concerned to demonstrate the social processes – including leisure practices – through which the collective identities of particular areas were forged. Although they have had little impact on the more explicitly defined sociology of leisure community studies did at least perceive leisure as part of a social process – as one of the ways in which particular ideas of community were realised and expressed. Within the increasingly powerful definition of leisure as an aggregate of individual leisure choices, this attention to the social processes involved in leisure has been lost. Leisure has increasingly come to be seen as an act of individual consumption and/or the satisfaction of psychological needs, in which the reality and potential of leisure as a collective 'coming together' has been suppressed. Community studies, whatever other limitations they had, were at least alert to this social dimension of leisure.

A parallel concern can be seen within the tradition of 'cultural criticism', exemplified by the work of Richard Hoggart and Raymond Williams. Here the working class community was seen as one form of a wider pattern of class based cultures. Where community studies stress leisure as a set of relationships *internal* to a social group, cultural criticism concerned itself more with the external relationships, with the processes of interaction and conflict between class cultures. Specifically there was an attempt to demonstrate how working class culture could not be viewed as a hermetically sealed entity – a 'life apart'. That culture had been formed, and was continually being remade, in conditions of cultural subordination. Writing in this tradition has emphasised culture as conflict, a conflict in which dominant culture strives to maintain its dominance, shaping other cultures in its image.

Both community studies and cultural criticism have remained largely marginal to the development of mainstream sociology, and their contributions to the study of leisure have remained undeveloped. But in the 1970s a different route to the study of leisure was opened up, with efforts being made to chart the study of leisure as a legitimate sub-area of sociology (alongside the sociology of work, the family, the mass media and so on). This characteristic academic process of dividing up the world into specific sub-areas of a discipline has particular consequences for how the 'sociology of leisure' is produced. Attempts are made to see whether the 'grand theories' of the discipline (functionalism, Marxism, interactionism) relate to leisure. This theoretical encounter is rarely a sustained one, while the main endeavour is to 'explain leisure', as a specific field of social behaviour. By starting from the problem or field to be studied, this sort of approach closes off the questions of the interconnection between leisure and other social processes, always leaving them to be studied 'somewhere else'. Consequently, the sociology of leisure demonstrates an obsession with defining leisure – as a way of establishing the legitimate boundaries of this (as opposed to other) fields of study within sociology. There are, of course, references across this boundary, leisure is considered in its relation to one or other of the other domains of sociology (leisure and work, leisure and the family, etc.), but such endeavours fall a long way short of conceiving leisure within a society understood as a complete structure. We must note one final general criticism of the sociology of leisure. Although there are many ritualistic acknowledgements that leisure is an arbitrary category (and its arbitrariness is regularly demonstrated in the struggle to define it) the *consequences* of sociologists adopting this category as the focus of their investigations is less discussed. The arbitrary *social* category becomes a suitable *academic* concept; the 'sociology of leisure' assumes that 'leisure' exists 'out there' to be studied as a real fact.

We suggest that the development of a sociology of leisure had been characterised by these tendencies – the loss of attention to the processes of class cultures and community; the failure to escape the limitations of a sub-area of a discipline, and the consequent absence of any structural analysis of leisure's place in the whole society; and finally, the ease with which the commonsense category of leisure is treated as an adequate concept through which sociological analysis can be carried out. These elements seem to us to form the fundamental assumptions which organise a 'sociological consensus' about leisure. Within this, it is true, there are very divergent approaches taken by different authors. But, as we hope to show, these differences take place *within* this wider set of assumptions about what the sociology of leisure is. Our critique, then, of the existing wisdom in this field has two purposes – to offer a critical assessment of the different substantive arguments about leisure, and to highlight the limitations imposed by these assumptions about the field of leisure itself. To achieve this, we have selected four texts. We decided not to include consciously designed textbooks. These tend by their nature to be agnostic, to review the arguments without particular professions of faith, even if parts of the catechism keep slipping through. We chose instead to select books which had some original research content, aimed to develop a theoretical argument and had come to be recognised as major works in the area. We review them in chronological order by date of original publication since any book is a creature of its time and later works may seek to develop or refute earlier ones. For each book we initially provide a summary of its argument. To those who have already encountered the texts, this may seem a tedious enterprise but not all our readers will have done so. There is also – or ought to be, at least in academic life – an obligation to state what is taken to be the essence of an argument, before its status can be evaluated. Such an evaluation follows the summary of each text. Thus our own perspective will begin to emerge as an accumulation of arguments about existing studies and be further consolidated in the rest of the book. That is our understanding of how critical thought does and should work. Existing work cannot be regarded as irrelevant; it has to be engaged in the act of criticism, on which, our prologue ended, we now commence.

Stanley Parker

Occupational hazards

Stanley Parker's interest in leisure seems to have grown out of a concern with the implications of the experience of work for life outside the workplace. This concern is evident in the title of his book *The Future of Work and Leisure* first published in 1971, subsequently revised as *Leisure and Work* for publication in 1983.

His starting point is that leisure cannot be understood apart from work: 'the problem of leisure is also the problem of work' (p. xii, 2nd ed.). Thus the sociology of leisure must recognise the salience of the experience of work for leisure. Work, for many, remains characterised by boredom, alienation and powerlessness. Leisure cannot compensate for these negative attributes and may actually reproduce them. Leisure is defined as against work, as freedom from it. The result is a continuum of categories of activity: work, work obligations, physiological needs, non-work obligations, leisure. Leisure can be measured not only by the time set aside for it but also by the sense of freedom involved. 'Leisure is time free from obligations either to self or to others – time in which to do as one pleases.' (*Leisure and Work*, Allen & Unwin, 1983, p. 10)

There are, Parker notes, various groups to whom the model does not directly apply, since they do not have paid work to structure their leisure. Marginal examples are prisoners and the idle rich, more substantial ones those of housewives, the unemployed and the retired, together a category of the unwaged to whom Parker devotes a separate chapter. For the rest, the model is held to be generally applicable. The work–leisure relationship is basic to the nature of industrial society and peculiar to it, sharpening boundaries between categories of experience which are less distinguishable in non-industrial societies.

So it is the experience of work in industrial societies which forms the context for the experience of leisure. Work may offer some potential satisfactions: the exercise of creative and technical competence, the use of initiative, the involvement in groups directed to a common goal. It may alternatively, or even simultaneously, produce dissatisfaction with repetitive, fragmented and meaningless tasks, in conditions of insecurity and insubordination. The hierarchy of occupations can be understood in terms of whether satisfactions or dissatisfactions predominate. Many, perhaps the majority, do experience work as a form of oppression but a fortunate minority find fulfilment. There is, however, a third pattern, where work produces no strong feelings of any kind. The predominant experience is one of detachment. This group may be on the increase as a result of changes in the occupational structure. Deskilling through automation may undermine the autonomy of some jobs, while the growth of the service sector increases the autonomy of others.

Thus, for the individual and the society, leisure is shaped by the *reaction to work* and this influence predominates over other factors, such as class and gender.

But the work–leisure relationship cannot simply be 'read off' from a particular occupation. It is necessary to specify the nature of the work experience, which may differ within and between organisations. There are also other, non-work, variables, such as level of education, which may again shape the functions an individual will look to leisure to fulfil. Nevertheless, a number of criteria can be used to identify patterns of work–leisure relationships: the similarity of the content of work and leisure, how sharply the boundaries are demarcated, where central life interests are located. The dominant patterns are those of extension, opposition and neutrality. For each, Parker offers a pen portrait, drawing on his own material from a survey of several different occupational groups.

In the *extension* pattern, work and leisure are similar in content and weakly demarcated. Work is the central life-interest and saturates leisure time, since occupational life involves autonomy and challenge, moral commitments and social relationships which are seen as contributing to personal development. This pattern is found in its purest form, where work and leisure become virtually indistinguishable, as in the lives of residential social workers interviewed by Parker. But other groups of highly educated people share the same opportunities for fulfilment, such as successful businessmen, doctors, teachers and the one working-class figure, the craft worker.

In the *opposition* pattern, leisure functions as a contrast to work. The activities pursued are sharply differentiated from those of work. The prison of work is endured as a means of realising the freedom of leisure. Work activity does not encroach upon leisure except as overtime. This polarisation of work and leisure is characteristic of those in low status occupations. Except in the special cases of occupational communities, such as in mining or fishing villages, friends will not be drawn from the workplace. This polarisation of work and leisure is characteristic of low status occupations, especially those involving routine assembly line work.

In the *neutrality* pattern, the effect of work on leisure time is weak. Leisure is not an extension of, or opposition to, work but more free-floating and independent. There is a tendency for leisure to be seen as the more fulfilling of the two and work is often seen as a means to another end. Work may often be boring and routine, but not personally damaging. Neither the activities nor the relationships of work extend into the home. This group has relatively more time to spend on leisure than the others and tends to seek entertainment. Occupations requiring some limited education beyond school fall into this category – minor professionals, technicians, intermediate managers and clerical staff, of whom the bank clerk acts as the symptomatic figure.

The association between certain occupational groups and these models of work–leisure relationships is not fixed: 'It is not claimed that certain occupations and certain types of work–leisure relationships always go together' (p. 93). Variations will exist and there may even be situations where leisure affects work but in general, because 'the work sphere is more structured and basic to life itself' (p. 111), work is the crucial determinant. Thus Parker is much concerned with any implications of the new technology for work, leisure and their interrelationship, though he remains sceptical about whether its potential is either as radical or as positive as is often made out. For him, the essential policy choice remains that between 'segmentalist' approaches which try to reform leisure whilst leaving work intact and more 'holistic' approaches which seek to improve the quality of both work and leisure. The kinds of choices made by individuals and planners of the future may depend on the extent to which education gives them skills in, and understanding of, leisure.

A worked-out theme

Originally written as a Ph.D. in the late 1960s, Parker's model requires adaptation to the rather different conditions of the 1980s. The second edition has been revised to take account of such relatively recent developments as mass unemployment, the microelectronics revolution and the influence of feminism. Each of these, in rather different ways, has questioned the necessary centrality of paid work. Nevertheless, Parker's insistence on the importance of work is a valuable one which others would have done better to pursue. He does not merely emphasise its pervasive influence on the rest of life; he constantly argues that for many it remains a fundamentally damaging experience from which leisure can offer only limited recuperation. His analysis of the meanings and experiences of work as the structure into which leisure is inserted does situate leisure, if only in the lives of male workers. That work has subsequently come to be eliminated and hived off from leisure analysis is no fault of his.

Because work is always psychologically present, even when physically absent, Parker is aware that his own definition of leisure as time and activity free from constraint describes what we feel about it rather than what it actually is. He recognises that the provision of leisure goods and services is no more in the control of consumers than work is in the control of producers. While this kind of argument is foreshortened in favour of elaborating the model, Parker's analysis remains alert to the gap between the illusion and the reality of freedom in leisure. In part this stems from Parker's insistence on an historical and comparative perspective on work–leisure relationships. Although not developed, the possibility of other ways of organising human life is not suppressed.

In the end, however, Parker's model remains more suggestive than definitive. Problems about its application might have been mitigated by more direct discussion of its status as a sociological 'ideal type': a model which may never be found in its pure form in real life but which provides a useful yardstick against which to measure identifiable patterns. Further, the model relies on a species of functionalism. Functionalist theory follows an analogy with biology by assuming that the existence of any social pattern or activity can be explained by the function it performs in maintaining the equilibrium of the individual and/or the society. Parker's functionalism is weak but appears at crucial points in the argument. Ultimately, he is explaining leisure as a 'function' of work experience, whether the function is one of integration, opposition or neutralisation. In short, the same objections can be raised to Parker's work as to more overtly functionalist arguments, that it fails to allow adequately for human agency and tends to reduce social behaviour to the level of a cultural reflex, in this case to the influence of work.

Still more serious doubts may be entertained about the model's comprehensiveness. The negligible discussion of full-time housewives in the first edition is extended in the rewriting into a specific rebuttal of feminist criticisms that the model cannot be applied to women with major responsibility for the care of children and husbands. Parker argues that unmarried working women do fit the model, that women who do any form of paid work fit at least in part, and that even full-time housewives can be incorporated, if necessary by categorising most of their activities as what he calls 'non-work obligations' or 'semi-leisure'.

We find ourselves unconvinced. It does not seem to us useful to think of a married woman with children and a part-time job as in the 'same' position as a man with two jobs. There would even seem to us to be significant differences between the 'work' of a married woman without children and that of her husband, unless, as is infrequently the case, all domestic duties are shared. Nor is it in the end so much the applicability of the model to particular situations which is the problem. Rather it is that the working man's experience is taken as the norm and other patterns as more or less slight deviations from it. A satisfactory analysis of domestic labour cannot be achieved by seeing it as a variant of wage labour. The differences of responsibility, constraint and dependency are too great. We need to consider both waged and domestic labour in the definition of 'work' which shapes the significance of leisure. It is no solution to place domestic tasks half-way along the continuum between work and leisure; they do more than just fill the gap.

More is at stake here than where to situate full-time housewives in the model. For, as Parker himself emphasises, the role of mother/wife is a gender identity, quite different in kind from that which may be derived from paid employment. It is constructed through relationships with children and husband of a permanence and intensity for which there is no comparison in most work situations. Thus, to return to the model, we might say that the family is a missing link between work and leisure but even this would not be enough. We already know that the attitudes of girls towards education and women towards work are quite distinctively shaped by their view of what are or will become their priorities in life; what kind of leisure they expect and want, whether they feel able to lay claim to any at all once they have accepted the overwhelming responsibilities of motherhood, seem unlikely to be immune from the influence of gender identity. Whether we look at it as an aspect of social organisation, how gender roles are habitually arranged within the family, or as a psychological factor of self-perception, how men and women think about themselves as men and women, gender is an all-pervasive influence on work and leisure, however we define and sub-categorise the terms.

Both empirically and theoretically, Parker's model is therefore rather less than half the picture. Any hopes that subsequent portraits may present wider and deeper perspectives than those of Parker's snap-shot, are not to be fulfilled. Instead another distortion has been effected, by introducing the family portrait as the foreground, in the process blurring the background profiles of men and women at their various labours.

Michael Young and Peter Willmott

Keeping it in the family

The Symmetrical Family was published in 1973, with the subtitle 'A Study of Work and Leisure in the London Region'. Its main empirical base was a survey of 2000 adults from 24 boroughs in and around London. A team of interviewers administered a 113–question schedule covering housing, work, leisure, relatives and friendships, family roles and social class. Such questions aimed to discover both objective facts about respondents' circumstances and their attitudes towards them. A random sub sample were asked to complete diaries of how they spent their time, fifty of whom, identified as active in sport, were given additional special interviews. Further original evidence came from a group of managing directors contacted through a professional organisation and case studies of observation and interviews at four firms. Existing data, especially from the Census and other government sources, was also extensively used.

Young and Willmott suggest that this form of research represents an attempt to combine macrosociology with history in a way which complements their previous work which combined microsociology with anthropology. Their concern was to analyse the relationship between work and leisure, especially as affected by class, within an analysis of the historical process. Two particular historical trends are defined as central. One is what they call the 'principle of stratified diffusion':

The image we are trying to suggest is that of a marching column with the people at the head of it usually being the first to wheel in a new direction. The last rank keeps its distance from the first and the distance between them does not lessen, but as the column advances, the last rank does eventually reach and pass the point which the first rank had passed some time before. In other words, the egalitarian principle works with a time lag. The people in the rear cannot, without breaking rank and rushing ahead, reach where the van *is*, but, since the whole column is moving forward, they can hope in due course to reach where the van *was*. (*The Symmetrical Family*, Allen Lane, 1973, pp. 19–20.)

The principle operates as a result of industrialisation, enabling the mass production of goods and services; democratic processes, providing common welfare and related benefits; and the psychological disposition of society's members to want what those above them in the social structure already have.

The second critical factor is the evolution of the family, which Young and Willmott divided into three stages. In Stage one, (dominant in Britain until roughly the early nineteenth century) the family was primarily a productive unit. Then industrialisation required individual wage earners to produce away from their families, necessitating the 'disrupted' pattern of family life found in Stage Two, prevalent by the mid-nineteenth century. By the beginning of the twentieth century a third stage begins to appear in which 'the unity of the family has been restored around its function, not of production, but consumption' (p. 28). What are being described here are historical tendencies: a few Stage One families can still be found today (e.g. in farming); many working-class families are still at Stage Two; Stage Three is characteristic of the expanding managerial and professional class. Distinguishing the Stage Three family from its predecessors are first, its 'privatised' nature, centred more on the home than the community; secondly its 'nucleated' form, relatively more isolated from the extended family network; and thirdly, for Young and Willmott quite crucially, the lessening of 'role segregation' between husband and wife. The male breadwinner/female homemaker distinction is becoming blurred. Both may work and the allocation of tasks is less rigid. Some tasks are for the husband and others for the wife but an increasing number are shared. The overall task of 'homemaking' is achieved by more complementary and equal roles, 'opposite but similar', to define which Young and Willmott offer the term 'The Symmetrical Family'.

Changing ideas about the respective roles of men and women partly account for such changes, which are also underwritten by alterations in the occupational structure. More women are working and they are working longer. As if in recognition of this, men take on more responsibilities in the home: 'Husbands are more at work inside the home; wives more outside' (p. 264). For men, longer education and earlier retirement has contracted the span of the working life. Hours of work have not decreased but steadied at around 45 a week; the real change has been the expansion of holiday entitlement. Class differences have not disappeared; higher status groups derive more satisfaction, see greater opportunities for advancement and challenge, exercise greater autonomy, in their work than do manual workers, even though, physically and psychologically, they are more likely to take their work home with them. Changes in the nature of work, towards non-manual work in the service sector and away from manual work in manufacturing industry, make such work and the family and life styles which go with it, the norm to which others are moving.

Young and Willmott situate leisure firmly within the matrix of work and family life. They found that their informants defined leisure as the opposite of work, as an exercise of freedom and pleasure, though in practice many activities were situated midway between the poles of work and leisure. Some class differences were evident amongst men. Compared with lower status groups, those in high status occupations played more sport, read more and spent more time in the garden – though they spent less time with their children or tinkering with the car. Greater than these differences was a similar tendency amongst all men to spend more of their free time inside the home than out of it, especially at weekends. The key variable in explaining leisure patterns, more important than class or any other factor except age, was car ownership. Working class car owners were more like the middle class in their leisure habits than working class people without cars. From this, Young and Willmott deduce that the spread of car ownership is an important example of the principle of stratified diffusion at work in leisure.

Gender was one of the few factors which divided the extent and nature of leisure time. Working wives had rather less, full-time housewives rather more, leisure than men, but they spent it on a far more restricted set of activities than men, rarely going out without their husbands, and having few identifiable leisure interests outside the home. Social contacts were confined to relatives and women friends.

In general, then, leisure appeared as family-centred, even for those middle class men most active outside the home. More active and less passive leisure, more involving the whole family, is the new middle class pattern, to which, according to the principle, other social groups will increasingly approximate. The future of leisure, about which Young and Willmott bravely make a specific forecast in an appendix, is inextricably bound up with that of work and family. Changes in who works, where they work and how long they work will affect the opportunities for leisure. The more stimulating such work is, the more will people feel able to undertake stimulating leisure. The scenario is an optimistic one. Higher incomes, better housing, longer holidays, greater access to cars will all contribute to increasingly family-centred life styles. And it is in the family that those who may otherwise feel unable to realise their identities may find meaning and purpose:

> Whether or not leisure activities are a compensation to people who do not fulfill themselves in their work, the family certainly is. As a multi-purpose institution it can provide some sense of permanence and wholeness to set against the more restricted and transitory roles imposed by the specialist institutions which have flourished outside the home. The upshot is that, as the disadvantages of the new industrial and impersonal society have become more pronounced, so has the family become more prized for its power to counteract them (p. 269).

Homing in on leisure

In constructing the bare bones of Young and Willmott's argument, much of the flesh has been lost. The survey material is used to generate statistics presented in the form of tables which are more sophisticated in the way they are processed than comparable official figures. Though now dated, the text remains an important source of complex factual data about the ways one section of British society spend and think about their leisure time. If sometimes this mainly serves to substantiate what other writers and surveys have suggested, the scale and care of the survey give its evidence special credibility. Qualitative evidence is also used in its own right, not just as illustration of statistical facts. Unlike Parker, Young and Willmott recognise that women relate to work and leisure and family in ways quite different from those of men. There can now be little doubt that there is a substantial trend towards family-based leisure. Young and Willmott's work attempts to verify the trend statistically and offers an explanation based on a model rather more complex than that of individual consumer choice.

The Symmetrical Family is by any measure a massive contribution to the sociology of leisure. Our reservations about its status are three kinds. First there are some problems of methodology: with how their evidence was collected, particularly the survey technique and their choice of sample. Secondly there are theoretical difficulties, especially with the 'Principle of Stratified Diffusion' as a model of leisure development. Thirdly, and underlying the other two, is the problem of 'epistemology', that is, what kind of knowledge is relevant to the study of a particular problem. This surfaces most visibly in the way Young and Willmott think about the family.

Discussion of methodology can become quite technical and require detailed discussion of a kind which is not possible in such a brief review. We shall therefore indicate only some general reservations. We are primarily concerned about basic deficiencies of the kind of survey method adopted by Young and Willmott. The tendency is for their research method to frame potentially complex perceptions into propositions which invite obvious and superficial responses. We are not convinced that anything very enlightening is going to emerge from a question which asks interviewees whether they are very/fairly/not satisfied with their job. This also raises the ambiguity of being 'satisfied': satisfied compared with what? Nor is it very surprising that exactly half the respondents declared themselves 'very satisfied'. Asking people whether they are 'satisfied' with their job is rather like asking if they are happy. Saying that you are not, constitutes an admission that there is something deeply wrong in your life. Such questions have the answers built into them by the way they phrase the problem. They stimulate predictable responses. Even when further measures derived from similar questions about autonomy of work, career prospects and the relative satisfactions derived from work and leisure are added, we are no nearer to understanding the complexities of how people think about their work. Nor are there any, comparable questions, even at this low level of sophistication, about work in the home.

There are other ways of asking more open-ended questions, sometimes of a more oblique kind. The problem (for Young and Willmott) is that they do not easily yield neatly aggregated statistics and it may be this insistence on numbers as evidence which accounts for the persistence of this sort of survey method. There is always a gap between what people say and what they actually do and no study of work or leisure can afford to take what people say at face value, especially when the answers are contained in the questions.

Even if some sort of survey and its quantified results are admitted to have validity, there are difficulties in the sample selected. Young and Willmott concede that the number of the original sample they could *not* contact includes a disproportionate number of young single people of both sexes and those in unskilled occupations. Consequently there is an under-representation of social groups whose leisure patterns are *least* likely to be those of the symmetrical family. Compared with the rest of the nation, the South East is more middle class and less working class, to an extent which makes the discovery of a predominantly middle class life style a self-fulfilling prophecy. This does not overly trouble Young and Willmott. The South East is part of the vanguard: what London does today, the nation will do tomorrow. It represents the geographical dimension of the Principle. This confident suppression of the imbalances in prosperity between regions and the distinctiveness of regional cultures can only be validated if the Principle really holds. Unfortunately, such validation is difficult, since the sources and kinds of data they use seem to have been designed to prove that the Principle works.

The onward march of history

The basic tenets of the Principle as a theory have already been
explained as dependent on industrialisation, democracy and
emulation. The objections to this model are so manifold that it is
difficult to know where to begin. It is not clear, for example,
whether this is an extrapolation from the recent past of British
history into a present and future which is peculiar to this country
or whether it is a theory of industrial capitalism in general. Even
for Britain, the account of history embodied in the principle is
naive in the extreme. Industrialisation and democracy are not
finished states but continuing processes: they involve not diffusion
but contest and struggle. Emulation is not a universal human
characteristic but a set of attitudes and behaviours necessary to a
high consumption economy, continuously induced by powerful
instruments of persuasion. What we have in the principle is a
Fabian view of history: foreshortened, optimistic, commonsensic-
al, happily producing a steady flow of improvement. We shall try
to show in the next chapter how this view of history is inadequate
to explain the full complexity of historical evidence.

For the moment, it is worth noting that the recession of the
1970s and 1980s casts some doubt on this steady growth of
progress. To pursue Young and Willmott's analogy of the marching column, it looks as though someone has sent down orders for
those at the rear to walk backwards for a while.

Young and Willmott's version of family history is equally
oversimplified as an examination of recent work in the area would
show. There are also problems with their sanguine conclusions
about the family as the focal point of contemporary society. While
leisure becomes more 'family centred' for those in families, there
are increasing numbers of people who live in households which do
not resemble the conventional family in Young and Willmott's
portrait. The diversity of non-family life styles (single people,
single parents, childless couples, collectives and so on) disappears
in the search for 'symmetry'. We must also doubt whether changes
in family relationships (especially concerning the sexual division of
domestic labour) have been of the scale which Young and Willmott suggest. Their own evidence can be interpreted as showing
only marginal changes, and this interpretation would be closer to

other studies which have pointed to the continuing inequalities in the distribution of domestic responsibilities.

But empirical trends apart, there are serious questions to be asked about the quality of their understanding of the family. Both description and analysis are superficial. In particular, family life is understood neither as a structural set of relations within contemporary society nor as a set of cultural relationships which each family makes anew in its own image. The family hangs suspended in space, a dislocated variable related to neither the life of society nor that of individuals. Understanding the family is not easy. We all know too much about our own experience, too little about the experiences of others, though some beginnings of more systematic analysis have been made.

The idea that the family is primarily a unit of consumption is taken as self-evident, with little examination of why or how such a definition has come about. That this consumer role is economically and politically structured by processes *outside* the family is hidden from view. Thus it is no coincidence that the isolated home-centred family is the most appropriate life style for an economy which demands labour to be geographically and socially mobile. Especially in the middle class, families rarely live in any neighbourhood long enough to develop any but the most tenuous of links outside the home. Home centredness may be an active choice but it is one made within constraints of the social structure which Young and Willmott do not begin to acknowledge.

The impact of social forces on the internal dynamics of the family – on the ways roles and relationships are experienced – also needs more consideration. If the family is, as Young and Willmott suggest, a refuge, it is worth asking about the status of the refugees. Despite their massive survey, Young and Willmott can only speculate about the precise attractions – the social meanings – of family life. We do, however, know rather more of the hidden costs which the maintenance of this refuge imposes on some of its members. The growing body of evidence about familial violence and about mental illness among women in families suggests that this particular refuge may not be the safest of retreats. These contradictions between image and reality are not explored by Young and Willmott. The family dominates their vision of leisure unproblemtically. By contrast, the work of the Rapoports promises a more profound analysis of the relationship between the family and leisure.

Robert and Rhona Rapoport

Peddling the life cycle

The concern of Young and Willmott with the family as a critical variable in understanding leisure patterns is taken a step further by Robert and Rhona Rapoport in their book *Leisure and the Family Life-Cycle* published in 1975. Reviewing some of the models previously advanced to analyse leisure, they argue that social life needs to be understood along the three planes of work, family and leisure which intersect in ways which change during the life cycle. It is the life cycle which has been under-emphasised as an explanatory variable, one of increasing importance as social change renders less powerful the influences of age, class and sex. These have become secondary processes modifying the primary factor of the life cycle.

The life cycle is 'based on relatively constant preoccupations arising from psycho-biological maturational processes' (p. 14). Every stage in the life cycle produces such preoccupations – 'less or more conscious mental absorptions' – but their nature is distinctive to each stage. Preoccupations produce sets of interests, potential motivations, which then ideally find expression in specific activities. It is the match or lack of it – between preoccupations, interests and activities which for individuals and societies constitutes the problem of leisure.

Each of the four life cycle phases – adolescence, young adulthood, establishment and retirement – has sub-phases according to developments in work and family life. The Rapoports devote a chapter to describing each stage and its sub-phases illustrated with case histories, concluding with a consideration of the policies necessary to meet the needs of those at this stage of the life cycle.

Thus for 13 to 19-year-old *adolescents*, the central preoccupation is with 'the quest for satisfying personal identity'. Its many facets – physical, social, mental, moral – explain the adolescent interest in trying out new experiences. School, family and leisure are the areas for the exploration of identity, and finding outlets for this exploration is the perpetual problem of adolescents and adolescence. Facility provision for such a group, argue the Rapoports, must be flexible and provide opportunities for adolescents to generate their own activities as well as participating in those provided by adults.

Entry into young *adulthood* is marked by leaving school in the late teens and extends into the mid-twenties, including the very early stage of marriage. Young adults are less concerned with individual than social identity, preoccupied with 'identification with social institutions'. Attachment to roles and intimate relationships becomes evident at work and in the home but their real interest is in heterosexual relationships, and the prospect of marriage. Some may delay or reject such a commitment, but most wish to become part of a couple, often sacrificing other interests to concentrate on establishing this identity. This 'privatisation of interests' is particularly restricting for women, thus storing up potential problems for later life when the family can no longer provide a sufficient sense of identity.

The *establishment* phase covers most of adult life from the mid-twenties to the mid-fifties. Earlier phases have been rehearsals: this is the actual performance. The major preoccupation is with making 'satisfying life investments' in personal relationships and material possessions which the majority realise through home and family life. With the birth of children, life becomes not just home but child-centred. For the woman this becomes a virtually exclusive life interest. The man maintains an alternative set of interests in work but his non-work leisure time is increasingly family-centred. As the children grow up and their departure becomes imminent, the man may be able to expand his work interests to fill the vacuum, but for the woman this readjustment is more difficult, especially if her return to work is delayed and partial. It is women over 35 and not working who are as a consequence most vulnerable to stress and depression. Such groups need to be rescued from their sense of being redundant and planners could do worse than to make these some of their target groups.

By the *mid-fifties* children will have left home and work will be decreasing in importance. The consequent preoccupation is with 'achieving a sense of personal integration of personal meaning and harmony with the world around one' (p. 270). If work, family and leisure are the three props to identity, the prospective removal of the first two places undue strain on the third. At a time when economic, physical, and psychological resources are contracting, the adjustment is far from easy. Leisure has to become the whole of life and recognition of this should underlie leisure policies. Integration with welfare and educational provision should be designed to offer a comprehensive set of activities for this increasing proportion of the population to create for themselves new social roles and fulfilling identities.

In their penultimate chapter, the Rapoports identify a divergence between the kinds of policies they advocate and those which dominate current leisure policy. As a result of its rapid expansion, leisure provision has become excessively institutionalised, concerned to install specialist facilities rather than flexible leisure bases. Planners are obsessed with creating controlled situations when the real challenge lies in the 'complexity, ambiguity and uncertainty' inherent in providing for leisure.

Such planning could contribute to the new culture of a post-industrial society, to which the concluding chapter is devoted. As a moral revolt against the excesses of bureaucratic industrialisation, people will reach back to rediscover the virtues of preindustrial society and seek to combine them with the material benefits of industrialisation. Current emphases on achievement, competition and short term planning will be challenged by the alternatives of self-actualisation, cooperation and comprehensive provision. In encouraging and facilitating this 'cultural revolution', planners potentially occupy a strategic role.

The generation game

Leisure and the Family Lifecyle is not an easy book to read, being long and repetitive. This may help to explain why it has not achieved the prominence of other texts reviewed here. It still remains an important book, the merits and deficiencies of which are worth assessing. One of its great strengths is a refusal to accept that leisure is by definition a sphere demarcated from the rest of life. The insistence on the interaction of influences from work and the family with those of leisure, breaks down the barriers which both sociological theory and leisure policy have created to shut out the rest of social life. Thus, the Rapoports do come close to recognising that leisure models based on the market provision of goods and services – leisure as commodity – are inadequate to conceptualise the exploration of meaning and identity – leisure as culture.

Even their view of the family is more dynamic and complex than that which stems from the stereotype of the consumerist family. Marriages exist before and after families, teenagers still live within them; the family is a constantly changing formation. This sense of variation over time of family life is accompanied by a willingness to assess the losses as well as the gains of living in and through the family. Changes have to be managed, not always successfully. The excessive privatisation of early marriage, the arbitrary narrowing of women's identities around the mother role, the psychological as well as physical pain of old age, constitute a consistent recognition that family life has its own problems.

The problems and experiences of women are given equal attention to those of men, representing a considerable advance over the work of Parker and even that of Young and Wilmott. In their discussion of parts of the life cycle, immediately before and after marriage or at the point that children leave home, there is an explicit recognition that existing stereotypes of sex roles within the family demand excessively damaging sacrifices for women. If the role of gender remains largely untheorised and never achieves more than the status of a variable within the life cycle, women are present in this book in a way rarely found in the sociology of leisure.

Other groups marginalised by standard leisure analysis are also given overdue attention. The late middle-aged and elderly, for example, are largely ignored by commerce and defined by public provision as a species of social problem to be remedied by the welfare services. That their problems find private and individual, rather than public and collective, expression has been too easy a reason to ignore the complexity of their needs.

These emphases of the Rapoports – on leisure as related to other spheres of life, on the inadequacies of the consumer model, on variations and paradoxes in family life, on the costs of motherhood for women, on the unacknowledged problems of ageing – give their work a distinctive and positive quality. The problems arise, as they have done before, over method, theory and history.

In their discussion of the elderly, the Rapoports argue that we actually know little about the experience of growing old, and need to explore how individuals feel about it, to obtain a 'phenomenology' of ageing. Yet, for us, such understanding of this or any of the other groups is scarcely advanced by the Rapoports own attempts to grasp how people construct meanings out of their daily lives. The biographical case studies or 'vignettes' which appear in each chapter serve neither to portray patterns within groups nor to render the texture of individual lives. Placed alongside the theory, they act as descriptive illustrations of it. The problem in part is that they do not statistically represent the group which they allegedly belong. We know not how they were contacted or interviewed. Neither do they fully represent themselves. The construction out of interview material, even that used verbatim, comes across as curiously flat, as if only the surface of identity is being revealed. Occasionally flashes of the underlife become visible as in the insistence of several adolescent interviewees that they positively enjoy 'mucking about', an activity difficult to fit into the Rapoports model of this phase of life.

The empirical evidence offered is not sufficiently convincing to compensate for deficiencies in the theory. Both its relationship to other theories and its fundamental basis remain unclear. In the introductory chapter, the Rapoports suggest that the concept of the life cycle is a useful supplement to existing theories of occupational factors and social change, as developed by Parker and Young and Willmott respectively, but it is hard to resist the impression that ultimately the life cycle displaces rather than supplements other factors, since the cycle is held to be more deeply rooted in basic human development:

> The contribution that we seek to make ... is to suggest a perspective that supplements rather than replaces the perspective of social class and social change already mentioned. This is the perspective of the human life cycles. Based on relatively constant preoccupations arising from psycho-biological maturational processes, this perspective cuts across and underlies class and cultural patterns (p. 14).

A concordance between psychology and sociology is long overdue but we doubt the success of this one, particularly since it places biological processes at the heart of its understanding of the life cycle. For example, the Rapoports' account of adolescence argues that:

> the developmental processes in adolescence are biologically rooted. Their manifestations vary by sex, class, locality, educational experience and subcultural style of life (p. 32).

Our own work on youth, and that of many other authors suggests that, to the contrary, adolescence as a stage of life is relatively recent *social* construction, and is powerfully shaped by class, gender and race. Rather than overriding these influences, it is actually constructed and experienced through them. What is really being proposed here is no more than a slightly more sophisticated version of the theory that the principal stratification in society is that of age.

We do not doubt that age is a factor to be taken into account in leisure analysis. It remains one major determinant of the pattern of activity participation. However, other theories of stratification cannot so lightly be dismissed, as in the Rapoports equation of a Marxist perspective with a *Pravda* review of a Mary Quant exhibition or what amounts to a complete silence on feminist approaches to the family. The construction of their own theory ought to require serious engagement with alternatives. Consequently, they do not realise that, if age takes us through the stages of the life cycle, with fluctuating relationships between work, family and leisure, the question arises as to *why* these experiences change. The possibility that society *constructs* age, through its organisation of education, housing, retirement and its images of youth and maturity, has been lost. The key processes are being held to be biological and psychological; social determinants have vanished. Their disappearance is presented as the result of social progress:

> The variables which have been productive in social research for detecting and analysing patterns are losing power as predictors to the extent that age, sex, social class, standards of housing and education become less divisive (p. 23).

The inclusion of age as less relevant seems to us a contradiction since it is age that appears to be the nub of the argument.

The more general confident image of a progressively more equal society seems to us a travesty. Such moves towards greater equality as have taken place in the last thirty years are relative and superficial. More absolute and deep-rooted inequalities remain. Since the Rapoports do not offer any support for their own assertion, we do not feel obliged, and do not have the space, to offer evidence for ours. The mistake here is not only to ignore whole areas of inequality but to confuse structure with culture. The appearance amongst previously divided social groups of a common life style around the nuclear family is held to signify the abolition of inequality. This is to misunderstand the nature of stratification. It is not a matter of differences in life style or values but of inequality in the material and cultural resources which groups can control to realise *any* kind of life style.

The Rapoports' view that the life cycle is the principal determinant of leisure can only rest on the assumption that social development has rendered obsolete not only pre-existent forms of stratification but also the theories which emerged to explain them. In this double refutation of history and theory, they are not unique. The work of Kenneth Roberts works in a different way to achieve the same end.

Kenneth Roberts

A singular case of pluralism

Contemporary Society and the Growth of Leisure (1978) is different from the other books we have been examining since it is not an empirical study. It is rather concerned with establishing which theoretical terms can most usefully be applied to leisure analysis. The four-part structure begins with problems of defining leisure and tracing its historical growth; moves on to consider various ways of theorising leisure; examines the relationship between leisure and the influences of work and family; and concludes with an attack on prophecies of the 'leisure society' and their assertion of the need for comprehensive planning for leisure.

Roberts follows Parker in defining leisure as an area of relative freedom and which has been increasing in the post-war period as a result of demographic and economic change. It is this 'growth' in leisure which, Roberts argues, serious analysis must seek to explain. If not all groups participate equally and some remain seriously disadvantaged, the underlying tendency is for leisure to grow, which even an economic recession may fail to reverse.

Thus Roberts poses the question of what kind of an approach can best explain the fact of this growth and the specific forms it has taken. Four such possibilities are outlined: recreation research, mass society theory, models of class domination and the scenario of pluralism.

Recreation research is argued to be deficient on a number of grounds. It operates with a definition of leisure narrowed around recreation, thus ignoring what Roberts calls the 'big five' leisure activities: watching television, drinking alcohol, smoking tobacco, betting and making love. He argues that the application of a simplistic model of supply and demand pays little or no attention to the complexities of leisure motives, for example failing to see how demand for a particular activity such as sport may be activated as much by the opportunity it provides for socialising as by its intrinsic appeal. In such demand focused research, individuals are atomised, removed from the context of their wider life styles which shape the meaning of leisure and its constituent activities. Finally, recreation research habitually justifies itself in terms of its contribution to improving the quality of life, a claim which remains unproven.

Mass society theory is found equally guilty of reductive approach to leisure. Postulating the existence of political and economic élites controlling means of mass persuasion, it sees leisure as an area of mass conformity, where individuality is suppressed and genuine quality sacrificed to mass appeal. Roberts criticises the way this approach reduces people to the level of automata, ignoring the active nature of uses made of the mass media and related leisure forms. Mass society theory makes use of dubious qualitative judgements which upon examination have no objective basis and merely reflect the cultural preferences of the evaluators.

Traces of mass society theory are to be found in the ideas of *class domination theorists*. They too see the media as a form of social control, though they are less concerned with discovering conformity and mediocrity than with ideological legitimation. In one version the media are seen to operate with a view biased against any ideas inimical to the existing social order. In another the bias is more implicit, consisting of an endorsement of a consensual view of the world, indirectly reinforcing dominant ideas. In a more general and complex argument, leisure as a whole is perceived as part of the process of cultural reproduction. Institutions socialise the population into acceptance of existing norms and values. Ideals favourable to the continuation of society as it exists are reproduced as apparently natural and spontaneous acts of individual choice. Far from realising freedom, leisure reflects alienation from the social structure: a vain attempt to recapture meaning through the consumption of leisure commodities.

Roberts has little time for critics of the media. Accusations of bias cannot account for occasions when the media discuss problems and uncover scandals which government and business would rather suppress. The appeal to consensus is necessary for meaningful communication to exist at all. If the media have prejudices, they merely reflect those of the general public. The description of leisure as 'alienated' is impossible to verify, depending on prior theoretical assumptions and a patronising view of most others in society. Some concessions are made to the theorists of cultural reproduction, though even they mistake mechanisms of social integration for forms of social control:

> the class domination theory tends to increase its own credibility when it disclaims conspiratorial implications in preference for identifying the latent, usually unintended social structural consequences that inevitably accompany the leisure that can be developed within a given type of society. (*Contemporary Society and the Growth of Leisure*, Longman, 1978, p. 21.)

Even the most sophisticated versions of class domination theory cannot account for the variety and complexity of leisure forms. The policies of central and local government go beyond, and in different directions to, what might be required by the need to control leisure activity. Business interests cannot control leisure, however much they would like to. Indeed, their problem is that the level and nature of consumer demand is continuously running out of their control. The only theory which can explain leisure is a pluralist one.

In Britain and other Western societies there exists a variety of taste publics that possess contrasting interests generated by their different circumstances. ... In recreation and other spheres the public uses its leisure to nurture life styles that supply experiences which the individuals concerned seek and value. ... This is the reality of modern leisure, and theories that fail to spotlight this aspect of reality prove only their own need of revision (p. 86).

Leisure is not alienated but anomic. Traditionally regarded in sociology as a pathological condition, in which moral and cultural rules are absent, this is, for Roberts, a positive attribute, since individuals can realise and implement the values which most suit them.

The *pluralist model* does not, however, assume that leisure is completely free from other influences. Roberts follows the Rapoports in arguing that membership of social networks is a crucial factor. The most important of such networks is the family. It is the situation in which most leisure takes place, it provides a set of interests with reference to which leisure choice is exercised. It is also the explanation for the greatest single inequality in leisure, that between the sexes. It is not the activity of leisure planners which has the greatest effect on leisure opportunity but the standard of living in the average home.

Acknowledgement of the increasing importance of the family has jeopardised those models of leisure which assume the centrality of work. At any one time, more than half the population are not in paid work and even those who are appear to carry little of its influence into their leisure. Work is essential to material existence but has little influence on the pattern and meaning of leisure activity. Roberts believes it is equally mistaken to argue that leisure has come to be the dominant experience in society, since while it may be dependent of most outside influences, leisure itself is *contained*. It remains important to individuals and to the survival of the social structure, but it does not and cannot replace work or change the nature of political priorities.

Finally, and it is in some ways his greatest unorthodoxy, Roberts refutes the advocacy of comprehensive planning policies. They are unviable, since leisure need and demands are volatile; and undesirable, since it may deprive the individual of that freedom of choice essential to leisure. The most planning could and should do is compensate for deficiencies in the mixed economy of leisure, especially by providing for disadvantaged groups. But in the end, the future of leisure is best determined by the exercise of consumer sovereignty.

Missing links

Contemporary Society and the Growth of Leisure is a contentious book. The explicit intention to encounter and evaluate leisure theory requires confrontation with a series of positions in which issues cannot be fudged. The resulting clarity of Roberts' own perspective is a welcome change from those who ritualistically gesture towards other theories but manage to avoid discussing them in any detail. While others inhabit the terrain of the consensus, oblivious of their neighbours, Roberts sets out to erect a boundary fence: this is our land, this is where we stand. He is therefore less interested in peaceful coexistence and actively resists the claim of others to some part of this territory. As squatters on the leisure frontier of sociology, our interests are clearly opposed to his.

There are still some points of mutual agreement. His demolition of the simple-minded approach of recreation research seems to us admirable in its execution. Whatever else we differ about, we share his rejection of the terms of their argument, if it can be dignified with such a term. For rather different reasons, we also share his suspicion of comprehensive planning, at least without a much greater sense of the need for participation. We also share his suspicion of much of mass society theory with its conspiratorial overtones and contempt for the common people (though we do not agree that all evaluation is invalid or that Raymond Williams is a mass society theorist).

The essential point at issue is deceptively straightforward. Roberts subscribes to a pluralist model of society; ours is a variety of the class domination theory he seeks to discredit. Even here some points may be agreed. We too are suspicious of theories of conspiracy, whether perceived in corporate business or the apparatuses of the State. We also concede that class domination theories have so far failed to offer an adequate account of leisure. But we do think they have the capacity to do so.

Short of a point by point refutation of Roberts' argument all we can do is to concentrate on three ways in which, with no small help from some of its cruder exponents, the theory of class domination

is misrepresented and misunderstood. The first is Roberts'
assumption that the test of class domination theory is whether it is
a useful predictor of leisure behaviour. If it can be shown to be of
little use, it can be discounted. But it is incorrect to expect an
immediate correspondence between the existence of a subordinate
class and any form of social behaviour, whether it be leisure,
family life, politics, religion or anything else. Class domination
theory is concerned with issues of ideological conflict and cultural
domination precisely because it does *not* accept that there is a
direct correspondence between class and culture. Secondly,
Roberts is quite silent about whether class is a useful concept at
all. It would be possible to argue that class is but one factor
amongst many, a familiar pluralist position, or that its salience for
leisure is quite limited compared with other parts of life, such as
political allegiance. Roberts argues for neither, thus apparently
wishing away the existence of class. Even the weakest form of class
analysis in sociology, the occupational gradations used by Parker
and by Young and Willmott, register that class may be a form of
inequality which may underlie common aspirations and life styles.
The 'disadvantaged groups' referred to by Roberts seem to
constitute a residuum, who, for one reason or another, have been
left out of an otherwise classless social system.

Thirdly, Roberts assumes that the test of class domination
theory is whether or not it can explain 'leisure'. The difficulty here
is that theories may seek to explain different things. One central
aspect of Marxist theory (to give it its proper name) is its
commitment to distinguish between the surface appearances of
society and the hidden structures and processes which lie behind
these appearances. Roberts, like the other authors we have
considered in this chapter, treats leisure as an obvious category of
social life. He takes that category as the focus of analysis. We are
rather more sceptical. Leisure as a social category is the product of
historical development – it is the result of other processes which
are *not* leisure. Because of this scepticism, we are concerned to
look beneath the surface of leisure and examine these other
economic, political and ideological processes which have produced
it. In this sense, there can be no 'Marxist theory of leisure' to set
directly opposite Roberts' pluralist theory of leisure. Where
Roberts is content to examine the internal pattern of leisure, a
Marxist theory must seek to understand its interrelationship with

other elements of the society. We do not accept that leisure can be abstracted from these relationships for the purpose of study.

These, then, are our preliminary reasons for wanting to return to what Roberts calls class domination theory. But we must also enter some objections to his own theoretical position – that of pluralism.

A basic one is that since everything is related to everything else, any kind of causal explanation becomes virtually impossible. Every instance is unique to a time and place. Patterns only exist as the aggregate of accidental individual behaviour. Roberts, for instance, sees leisure as socially and historically constructed 'by attitudes and values that are invariably rooted in the surrounding society' (p. 36). But where are they rooted? The answer is everywhere and nowhere in the flora and fauna of society. In this sense pluralism is not a theoretical argument at all, but an abdication of it. If it is unreasonable to search for the Holy Grail of The Single Cause, at least some causal pattern should be offered. In practice, Roberts begins and ends with the individual, situated in social networks to be sure, but otherwise untrammelled by determinants of conduct. This does not mean that leisure behaviour is completely free: 'Unmitigated individualism is a sociological impossibility. Leisure means that the social system can tolerate more "play" or "looseness" and accommodate more cultural diversity than was possible in previous eras (p. 137).

Our disagreement with such statements is not merely with their empirical accuracy, that in fact there may now be *less* cultural diversity than at any time in the last hundred years. More serious is the inability of the pluralist perspective to tell us anything about leisure other than how complex it all is. Leisure and the family, we are told, exert a reciprocal influence upon each other: when or how this process started is not apparently relevant, nor is the possibility that changes in both might have 'determinations' elsewhere in the structure of society. We simply dissent from a model of human behaviour which explains social life as the aggregated or individual choices made within social networks, somehow shaped by the interplay of free-flowing variables.

We are offered no way of grasping the social totality of which leisure is part. Instead, we are told that the movement of society is inconstant; at different times and in different places, different parts of the social structure influence outcomes. The tenuous grasp of this perspective on any conceptualisation is revealed by its collapse into functionalism when challenged. In reply to the assertion by class domination theorists that contemporary leisure is indelibly marked by the institutions, experiences and ideas of industrial capitalism, Roberts argues that leisure is always related to the social system because it invariably has similar functions to perform.'The truth is that leisure, or alternative forms in which play may be institutionalised, performs comparable functions in all societies' (p. 79). Yet, if we ask about how the 'functions' of leisure relate to those of other parts of the social system, the answer is that they coexist as complementary but independent forces: 'Leisure has developed alongside work and functions alongside it in identity formation and maintenance' (p. 144). Modern society is unique in the tendency for leisure to be independent of other social forces: 'contemporary societies are sufficiently loose knit systems to make the primary relationships amid which individuals experience life substantially independent of the larger political economy' (p. 123). Yet, and the paradox does not trouble Roberts, it is the dependence of leisure on a major aspect of the political economy, the market, which guarantees its freedom: 'Despite its imperfections the market remains one of the most effective participatory mechanisms devised for modern societies' (p. 158).

Confronted by the intricate patterns of contemporary leisure preferences, pluralism abdicates any attempt at explanation. Other than the family, it is difficult to find any factor which significantly affects individual choice in the market-place. Hence all 'grand theories' are to be rejected. Leisure is, by definition, that part of life least affected by political and economic structures, which is both its psychological attraction and sociological strength.

Countering such a position is one task of this book. Here we can only suggest that such a theory cannot even manage to explain what Roberts castigates recreation researchers for ignoring: the persistence of the 'big five' leisure activities of smoking, drinking, watching television, gambling and making love. The implication of the pluralist position is that these dominant leisure interests represent the aggregate of individual choices, affected more by social networks than political, economic and cultural characteristics of society. This does not seem to us to be a tenable position. With the possible exception of sex, all these activities are defined by class membership. If not the level of participation, then its form, is given class meanings. Members of all classes may drink, smoke, gamble and watch television but where, when, how, and why they pursue such activities have particular cultural meanings shaped by the social groups to which they belong. Bitter is not the 'same thing' as burgundy, nor bingo as *chemin de fer*. What is true of class is even more so of gender. Again it is not the rate of participation which is the issue, though gender differences in these are real enough. It is rather that the meanings of the activity and hence its correct form, are prescribed by definitions of gender-appropriate conduct. 'Real, feminine' women do not drink pints of beer, smoke pipes, bet on horses, watch war films or 'have a little bit on the side'. The search for sociability which Roberts suggests may underlie major forms of leisure activity, is similarly inflected in different ways by both class and gender.

In the pluralist model, social networks replace ideological influences. Our argument would be that they stand in for them. They mediate individuals and social structures. Members of the family socialise each other into sex roles. These cannot exist without the family and are continuously reproduced within it. But they also exist outside it, in the organisation of the economy and prevailing ideologies of sexuality. In this way social networks do not establish independence from the rest of society but disguise a more subtle dependency. Influences outside leisure shape and structure not only the physical and temporal limits within which leisure operates but also the institutional forms it assumes and the cultural meanings it carries.

Where do we go from here?

We have discussed these texts in order of their date of publication to see what sort of development has been taking place within the sociology of leisure. Such movement as there is, seems to us to be largely backwards. These efforts to create a sociology of leisure are typified by a double retreat. On the one hand there is a withdrawal from the attempt to grasp leisure as a social process which was implicit in studies using the concepts of class culture and community. On the other, there is a withdrawal from any attempt to grasp the positioning of leisure within an overall social structure. Instead, work, the family and leisure are constantly invoked as the cornerstones of modern life. In this shrinking vision of society, any analysis of the totality of economic, social, political and ideological patterns and processes has been lost. Instead, the microcosms of our own lives as we work outside (and, occasionally, inside) the home, bring up our children and take our pleasures are reflected back to us as adequate accounts of what society is. That power, goods, cultural resources and identities are socially produced and unequally distributed is hidden from view. Our own blindness to the social forces which organise our lives is here turned into a sociological truth.

Just as any sense of social structure is obscured, so is any active sense of culture. If societies are made by humans, under conditions imposed upon them, they are nevertheless *made*. This process of cultural creation – the meaning with which people invest their actions – is also absent from this sociological consensus. Instead, we are offered leisure as a reflex of work (Parker); leisure as a spin-off from middle class life styles (Young and Willmott); leisure as an aspect of psychobiological maturation (the Rapoports); and finally, leisure as the embodiment of pluralist diversity (Roberts). Agency – the active creation of patterns of behaviour and meaning – is left to reside only in the individual, exercising consumer choice. There is no sense of *social* agency within leisure; and no sense that the processes which impinge upon leisure in these accounts (work, the family, the life cycle, the market) are themselves social processes, requiring human agency to reproduce or change them. They appear as inevitable external determinants confronting individuals in leisure as so many sociological 'variables'. We would want to argue that, on the contrary, these are social processes, open to action, conflict and change – rather than the natural, inevitable or universal backdrop to leisure. Work – and the social division of labour into classes and genders that structures what work means for us – is organised and changed through human agency, through the decisions of possessors of capital, through the actions of organised labour, and through discrimination on the basis of race and gender in employment. The family (always changing but somehow still the same) continues because it is supported by powerful social forces, offers powerful promises, and remains a way of meeting some human needs for which no other outlets may exist. For all of the variables, or institutions, on which the sociology of leisure touches, we would want to insist that an adequate analysis has to deal with the double movement of constraint and creation. People do make choices (and not only in leisure), but these choices are made within the structures of constraint which order their lives.

This twin consideration of society as both a system of structures and processes and a constantly recreated set of meanings and social practices brings us back – as it must – to the question of history. The texts we have examined vary in the extent to which they separate leisure historically. For Young and Willmott it provides the initial theoretical framework (the principle); for Parker and Roberts it is a warm up exercise before the main event; and for the Rapoports it is a footnote on social change. In spite of these differences, there is a common view of history which can be discerned across these texts. All share the view that leisure has developed in a linear fashion. The history of leisure marches to a steady beat, growing all the time in its social salience. Here, history is used in such a way as to destroy itself. These histories of leisure have the peculiar effect of dehistoricising leisure – that was the past, but it is over and done with now. History is a mere preliminary, necessary to get us to where we are now, but now we have arrived, we can get on with the serious business of the present and the possible future (the subject of an obligatory concluding chapter). In this way the past is disconnected from the present. What we need to know is that 'things have changed'.

We take a very different view of what the relationship between theory and history should be. We remain committed to C. Wright Mills' axiom that 'the sociological imagination enables us to grasp history and biography and the relation between the two within society. That is its task and its promise'. We believe that the sociology of leisure has abandoned that task and reneged on that promise. In the following chapter, we return to that task, initially by retracing the historical dynamics through which the leisure we now know was created.

Further reading

The principal texts discussed and relevant work by the same authors are as follows. Stanley Parker: *Leisure and Work* (Allen & Unwin, 1983) is a revised edition of his earlier *The Future of Work and Leisure* (Paladin, 1972). He is also the author of a standard textbook *The Sociology of Leisure* (Allen & Unwin, 1976). Michael Young and Peter Willmott's *The Symmetrical Family* (Penguin, 1975) can be usefully set alongside some of their earlier work, in particular their classic *Family and Kinship in East London* (Routledge & Kegan Paul, 1957).

In addition to their *Leisure and the Family Life Cycle* (Routledge & Kegan Paul, 1975), Rhona and Robert Rapoport have also produced a study of middle class couples, *Dual Career Families* (Penguin, 1971). Some of the arguments of Kenneth Roberts' *Contemporary Society and the Growth of Leisure* (Longman, 1978) have also been presented in textbook form in his *Leisure* (Longman, 2nd ed., 1981). He has also written *Youth and Leisure* (Allen & Unwin, 1983).

The state of leisure studies before the publication of these books may be gauged from an encounter with any of the following: E. Larrabee and R. Meyersohn (eds), *Mass Leisure* (Glencoe Free Press, 1958), J. Dumazadier, *The Sociology of Leisure* (Elsevier, Amsterdam, 1974) and M. Kaplan, *Leisure: Theory and Policy* (Wiley, New York, 1975).

British working class community studies are well represented by N. Dennis, F. Henriques and C. Slaughter, *Coal is Our Life* (Tavistock, 1969); B. Jackson, *Working Class Community* (Routledge & Kegan Paul, 1968); and K. Coates and R. Silburn, *Poverty: the Forgotten Englishmen* (Penguin, 1970). The tradition of cultural criticism focused on leisure in R. Hoggart, *The Uses of Literacy* (Penguin, 1958) and R. Williams, *Culture and Society* (Penguin, 1962). For an evaluation of these two traditions see C. Critcher, 'Sociology, cultural studies and the post-war working class', in J. Clarke, C. Critcher and R. Johnson (eds), *Working Class Culture* (Hutchinson, 1979).

3

Passing the time away: the historical development of leisure

The demand for amusement is not less noticeable than that for holidays, and supply follows. To 'what shall we eat, what drink, and wherewithal shall we be clothed?' must now be added the question 'How shall we be amused?' To this an answer has to be found. Even to the police it is a problem. (Charles Booth, in A. Fried and R. Elman (eds), *Charles Booth's London*, Penguin, 1971, p. 258.)

A brief case for history

We concluded the last chapter by arguing that the sociology of leisure had failed to situate leisure within the structural and cultural processes which constitute society. Our remedy for this is not to construct a complex theoretical model of the social system. The ultimate test of the abstract concepts of any grand theory – even of Marxism – must be their value in studying real historical processes. Our aim in this chapter is to use an examination of the history of leisure in Britain in the last two centuries to develop the alternative view of leisure. What we mean by structural and cultural processes, and leisure as a site of social conflict can be clarified through an historical analysis of leisure in British society.

We have been arguing against the representation of the history of leisure as a steady growth providing expanding possibilities of leisure for 'the people'. It is simply inadequate to suggest that industrialisation created leisure, which has subsequently grown to today's level. In fact, industrialisation in Britain began by *des-*

troying leisure. When leisure re-emerged, it was given very particular social forms, which need to be understood as the outcome of a continuous struggle between dominant and subordinate groups. If leisure was an achievement, it was achieved not by some abstract process called 'industrialisation', but by the struggles, conflicts and alliances of social groups. Both the right to leisure – and the ability to pursue certain forms of leisure – are products of this history of conflict.

As in the discipline of sociology, 'leisure' was until recently a marginal category in historical studies – appearing primarily in the guise of histories of 'manners' or 'taste' among dominant social groups, in which the bulk of the population at best played the role of passively admiring onlookers. Even the more radical historians concerned with developing a class history of Britain tended to invert dominant models of economic or political history, substituting the standard of living of the common people for the analysis of industrial expansion, or the activities of trade unionists or socialists for the analysis of party fortunes. The publication of Edward Thompson's *The Making of the English Working Class* (1963) marks the emergence of cultural history. Everyday life became more than the cold indices of the standard of living; class consciousness was understood to take forms other than political or trade union organisation; and perhaps most importantly, ideas about class conflict were extended beyond the issues of economic and political power to encompass struggles over the cultural legitimacy of images, definitions, meanings and ideologies embedded in social behaviour. Subsequently, Thompson's pioneering work has been elaborated, especially for the nineteenth and early twentieth centuries. Our account which follows is heavily dependent on this body of work, and other more specific studies.

We hope that our account reflects the strengths and significance of this work, but it must also necessarily reflect some of its weaknesses. First, attention has been very much concentrated upon working class leisure. Given the persistent absence of the working class from much conventional history this focus is perhaps not surprising. Nevertheless, other classes and strata have their own leisure histories, which are poorly represented here. These other trajectories appear mainly in terms of their impact upon working class leisure forms.

Secondly, even within this focus, this history is selective – being focused primarily on *institutional* forms of leisure practice. It deals with formal, or relatively organised leisure, rather than the informal or unorganised. This dimension of unorganised, informal and private leisure (including much of domestic life) is a significant gap in the history of leisure. Much of the day to day fabric of life has eluded historical analysis.

Thirdly, and as a result of these first two points – the history of leisure is predominantly a history of *male* leisure. Here, as elsewhere, women remained 'hidden from history'. For most of the nineteenth and twentieth centuries, it seems that the sexual division of labour has had profound consequences for leisure as well as the organisation of work. Working class women, in particular, appear to have been excluded from most forms of organised leisure, even where they possessed the time and economic resources to pursue it. For women, time has been predominantly structured around the family, and women's free time seems to have been woven into the private spheres of family, street and neighbourhood rather than the public worlds of institutionalised leisure. The emergence of historical studies directed at the uncovering of women's economic, social and political lives promises to remedy this absence, but for the present we are forced to accept that the account we offer in this chapter is dependent on sources in which women form a missing dimension. In Chapter 5, we have tried to examine the contemporary dimensions of leisure where the current consequences of the historical development of this sexual division of labour are, at least for us, more visible.

This explanation for the absence of women, focuses primarily on the subject matter of historical research – the attention to public rather than private forms of leisure. But we are also aware that history, like other domains of academic knowledge, is, and has been dominated by men and their concerns. If women are hidden from history, this is also the product of male historians covering them with a cloak of invisibility in the organisation of their research and writing.

Finally, as if the over-emphasis of this chapter on the working class, institutional forms and men were not enough, we must also acknowledge that the quality of historical material deteriorates the closer we get to our own time. There has been little of value written on the history of leisure in the post-war period, while the position of the interwar years is scarcely any better. If sociology

has seemed too anxious to dispense with the past, it may also be
said that history has appeared equally reluctant to build bridges to
the present.

Despite these extensive qualifications, we believe that there is
much of value to be gained from the work of the cultural
historians; and an historical perspective, however limited, is vital
to our attempts to establish a critical approach to the study of
leisure. Before presenting our account, however, we must draw
attention to one final issue – the problem of how we present our
account of the last two hundred years of British leisure.

Even if we had the space, we could not write a leisure history of
the last two hundred years of British, or come to that, English,
society. Nor are we confident enough in our grasp of historical
development to identify critical periods. So we have decided on
the crude and arbitrary method of slicing through historical
development at forty-year intervals. We thus discuss in turn the
1800s, 1840s, 1880s, 1920s and 1960s. Decades are convenient if
theoretically dubious ways of dividing history. This method
seemed to us to enable reasonably detailed discussion of empirical
data and to incorporate most of the periods in which the history of
leisure reveals significant influences.

The 1800s: 'Merrie England'

In looking at British leisure in the 1800s, we immediately encounter some problems of terminology. The temptation is to label such
a society and its popular culture as all or any of preindustrial,
rural, traditional, in contrast to the industrial, urban modern,
society which we know follows it. The problem with such labels is
that while they enable us to identify real and dramatic changes,
they often disguise the process of change, which is more complex
and uneven than a simple transition from, for example, a society in
which most people live in the countryside to one where most live in
towns or cities. Cities existed before industrialisation, and villages
after it. This is not to suggest that there are no quantitative and
qualitative differences between country and city life but they are
often more complex, especially in their implications for popular
culture, than any simple notion of urbanisation would have us
believe.

So if it is said that Britain was in 1800 still a preindustrial, rural and traditional society, that must not imply a static society, unchanged and unchanging. The eighteenth century, especially towards the end, experienced change in its economic political and cultural organisation. The task, therefore, is to identify both continuity and change.

The most important point to establish about leisure in the 1800s is that as a category of experience it would have been less easily recognisable. The term 'leisure' differentiates employment from free time with a sharpness which does not accord with the experience of daily life at the end of the eighteenth century. People knew when they were working and when not, yet the boundary was often negotiable. It was not set by the dictate of mechanised production or by the physical limits of factory or office but by the command of custom and the rhythm of the agricultural year. The orientation was to the task in hand rather than to fixed periods of time. The nature of work supported this structure. For the labouring class work on the land, for themselves or others, was frequently mixed with some form of cottage industry, often involving the system of 'putting out' where, especially in the cotton industry, weaving and spinning would be contracted between families and middlemen. This gave some flexibility since the family could vary the intensity of work within the period agreed for production. Agricultural work was itself seasonal. Peaks such as harvest time might be followed by periods of relative inactivity. Thus work, whilst arduous, was varied and variable: time could be taken out to attend to domestic or cultural matters. Drinking on the job was common, especially in skilled trades where guilds protected traditional ways. Particularly notorious was the habit of 'Saint Monday'. Obliged to work Saturday, workers would absent themselves on Monday to claim extra leisure. It was a more general complaint of more profit-conscious employers that labourers would only work for as long or as hard to earn sufficient for themselves and their families. Given the choice they preferred to play or rest rather than toil for extra money. The fluidity of the boundaries between work and leisure was apparent in the street culture of village and town. Workshop and tavern opened side by side on to the street. Drinking, producing, bargaining, passing the time of day, all contributed to a common flow, eddying around street traders, itinerant salesmen, balladeers. Here work and leisure intermingled, both aspects of a life which was, above all, *public* in its orientation and presence. Not for nothing was one place of amusement referred to as the 'public house'. In its more common form of tavern or alehouse or inn, it provided a location for political and economic as well as purely pleasurable activity. Beer was supplemented by conversation, indoor and outdoor games. Publicans were the main leisure entrepreneurs, it being a profitable expectation that they should organise human and animal sports for their clientele.

Market day intensified such activity; so too did fairs, wakes, and holydays, which existed to an extent and in a form not seen since. Christmas, Good Friday, Shrove Tuesday, May Day, St Valentine's Day – Christian religion, pagan tradition, political celebration, severally and together, occasioned public festivals and carnivals, often involving elaborate ritual, invariably fomented by alcohol. These often provided the context for sport of all kinds: football, cricket, pugilism, wrestling, footraces, cudgelling, bellringing, horseracing and animal sports: bullrunning or baiting, bear and otter baiting, cock throwing and fighting, dog fighting.

Violence and brutality were indeed major features of popular culture. Life, on or off the streets, was often nasty brutish and short. In society as a whole, violence for individual, moral and even political ends was common, if spasmodic. In times of economic or political crisis, riot was often the only perceived resort for the population at large. And yet, violence was nearly always eventually contained, both politically and culturally. Popular culture, in all its forms, was endorsed by those who in retrospect might have seemed most threatened by it: the aristocracy and the gentry. Popular culture at the turn of the century cannot be understood without reference to the sources and nature of this patronage.

As Tory traditionalists had begun to argue, the promotion, or at least toleration, of popular culture was a vital part of complex structure of social control. The rulers of Britain were rurally based, dependent for their authority as much on consent as coercion. Popular culture was part of a negotiated if inequitable settlement. Patronage was also self-interested in another sense, since frequently local landowners were not themselves averse to eating, drinking, betting and ribaldry. In this sense popular culture was the culture of the whole people, a culture which negotiated a tenuous 'Englishness', a unity, out of the complex divisions of class, gender and region. The leisure of the labouring masses was, at least at holyday time, the leisure of the ruling oligarchy. Thus, custom, self-interest and inclination were powerful supports to patronage.

However, not all authority approved. Puritanism had been a major force in seventeenth century England and Methodism was shortly to break out like a rash on the body of the Church of England. In between, moral sobriety was frequently invoked on a local scale, sometimes with some effect on popular culture. These attacks and prohibitions prefigured later more systematic attacks. For example, throwing at cocks was banned in Worcester in 1745, Bewdley and Kidderminster in 1750, and Liverpool in 1778. In 1780 London magistrates banned the playing of skittles outside taverns. Additionally there were sporadic attacks against football, horseracing and fairs. Towards the end of the century especially, developments in the economy, in politics, in religion, and in the leisure of the non-labouring classes began to shape more stringent attitudes towards popular culture.

Central to this was the enclosure of common land. Piecemeal enclosure had gathered pace in mid-century and agitation by agrarian capitalists produced the Enclosure Act of 1793 which broke through existing legal impediments. This increasing privatisation of land had clear implications for popular culture since it removed some of the most strategic sites of customary activity. It also impoverished strip farmers, cottagers, and squatters who depended wholly or in part on the grazing and foraging rights on common land. Some joined the swelling ranks of the paupers who, socially and economically offensive to payers of the poor rates, were subject to an increasingly draconian Poor Law.

Enclosure and changes in the Poor Law were part of a general trend towards legal suppression of customary economic and cultural rights. Game Laws against poachers, a stricter interpretation of what constituted 'theft from the workplace', a savage penal code, Combination Acts in 1799 and 1800 aimed at aborting embryonic trade unions – all these constituted a tightening of control over the common populace, in public and in private. The unrest of the 1970s in the form of food riots and the spectre of the French Revolution hastened the impetus towards a tighter control of social life.

To economic and political factors must be added that of religion.

Methodism grew from an estimated 24 000 members in 1767 to 77 000 in 1796. If hardly yet a mass movement, it was beginning to affect attitudes towards popular culture, as was middle-class evangelicalism. A Royal Proclamation for the Encouragement of Piety and Virtue of 1787 had mainly exhortatory effect, but its title caught the new tone nicely. More ominous were the activities of the Society for the Suppression of Vice which by the turn of the century was instigating local, but largely successful, prosecutions for infringement of laws governing the Sabbath.

More subtle than any of these influences, yet of equal signi-ficance for the future of popular culture, was the move within at least some sections of the ruling classes, to adopt a pattern of leisure activity which deliberately eschewed contact with the lower orders. Its forms were as yet disparate. Shooting, hunting, and horse-racing (the major flat race classics dating from the 1770s onwards) were more exclusive developments of traditional rural activities. Meanwhile for the increasingly influential urban bourgeoisie, the theatre, literature, seaside holidays and music hall denoted more rational forms of leisure which depended for their decorum on the exclusion of the mass of the populace. If the land was closed off from the common people, so too were the new forms of leisure, if only because most were too poor to purchase in a burgeoning commercial market of upper class leisure.

These forces were assembling but did not yet constitute an army. Missing as yet was the heavy artillery of factory discipline which would destroy the nature and rhythms of work on which this popular culture was founded. Even the 'take off' into industrialisa-tion evident from the 1780s was confined to particular localities and industries. Much of the existing economic structure remained, like the social structure, largely untouched. Agriculture's propor-tion of the Gross National Product was decreasing, and the economic axis was tilting away from the southern counties towards the towns of the north. Yet in 1800 fewer than one in five of the population lived in towns of more than twenty thousand inhabi-tants. In the 1800s, British society was in a transitional stage, just embarking on the early phases of capitalist industrialisation. The early nineteenth century was to bring dramatic transformation of the form, context and content of popular culture, imposing very different parameters of time and space, rhythms and routines, behaviour and attitude, control and commerce.

The 1840s: 'hard times'

The 1840s were a period of deprivation for what were coming to be defined as 'the working classes'. Economically, they had their first exposure to the cycles of depression which were to prove endemic to capitalism. Politically, they suffered a series of defeats and were ultimately unable to wrest any power from the new bourgeois class who allied with the aristocracy to dominate the state following the Reform Act of 1832. Culturally, they were deprived of most of their customary pleasures and habits and provided with few viable alternatives.

Britain was emerging as an industrial and urban society. In 1851 for the first time the majority of the population lived in urban environments; by the same date 20 per cent of the population was still employed in agriculture and a further 10 per cent in domestic service, but 30 per cent now worked in manufacturing industry. The discipline of the factory was becoming the typical experience of the wage-labourer and it was quite revolutionary, with a six-day 70 hour week for man, woman and child labourer alike. To break a workforce into this new discipline it was necessary to transform the whole of their lives, even that small part spent outside the factory walls. Control was easier if 'suitable' modes of conduct could assume the form of ingrained habit. Holidays, a threat to profit and an invitation to vice, were a particular target. By 1834 there were just four Bank holidays when some eighty years before there had been seventeen.

If opportunities for leisure decreased, so did legally permitted outlets. There is some dispute amongst historians as to exactly when, and with what effect, a wholesale attack on the customary pastimes of the people took place. But there is agreement that such an assault happened and that it reached a pitch of intensity around the 1840s. The increasing success of this suppression of popular culture was due to the formidable combination of punitive legislation and effective policing through which it was exercised.

Three acts of Parliament may serve as examples. The Poor Law of 1834 had cultural as well as economic effects. Its provisions could be and were used to control and eliminate the infra-structure of popular culture. Travelling balladeers, entertainers and itinerant salesmen, could from this point be defined as vagabonds and be returned to their parish of origin. In 1835 the Highways Act was designed to clear the streets of nuisances, in the definition of which football players and street entertainers or traders rated highly. In the same year the Cruelty to Animals Act was passed. Confined to domestic animals, so as not to interfere with their lordships' predilection for huntin' shootin' and fishin', this was specifically aimed at popular animal sports. Such legislation was rigorously enforced by regular police forces which began to appear in many towns and cities from the 1830s.

This portrait of a sustained and largely successful onslaught on the amusements of the people has led some historians to portray the 1840s as a 'bleak age', bereft of any chance to play. More recently others have argued that this is an oversimplification, since this period also contains much evidence of indigenous working-class cultural activity. Friendly Societies, the Co-operative movement, Chartism, and Owenite socialism hardly indicate a working class shorn of initiative. Even in more narrowly defined leisure activities, strategies of avoidance were available. Many activities declared illegal, such as cockfighting, simply went underground. Others survived in muted form, even in the absence of patronage and the presence of hostility; among these were fairs and pugilism. Some, to which no moral objections were raised, actually gained in popularity; such was the case with cricket, for which occasional five-figure crowds were recorded from early in the century. There were also some successful innovations often mixing the old and the new: popular theatre, pantomime, the circus and from the late 1840s, railway excursions.

Yet many of these remained exceptional, in the nature of special events. For more routine leisure, the mass of the populace was driven back to the tavern. This sole surviving institution of popular culture offered, in addition to the relief of alcohol, heat, light, sociability, reading, games and animal sports. After the Beer Act of 1830 publicans sought to extend the range of amusements to compete with gin houses. In particular they sought to offer organised entertainment. The 'free and easies' and saloons, so important to the later development of the music hall, date from this period.

Not all members of the ruling groups were content with a situation where the free time of the workforce, such as it was, might be exploited by the merchants of drink or the messengers of socialism. Paternalist attempts to provide more respectable yet viable alternatives met with mixed success. The Sunday schools began to extend their originally rather narrow religious brief to incorporate temperance parties and outings, which met positive responses from parents and children. The Mechanics Institutes, however, were less sucessful. Neither the high cost of subscriptions nor the censorship of literature and lecture content were appreciated by their potential public. Yet such moves did indicate the beginnings of a shift of attitude amongst at least some sections of the bourgeoisie. 'Rational recreation' became a slogan, if not for an organised movement, then for a slowly diffusing mood. In addition to what were often local initiatives, legislation began to appear, designed to enable local authorities to levy a rate for a number of leisure provisions. The Museums Act of 1845, the Baths and Wash-houses Act of 1846, the Libraries Act of 1850, had little immediate impact, but the way had been cleared for local councils to act, if and when they wished. And since the Ten Hours Act of 1847 aimed at controlling conditions of child labour had some effect on adults' working hours, some signs of improvement were evident.

The pattern, then, is complex. Many traditional amusements were suppressed, yet some continued and others actually grew. In and around the pub, small-scale entrepreneurship anticipated later commercial exploitation of the working class market. Municipal initiatives were as yet few but the incorporation of leisure into the evolving scope of local government had been started.

The precise impact of the attack on popular culture and the extent to which it was circumvented remain a matter for some substantial historical debate. Yet looking overall at the trends evident by the 1840s, the clearest impression is of the wholesale changes in the rhythms and sites of work and leisure enforced by the industrial revolution. It was during this period that what we have come to see as a discrete area of human activity called 'leisure' became recognisable. But, contrary to the account offered by sociological orthodoxy, it did not develop in any simple linear fashion, as an aspect of industrialised progress. It was enforced from above as a form of social control, by magistrates, clergymen, policemen, millowners, poor law commissioners. Its rationale was in the end, despite religious and moral camouflage, that of the economic system. It concerned, most simply, the taming of a workforce. There may even be in qualitative terms a loss here: leisure becomes demarcated from work as a reaction to, and compensation for it. This antithesis of work and leisure, from which so many contemporary accounts begin, is not a given social fact, but an historical creation. That people may gain in leisure satisfactions they do not derive from work is not a psychological but an historical phenomenon. The form industrialisation took in the mid-nineteenth century ensured that what was an artificial imposition would be taken for granted by succeeding generations, including some of its most influential scholars of leisure.

One key element in the construction of this segregation of work and leisure is the changing status of the family in different social classes. In this period, it is possible to trace the emergence of the Victorian ideal of domesticity within bourgeois culture. The affirmation of the home-as-haven to be tended by the women, awaiting the return of her husband from the male worlds of business and politics, shaped both bourgeois family life and its aggressive public ideology.

Within the working class, the growing concentration of production in factories eroded the operation of the family as a producing unit. It is also a period in which women workers came increasingly to be seen as a source of competition by the male working class. There was a sharpening of attempts to demarcate 'women's work' (e.g. in clothing) from the occupations and trades which were exclusively male.

In these different class contexts we can discern the outlines of a sexual content to the separation of work and leisure, based on the equation of work with paid employment as a masculine sphere, and the home as the private sphere of femininity. Thus the distinction between work and leisure, and between public and private spheres were inflected with the imagery of gender difference: work–public–male versus home–private–female worlds. We have already seen the trouble which this 'layering' of different meanings which surround work/leisure has caused for contemporary theories of leisure. In this historical period, we encounter them at the moment of their formation. The struggles to define the boundaries of these separate spheres have not yet been won, but the lines of demarcation have been drawn on the map of British society.

The 1880s: 'Coronation Streets'

Contemporary observers and subsequent historians were struck by the absence of leisure time and opportunity in the 1840s; by the 1880s it is the expanding presence of leisure which has been most noted. The orthodox portrait of leisure in and around this period situates recognition of the right to leisure and provision of the means to enjoy it as a symptom of the increasing confidence and democratisation of Victorian Britain. The emphasis is on the growth of leisure under exceedingly favourable conditions: shorter working hours, slowly rising standards of living, a greater municipal provision, proliferating voluntary activity, commercial innovation.

But, once again, this model of simple linear growth disguises a multitude of influences and cross-currents, especially hiding from view versions of leisure at variance with that which was eventually to dominate. Above all, this evolutionary account does not explain the apparent change in the attitude of ruling groups towards popular cultural activity. What happened to the stern nonconformist conscience so that by the 1880s it was prepared to contemplate, if not with a smile then at least without a frown, such disparate but widely enjoyed leisure activities as railway excursions, the music hall and professional football?

At least four essential processes were at work underneath the superficial expansion of leisure opportunities from the 1850s and 1860s onwards. The first was a significant reorientation of middle-class leisure which, sometimes by accident sometimes by design, was extended downwards into the working classes. The second was the expansion of local government into the area of leisure provision and control. The third process was a new kind of commercialism: new in its dependence on heavy capitalisation, mass audiences and formal licensing. The fourth, often present within the others but more rarely achieving a degree of autonomy, was the attempt by the working class to organise leisure according to its own values and aspirations – or at least those of its adult male members.

In 1851 Britain had become statistically an urban society. By the 1880s, not individual towns and cities, but conurbations had come to dominate: in 1881 two-fifths of the English population lived in the main six conurbations (London, South East Lancashire, the

West Midlands, West Yorkshire, Merseyside and Tyneside). Three-quarters of the population lived in families whose principal wage earner was of the manual labouring class. Despite the already evident tendency of the capitalist economy to cycles of expansion and depression, real working class incomes rose by 40 per cent in the fifteen years after 1860 and by another 50 per cent by the turn of the century. Diet improved with spending power: meat, fish and fruit might now be afforded. Multiple stores, including the Co-operative Society, expanded to take account of this new if marginal element of disposable working class income. There was even the first mode of transport designed specifically for a working class wanting, and able to pay for, short distance travel – the tram.

There was also now greater national uniformity in the regularity and duration of employment which further institutionalised the demarcation between work and leisure. Yet even here, ambiguities arise over any simple interpretation of these tendencies as a kind of progress, much less as a result of upper class generosity. The Bank Holiday Act of 1871, extended in 1875 and afterwards, is often portrayed as an altruistic or concessionary gesture, yet it was never originally intended to apply to the whole community but to bank workers. The extension to other trades was not disinterested. Like the Saturday half-holiday which spread from Lancashire in the 1850s, it could be understood as a sophisticated strategy to control absenteeism, especially the obdurate tradition of Saint Monday. The concession of defined periods of free time had, as its price, the tightening of control over work attendance. Similarly, the Factory Acts of 1850, 1867, and 1874 did protect workers, especially children, in many trades from the twelve hour day, yet such measures were not opposed as strenuously as they might have been by employers, precisely because they now recognised that profits rested as much on the intensity with which labour could be exploited within a fixed time as on the length of the working day. 'Productivity' emerges as the new goal of the capitalist and his managers in this period.

The reasons for the concession of leisure time and opportunities were ambiguous and contradictory, the consequences frequently unforeseen and unintended. This was also true of the first of the four processes underlying leisure expansion: the reorientation of 'bourgeois' leisure. The working classes benefited from new attitudes towards leisure which first originated within the ruling class towards its own free time. The concession to the majority of the population of public leisure activity was possible only because the powerful minority had first made the concession to itself. In their early nineteenth century attempt to differentiate their life style from both the decadence of the aristocracy and the brutality of the common people, the industrial bourgeoisie had become prisoners of their own morality. Sobriety, thrift and domesticity left little room for any morally legitimate forms of public leisure. Bourgeois leisure had been forced to become privatised; entertainment was home-based, centring on religion, reading and music, occasionally supplemented by annual holidays at the seaside. While this was held to be sufficient for the bourgeois woman and girl and while adult males could absorb themselves in their work and obtain illicit pleasures elsewhere, the problem of young bourgeois males proved more intractable. It was as an outlet for their pent up energies and as part of a more ordered pattern of socialisation that organised sport emerged.

The roots of organised sport in the public schools have been well documented. The encouragement of organised sport was simultaneously a means of controlling the characteristically anarchic behaviour of public schoolboys and of redirecting the public school ethos towards a model of what would subsequently be defined as 'muscular Christianity'. Thus both the traditional clientele of the aristocracy and the new market of the sons of the bourgeoisie could be retained for the public schools, refurbishing an image tarnished by low morality and dubious academic accomplishment.

Football is the paradigm. It built upon a tradition of football which had persisted in public school cloisters long after it had been banished from the streets. The first set of rules was drafted at Cambridge in 1862, the Football Association was founded in 1863, a Challenge Cup inaugurated in 1872. With missionary zeal, ex-public schoolboys took the game out of the schools and into the cities, but in doing so lost their control over it. In 1885, after a protracted struggle, the FA was forced to recognise professionalism and in 1888 a Football League, based in the north and the midlands, was begun. Control passed to local businessmen, running clubs as a form of patronage for working class audiences. What had begun as a moral crusade had become in twenty-five years a form of commercialised mass entertainment. In the south, the 'amateur ethos' persisted longer, delaying the entry of southern clubs into the league. The Rugby Union, founded in 1871, so set its face against broken time payments (as incipient professionalism was known) that an alternative Rugby League was set up in the north in 1895.

Such examples have led to some simple interpretations of the growth of organised sport as an act of downward cultural dissemination by aristocracy and bourgeoisie. Yet some sports were not disseminated in this way: tennis, cycling and golf clubs aimed to exclude, not incorporate, working-class presence. Further, there is also evidence of the middle class appropriating for itself sports which had previously been the province of the working class. Such was the case with cricket. The inauguration of a county cricket championship in 1873 in fact represented a middle-class monopolisation of a sport which throughout the 1840s and 1850s, in the form of touring professional teams, had relied on working-class players and spectators. The 'heroism' of W. G. Grace was class-based, since his great achievement was to demonstrate that 'gentlemen' could consistently beat 'professionals', thus validating a class domination of county cricket which was to last until the 1950s. Similar patterns of middle and upper class domination of rules, organising bodies and ethos, even where many adherents were from the lower social orders, was present in such sports as rowing and athletics. Thus a patronising attitude towards working class participants was established, exacerbated if they had the temerity to earn their living through sport. This Victorian legacy of amateurism has been inherited by modern British sport, largely to its detriment.

Thus while organised sport was often advocated because of its potential to remove class differences and create common male fellowship, in practice it did not remove class differences but reproduced them with varying degrees of transparency. Where there were apparent class alliances around sport, they were rarely alliances of equals. In general terms it might be said that what the middle and upper classes brought to sport were primarily the resources of time, capital and organisational skill; the working classes brought energy, raw talent and a paying public. How such an alliance worked out depended largely on the reaction to pressures for professionalisation; the subsequent history of individual sports is shaped by the way in which this dilemma was handled.

Organised sport represented an innovation in male upper class leisure. There were complementary adaptations of existing forms towards a less repressive pattern. Religious influences, for example, withdrew from a position of implacable opposition to anything resembling enjoyment, to a point where they became advocates of Godly recreation.

Such developments represented both a loosening of control by the middle classes over their own leisure and a recognition that, if the working classes were going to have leisure anyway, it was better that it should be directed towards more acceptable activities. Throughout the 1860s and 1870s, groups of middle class reformers had come to see that it was not enough simply to forbid most forms of leisure, especially as this strengthened the attractions of the public house. Thus the emphasis shifted towards the provision of alternatives, designed to supplant more immoral forms. This advocacy of 'rational' recreation was an influential ideal, but its practical successes were few.

The enthusiasm for fostering 'rational recreation' within the male working class was paralleled by an equal enthusiasm for encouraging 'rational domesticity' among working class women. From the 1870s onwards, one substantial focus of philanthropic activity is 'home visiting' of the poor. Although most philanthropic societies were organised and run by men, the task of visiting was entrusted to women, who, it was believed, would be able to use the affinity of their gender to bridge the gulf of class. This form of philanthropy, aimed at assisting working class women to become more competent home makers, contained a complex paradox of class and gender. Although allowing bourgeois women a legitimate route of escape from the confines of the domestic ideal, this escape involved them in educating their working class counterparts in the virtues of that same ideal. Like the Mechanics' Institutes, the philanthropic societies were not completely successful in their 'civilising' task, creating a fund of working class hostility (among men and women) to moralising intrusion.

By contrast, some initiatives in the field of rational recreation met with rather more success, especially where they drew on existing elements of popular culture. Such was the case with music. The choral societies of the 1850s and the spread of the brass band movement, peaking in the 1880s, were often patronised by employers and churches as 'improving' forms of recreation. And they were extensively supported by working class men, for whom music in both religious and folk forms was far from an alien influence.

But the real success of the 'rational' recreationists, apparently without much working class support or agitation, was in the second process underlying the leisure explosion of the 1880s. This was the active involvement of the new local authorities in leisure provision. The enabling legislation of the 1840s was increasingly implemented in the subsequent half-century. In its earliest form, it consisted of donations of land and buildings to the council by local entrepreneurs or aristocrats. By the 1870s, corporations were actually purchasing land to provide open space and public parks. Parks were not all. Though by 1885 only a quarter of the population had access to a public library, there had been virtually none forty years before. Swimming baths were also appearing as badges of municipal enterprise. There were still severe restrictions on the use of such facilities: games were banned from parks and libraries' stocks were censored. But the principle of the public provision of leisure out of the rates and with little or no direct charge, had been established.

There was, however, another side to local government's involvement in leisure, which was in the long run to have equal importance to the provision of public facilities. This stemmed from the introduction of organised police forces under the Metropolitan Police Acts of 1829 and 1839, the Municipal Corporations Act of 1835 and the County Police Act of 1839. The effects of this, like other legislation, took time to become apparent. The control of crime was part of a wider brief to maintain public order. As defined by local magistrates this involved clearing the streets of nuisances. One of the biggest nuisances was popular culture.

The new police forces were regulatory and intrusive, constant watchers over working class life, especially that of the street. Their role as 'domestic missionaries', controllers of all forms of public cultural life, provoked some violent resistance, through the 1840s and beyond. But, more typically, there were attempts to evade police supervision by pursuing 'illegal' leisure activities at times and in places the police were unlikely to encompass. Yet the police were soon evident as a presence at almost any public activity – at fairs and wakes, at holiday times and resorts, inside pubs and music halls and, above all, on the streets. Those who regarded streets as thoroughfares and shopping parades now had the power to enforce this definition on the recalcitrant vestiges of popular culture, from street trading to children's games of pitch and toss.

In addition to this daily supervision, the police now gained additional power as a result of moves to license places of entertainment. The police, then and now, had this double function: not only could they immediately enforce an infinitely elastic set of laws but they could also object, on the vaguest grounds of perceived immorality or disorder, to the renewal of licences.

The shape of things to come

Licensing policies were a means of controlling and channelling the increasing commercialisation of leisure, which is the third process evident in the 1880s. To describe this as 'commercialisation' is too simple, since even the humblest street entertainer had always been involved in a commercial relationship with his or her public. What characterised the 'new' commercialism was its heavy capitalisation, the consequent need to control demand to guarantee profit, and its ultimate dependence on the State for legal sanction. A simple model of leisure growth cannot do justice to the complexity of this development, whose shape we can sketch by taking the music hall as an example.

Like almost every other leisure activity hailed as 'new', the music hall had its prototypes. Following the Beer Act of 1820, which has loosened restrictions on licensing, many 'drinking saloons' had sprung up. Catering for the 'lower' sort of customer, these included half-organised singing as an integral part of their attraction. By the 1840s publicans, realising the potential for increased sales, began to introduce 'penny gaffs' and 'free and easies', where organised music-based entertainment was designed to draw audiences and thus their drinking custom. That this function could be hived off from the public house was demonstrated by the success of the Bolton Star, the first specialist music hall opened in 1840, followed by similar enterprises in Southwark (1848) and Lambeth (1851). In the 1850s and 1860s greater capitalisation was evident, especially after limited liability companies were permitted in 1864. By 1866 London had 33 music halls with an average capitalisation of £10 000 and a seating capacity of 500, with between two and three hundred smaller halls in the provinces.

However, the authorities did not take lightly the spread of entertainment venues where large crowds habitually gathered. The potential for drunkenness, prostitution, ribaldry and even subversion was considerable. From 1860 the London Music Hall Proprietors' Association was formed to argue and negotiate with the licensing authorities. The precise details of this negotiation are too complex to relate here. But what emerged in the 1880s as the institution of the music hall was radically different from what had existed forty or fifty years before. Gone were drink, food and most of the prostitutes. Tables and chairs had been replaced by fixed rows of seats; and semi-professional and amateur performers had been supplanted by full-time professionals tightly controlled by contract, including guarantees that they would not include in their acts any material 'offensive' to political figures and institutions. In short, what had happened was that magistrates, police and music-hall proprietors had worked out an agreement to their mutual advantage. The more 'deviant' potential of the music hall, especially the behaviour of performers and audience, had been eliminated. In return, as it were, drinking saloons were systematically refused licences on the grounds of potential disorder.

Given the apparently insatiable working-class demand for entertainment, it suited both public and private interests to promote the most organised and orderly forms. The activity was licensed, specialised and professionalised; popular culture incorporated. Of course, it was not exactly how magistrates and moral reformers would have liked the working classes to have spent their time. The mixture of comedy and sentiment, acrobats and dramatic tableaux, audience vociferousness and communal singing had to reflect something of the texture of working-class experience. The result was hardly 'rational'. Yet it could be, and was, carefully controlled. Essentially the same model was applied to the similarly capitalised funfairs and circuses which institutionalised longstanding elements in popular culture. Thus as a form of heavily capitalised mass-based leisure, licensed by the State, the music hall, rooted in the past, pointed to the future.

If the elimination of drink from the music hall was one of the essentials in its taming, the elimination of drink from the lives of the working population proved more difficult than ever. Indeed, during the 1880s per capita drinking, drunkenness and Exchequer revenue (alcohol provided 43 per cent of all tax revenue in

1879–80) reached an all-time high. This was despite, or perhaps because, the pub began to lose many of its functions as a social as well as a drinking institution. After the mid-century attack on popular culture, the pub had become the locus for a range of activities, from animal sport to Friendly Society meetings. This spatial monopoly of the pub had been undermined by a number of the factors already discussed: alternative places of entertainment, public leisure provision, the increasing independence of trade unions, the prohibition of gambling and games. The police became an even more important factor after the Licensing Act of 1872, which gave magistrates absolute discretion over licensing, restricted late and Sunday opening, and increased penalties for drunkenness, serving children and the adulteration of beer.

The pub could not be abolished, if only because of the substantial political power of the brewing interests. But it could be, and was, policed. Its functions became much more specialised: singing and dancing did not disappear, but were muted. Fewer ancillary activities were evident: the pub's diffuse social role was becoming narrowed to the sale of alcohol. Customers who sought to extend sociability beyond limited forms would henceforth have to go to what middle class patrons, local government and the new leisure entrepreneurs between them provided in the mixed economy of leisure.

What is striking about this whole period is how little of the expanded leisure activity was indigenous to the working class. Then as now, no doubt, much leisure was informal, street and neighbourhood based, only partly visible to the historian. One exception proved the rule. The working men's club movement was a rare example of the fourth process in the leisure of the 1880s: working class self-activity. Even this had its roots in middle class patronage. The Club and Institute Union, founded in 1862 with 23 member clubs, was originally part of a movement led by one the Reverend Henry Solly, to wean working men off drink by providing attractive temperance clubs. Yet by 1875, after a protracted struggle, the leadership had passed into working class hands. Their quite different conception of the clubs was indicated by their immediate decision of that year to start selling alcohol, a move which ensured financial independence. By 1883 they had over half a million members. They remained, in ethos and organisation, exclusively working class male preserves. They often had a political edge soon to be blunted, not least by the conviction that 'politics' did not belong in an institution devoted to entertainment. This acceptance of the compartmentalisation of life-work, family and leisure in separate spheres – was a crucial outcome of leisure developments in the 1880s. That it could so successfully penetrate one of the few activities run by working class men for themselves, is a measure of its strength.

In subsequent decades, there were recurrent attempts to promote working class leisure activities which were public, self-organised and involved collective participation. The two main areas of activity form an interesting contrast with the world of the working man's clubs. One was education, where efforts at collective self-improvement took such diverse forms as the Plebs League and the Workers' Educational Association. The second was the efforts to escape the cities and gain access to the countryside through organisations such as the Clarion cycling clubs and the Ramblers' Associations. This thread of collective 'self-determination' in working class leisure was simultaneously tenuous and tenacious in the face of the growing dominance of state and commercial provision. Its appearances in working class leisure activity were uneven and fragmentary, but it nevertheless formed a persistently recurring theme in the way the British working class approached their free time.

Separate spheres

Thus, if we must talk about the 'growth' of leisure at the end of the nineteenth century, we should recognise the conditions under which this growth took place and how they affected the shape and nature of what grew. Leisure did not 'grow' because people had more free time or more money, along lines which now seem obvious. Leisure did not and does not have a trajectory of its own. All the processes we have identified as shaping the growth of leisure in the 1880s – the reorientation of middle class morality, the expansion of local government initiative, extensive entrepreneurship, rare instances of working class self-activity – reflected the economic, political and cultural ideas and institutions of a conurbated, industrialised, patriarchal and capitalist society. The pattern of leisure need not have been determined by these factors, but it was, in three main ways: it was *segregated*, *specialised* and *institutionalised*.

It was *segregated* in several senses. First it was segregated in time and space from the rest of life. Leisure was made to appear as compensation, retreat, escape from the material struggle to live. It was also class segregated: it is simply difficult to find any leisure activity which was not exclusively the province of one class or reflective, in however transmuted a way, of class antagonism. Next, and by no means least, it was sexually segregated. Public leisure, even where women were admitted, meant a leisure defined by and for men. While some women, perhaps the younger and unmarried, might have free time, it would appear that for most middle class women it was forbidden; and for working class women committed to the double time of waged and domestic labour, it was non-existent.

If leisure was segregated as a sphere, its component parts had become more discrete and *specialised*. Though music, drink and sexuality appeared in many different kinds of activity, increasingly one particular focus was exclusive of others. Pubs were places for drinking, music halls for being entertained, football grounds for getting excited, parks for walking. Some space had been reclaimed for leisure from the enclosure of industrialisation, but as a series of individual allotments rather than open and common ground.

This segregated, specialised leisure was highly *institutionalised*. The capital required to initiate leisure activities could only come from public corporations and private companies. While it is true that for many, then as now, participation in formally organised leisure was the exception rather than the rule and that the life of street and neighbourhood exerted its own kind of attraction, the major forms of organised leisure were outside the control of those who enjoyed them. Certainly no mass leisure form, from professional football to the music hall, could ignore the needs of its audience, but the essential relationship was that of provider and customer. This relationship was increasingly mediated through the activities of the State. That its emphasis had changed from control-through-prohibition to control-through-licensing did not diminish its significance.

Many of the particular leisure forms emergent in the 1880s were subsequently displaced. The Victorian heritage of leisure is not the music hall or football, but the overall definition of organised leisure as segmented, specialised and institutionalised. Leisure was made in the image of Victorian capitalism. It was to change as the image of capitalism changed, not without difficulty or contestation, but always within the limits of moral, political and economic control established in the 1880s.

The 1920s: 'love on the dole'

It is apparently a paradox of twentieth century social history that from the mid-1920s onwards, increased unemployment and poverty were accompanied by increased amounts and varieties of leisure activity. Yet the paradox is only superficial, for those experiencing increased hardship were often in different social and geographical locations from those finding new ways to have a good time. What sharply divided leisure experiences during the period was access to the leisure market. As heavy industry found itself unable to compete in a shrinking world market, investment switched towards light engineering, chemical and electrical industries oriented to the home market. In terms of both goods and services, leisure was moving from a peripheral to a central position in the economy. But not all could participate as equal consumers in the marketplace of leisure: inequalities between men and women, adults and young people, northerners and southerners, rooted in the economic and political structure, were carried over into leisure. In this brief review of leisure developments in the period, we shall look at the introduction of some new leisure forms, the persistence of some old ones, underlying patterns of inequality and the tension between private and public definitions in provision of leisure.

Something old, something new

The prototype of the new amusement was the cinema. Moving picture shows had begun to appear in music halls early in the 1900s and expanded in the next twenty years. The 'silents' established themselves as an integral part of working class leisure. In 1926, there were well over 3000 cinemas in the UK, with a cumulative weekly attendance of 20 million; half of the patrons attended twice or more a week. They were predominantly young, female and working class.

For this group the cinema was more accessible and appropriate than anything before: available locally in a continuous but changing form, romantic and respectable on and off the screen. It was the first form of entertainment to appeal to, and come to be designed for, the leisure needs of women. As interpreted by Hollywood moguls, their needs were for fantasies which confirmed rather than challenged the conventional female role. The escape routes led to a larger than life variety of 'women's concerns' – emotion, romance and tragedy. But the breakthrough involved in a provision of leisure which, even in this restricted form, identified women as an audience is not to be underestimated.

If the cinema largely displaced the music hall, it also built upon it as a cultural form. Comedy, romance and drama were still the essential elements of early films, supplemented by song and dance after the introduction of 'talkies' from 1928. The cinema was also even more capitalised than the music hall. Following an early burst of activity by individual entrepreneurs, the trend was towards circuits of cinemas organised centrally by a small number of distributors. The organisational model, in which production, distribution and presentation were increasingly controlled by the same agencies, was American – as were most of the films, despite attempts at legislation aimed at protecting the British film industry.

American influence on commercial leisure forms was ubiquitous. Music, for example, had already gone through the first stage of commercialisation, with the sales of pianos and sheet music. Now the gramophone and records, not beyond the means of a household with a regular wage-earner, transformed the potential public and profit. America provided the music (not least the black-rooted jazz and swing), the exposure of stars through films and, of course, the records themselves. Such music was not just to be listened to. The *nouveaux riche* experimented with new dancing styles. A less affluent but potentially as profitable market was reached by the dance hall or 'palais' though the largest of these did not appear until the 1930s. Radio made what the BBC defined as 'light' music habitually available in the home. The number of radio licences increased dramatically: under thirty thousand in 1922, over two million by 1926, over nine and half million by 1939. The effect of any mass medium is never easy to judge but what radio may have done was to give a focus for home-based leisure involving the whole family, thus reinforcing tendencies evident elsewhere in the society.

By the 1920s, the ideology of a 'woman's place' had been firmly reestablished following temporary need for women as waged labour during the war. Their enforced return to the home was spurred on by the deals made between employers and male trade unions to guarantee that men would be given 'their' jobs back when peace broke out. The virtues of motherhood and domesticity so powerfully stressed at the end of the nineteenth century were put temporarily in cold storage during the war, but 1918 saw them taken out, dusted down and put back into circulation. 'Homes fit for heroes' were to be made not just by government building programmes, but also by the careful attention of wives and mothers.

The significance of family centred leisure was fostered not merely by these economic and ideological imperatives, but also by the changing geography of cities where new house building began to create a growing separation between employment and home. Thus, social geography buttressed the ideological segregation of work and leisure, while the home itself required more intensive domestic labour, on the part of wives and mothers, to keep it 'respectable'.

The relationship between geography and leisure was also visible in another emerging family centred activity – the annual holiday. It was not until the 1930s that paid holidays enabled the mass of the population to have a 'week away', perhaps at one of the newly opened holiday camps, but most could and did manage day trips to the seaside: each Bank Holiday saw a massive exodus from the industrial areas to the coast. A little more margin of spending power for those in work combined with quicker and cheaper transport facilities. To train and tram were added the 'charabanc' and even the motor bike, though cars remained the monopoly of the rich. Cheaper and healthier were cycling, hiking and rambling, enabling exploration of the countryside, occasionally resisted by landowning interests.

Cinema, music and dance, radio, the annual holiday, did represent a transformation of leisure opportunities. Though they supplanted some existing forms, notably the music hall, they also coexisted with older forms of entertainment which expanded and changed in this period. The most important of these were organised spectator sport, betting, drink and more informal kinds of working-class culture.

Keeping spirits high

Spectator sport was now regularly attracting massive crowds. Even the unemployed might scrape together the entrance fee for a cricket match, though the social tensions, between members and spectators, gentlemen and players, North and South, showed that cricket divided Englishmen even as it united them. More transparently a male working class sport was professional football. Two divisions were added to the league in 1922, making it a genuinely nationwide competition, though Northern and Midlands clubs continued to dominate. The shift to the South was not apparent until the rise of the Arsenal, when spiralling transfer fees (though not wages), ground investment and tactically-based management anticipated the trends which were to dominate the post-war game. But its economic base was secure: at a first division match, 20 000 was a poor attendance and many attendance records were set in this period.

Technology and the market did produce innovations in sport, notably cycle and car racing. Speedway threatened to become a major spectator sport in the late 1920s. But more indicative of the state of organised sport was the introduction of greyhound racing, for this owed its rationale to a continuous and expanding element of popular culture – betting.

Gambling had always been an integral part of popular leisure but did not become habitual and widespread until the 1880s, when the telegraph and the popular press made horse-racing results immediately available and improved economic conditions increased discretionary spending power. The result was an increase in the pervasiveness of betting. Despite the Street Betting Act of 1906 which forbade (working class) off-course cash betting while permitting (upper class) credit betting, illegal street bookmaking flourished. By the early 1930s its annual estimated turnover was between three and four million pounds, though most wagers were only sixpence or a shilling a time. It had become Britain's second largest industry. Football pools were introduced in a form designed to evade the Football League's fixture copyright from the early 1920s; when the companies and the league reached agreement in the early 1930s between ten and fifteen million people a week were weekly sending off postal orders totalling £800 000 to the pools companies.

That other stalwart of popular culture, drink, abated from the extremely high levels of consumption evident before the First World War. Yet the pub remained a central focus of working class leisure. Its real competitor was the working man's club. Now almost exclusively entertainment centres and cooperatives for the purchase of beer, it seems to have been in the interwar period that these quasi-autonomous leisure institutions underwent their greatest expansion. In York, at least, they increased threefold in number and eightfold in membership between 1900 and 1940.

The working men's club was only the most visibly institutionalised form of culture common to the working class from the 1880s through to the 1920s and beyond. Pigeon-racing is an example of an organised part of this culture which expanded substantially in the first thirty years of the century. Less gender segregated were chapels and Co-ops which continued to exert their very different (if ultimately not uncomplementary) influences on working class life; the working class neighbourhood became, if anything, more homogeneous as the middle class began their flight to suburbia.

It's still the same old story

It is perhaps necessary to insist that the leisure market did not eradicate inequality, of which class was only the most obvious dimension. Minorities are always excluded from mass markets if they will not or cannot pay for what is on offer. Often such groups are not minorities at all, but made to appear so by a shifting definition of who the majority are. In the leisure pattern of the 1920s the numbers excluded for one reason or another, appear to constitute a good part of the population. Region, class and gender were factors which differentiated access to the market and demonstrated its partial scope.

The simple fact about the interwar economy – whose ramifications are still being worked through – was that the recession devastated some areas, while others were left relatively unscathed and even experienced economic expansion. So while cinemas and working men's clubs may have been as common in the North as in the South, there was an increasing differential in spending power between those on the dole, in insecure or poorly paid employment and those who in relative terms were better off, because they had jobs which were secure and better paid. The whole definition of what constituted a skilled job and the security and remuneration which went with that status, shifted away from the heavy industry towards the lighter industry of the South. An image of increased access to leisure goods and services must be heavily qualified by contemporary accounts of whole communities demoralised by unemployment.

Emergent inequalities between regions were reinforced by gradual changes in the class structure. There never seems to have been a period when it was not possible to argue that the upper reaches of the working class were, in terms of objective conditions or subjective identification, more like those above them than below them in the class structure. In the 1920s some specific changes in the occupational structure especially in the south indicated that manual labour, so often and mistakenly held to define the working class, was declining. The growth of professions, civil servants and administrators, middle management and the office staff who serviced them contributed to an increase in the 'salaried class' from 12 per cent of the working population in 1911 to 22 per cent in 1921. In a sense, it was this group which inherited the Victorian mantle of leisure respectability and rational recreation, just as their betters, or at least their betters' children, were abandoning it. The *nouveaux riche* young, financially secure physically mobile, reverted to what had been originally the aristocratic mode of conspicuous consumption. With access to a car almost anything was possible. Cabarets and night clubs, a merry-go-round of eating drinking and dancing, whirled them through the post-war period. Trips to the coast or continent became routine. With an indifference which now seems stunning, they pronounced the 1920s to be gay.

Neither the wealthy decadence of the *nouveaux riche* nor the working-class predilection for mass entertainment provided a model for the sober, industrious and often impecunious lower middle class. It was this group, in a sometimes desperate and not always financially viable search for respectability (so subtly evoked in the novels of George Orwell), which placed particular emphasis on the home: a modest, mortgaged suburban house with a garden, or at least as near to it as the family could afford. Hobbies, evening classes, church activities, gardening and do-it-yourself (encouraged by the introduction of plywood), the evenings spent round the radio, constituted a leisure pattern which was to become more influential after the next war.

The family orientation of this kind of leisure may have ameliorated the situation of some women; if they were tied to the home, at least hubby chose to spend much of his leisure time there too. But more generally gender remained a major source of inequality in access to and enjoyment of leisure. For the leisure market extended only to select groups of women; those with marginal spending power. Thus unmarried working girls and women may have been able to afford silk stockings and cosmetics, and had the time and energy to join their friends in the dance hall or cinema, at the pub or on the street corner. They may also have been allowed more freedom by parents gradually abandoning the more rigid aspects of Victorian values. Yet ironically enough many of these girls and women would themselves be employed in service and leisure industries, which were becoming the new sweated trades. The cinema usherette, working unsocial hours for low wages, suffering from boredom and sore feet, was a symptomatic figure – the invisible support of the glittering world of the 'dream palace'.

In any case this period of leisure freedom and consumption was all too brief. Despite a birth-rate falling steadily throughout the interwar period, marriage brought the acceptance of family responsibilities. Time, energy and money were in short supply, not to mention husbands' expectations and prohibitions. Home was where the woman belonged and had to be. The 'democracy' of leisure brought about by large-scale commerce had a place for the woman but only in the narrow role of domestic consumer.

This role of domestic consumer was coming to play a more significant part in the operations of British capitalism between the wars. The decline of traditional heavy manufacturing and the loss of export markets, coupled with the development of new technologies and a plentiful supply of cheap labour, produced an increasing variety of goods and services aimed at the home market. The mass production of relatively cheap clothing, food and household goods was accompanied by the 'retailing revolution' of high street multiple stores (Woolworths, Marks and Spencer, Sainsbury's,

Lipton's, etc.) and the expansion of advertising (£100 million by 1938). The 'home' market meant the home in both senses – and the woman (as keeper of the household budget) was groomed for the key supporting role in this change of economic direction.

The economically-rooted expansion of leisure in the 1920s was to extend into the 1930s and to expand almost beyond recognition in the 1960s. It did represent a significant shift in the extent to which mass market forces shaped the nature of leisure. Yet continuity was nevertheless apparent. If anything, the essential characteristics of leisure emergent in the 1880s, of segregation, specialisation and institutionalisation, were intensified in the later period. If they became more complex, less transparent in appearance, they did not diminish in significance.

First, *segregation*. Temporally, though cinema and radio extended into the weekday evening, the weekend – pay-day, the pub, football, dancing – remained the hub of leisure activity. The institution of the annual holiday reproduced symptomatically the division between work and life which leisure embodied: people would scrimp and save all year to 'let themselves go' for a week. Spatially too, leisure was separated from work, either in the retreat of home or in the places specially provided by private or public enterprise. Segregations of class and gender remained strong, supplemented by powerful regional differences.

Specialisation was a tendency reinforced by the concern with mass markets. Cinemas and football grounds were neither designed nor intended for anything other than specialised activities. Only reluctantly did local authorities admit that parks might legitimately be the place for the playing of ball games. Neither private capital nor State providers had any interest in providing flexible sites for leisure activity. Though street and community based leisure and some kinds of voluntary activity incorporated a variety of leisure forms, leisure institutions were increasingly aimed at attracting discrete bodies of leisure consumers rather than the public in general.

Finally, *institutionalisation*. The logic of the mass market was precisely to recoup profit through small returns on large numbers: football, the cinema, betting, even the sale of radio sets, rested on this premise. Hence new leisure forms were increasingly innovated, or at least exploited, by large scale business. While the state retained a regulatory role over licensing hours, censorship of films and supposedly over betting, and the police continued their constant supervision, government had clearly abdicated most direct power to commercial control. The level of public activity was strikingly low compared to preceding and succeeding periods. One notable exception was broadcasting, where fears of the crassness of American-style commercialism and its propagandist potential led to the creation of the nominally independent and avowedly paternalist British Broadcasting Corporation. Although, even here, the creation of a state institution owed much to the concern of radio manufacturers to ensure that a steady flow of programmes was available.

The control exercised by the average citizen over his (or more occasionally her) leisure remained apparently a kind of freedom: whether to spend it at home, in the community or to take advantage of what commerce or State provided. But *spend* it they must, and increasingly in ways mediated by the market. The control was increasingly that of the consumer: to pay or not to pay. By the 1960s, the capacity of the leisure public to pay, and what it could pay for, had been extended still further.

The 1960s: 'You've never had it so good'

To write historically about a period as close to our own as the 1960s is extremely difficult. The period merges imperceptibly into what we think of as contemporary society. There is a wealth of some kinds of evidence, especially from surveys of leisure expenditure and participation, yet virtually no collated evidence on equally important factors, such as ownership and control of leisure industries. Interpretation is consequently hazardous, not helped by academic divisions of discipline. The post-war period is too modern for the traditional focus of the historian; it has been dominated by sociologists whose grasp of history is frequently uncertain. The most that we can do here is to trace descriptively some of the significant changes in leisure during the 1960s and to relate them to some of the themes which have emerged from consideration of previous historical periods. Six such trends will be identified: the rising standards of domestic consumption; the family-centredness of leisure and the consequent decline of traditional public forms; the emergence of youth cultures; the establishment of ethnic leisure cultures; increased State activity within prescribed spheres; commercial domination of leisure institutions and services, on a scale and in an organisational form of a quite new kind.

More thematically, these may be interpreted through recognition of: the enduring differentials of leisure along the structure of class, gender, age and increasingly, of race; the primacy of the family as site and unit of leisure consumption; the interaction – mutually exclusive, jointly dominant – of provision by the State and commerce; the establishment of leisure, even in its most public form, as the extension of private consumption; the economic fragility of the 'consumer revolution' and the ambiguity of the values it sought to express.

In the years immediately following the Second World War, the leisure patterns of a society, released from the tension of war into the austere economic consequences, was a straightforward expansion of those activities inherited from the pre-war era. During the 1940s, both football and the cinema recorded their highest ever annual attendances; the pub, dance halls, and betting continued to be both communal and commercial; the annual holiday expanded under the influence of the Holidays with Pay Act of 1938, though most of the population still spent their holidays at home. Living standards, too, altered little, especially with the effect of rationing. Imaginative effort is required to appreciate that as late as the early 1950s, Britain was a land of austerity, of rationing of basic goods and import restriction; a Britain without detergents or synthetic fibres, where home ownership, central heating and even washing machines were the monopoly of the better off; a Britain whose educational and health systems were only slowly becoming comprehensive in their coverage; and where mobility for work or leisure was limited.

Fings ain't wot they used to be

To those who lived through or attempted to observe and record the late 1950s and early 1960s, the sense of change was sweeping and profound. It could even, in its more tangible manifestations, be measured. Ownership of consumer durables, the most obvious sign of what was to be called 'affluence', spread rapidly downwards, so that ownership, first of electric irons, vacuum cleaners, washing machines, then of refrigerators and televisions, became by the end of the 1960s the experience of a majority of families. Such families were increasingly buying their own homes on mortgages and the less affluent were removed from back street rented accommodation to council houses and flats. A car, too, albeit a second hand one, was a realistic aspiration for the statistically 'average' family by the early 1970s.

The newness, the sense of release and enjoyment, provoked by these changes were real enough, yet the economic base was old. It was essentially an extension, under even more favourable circumstances, of the realisation, first evident in the 1880s and growing apace in the 1920s, that the working class was a potential market for more than just the essentials of existence. The twin strategy of advertising and credit terms had already proven its worth. Both were rapidly expanded to the point where the whole nation was in hock: in 1958 the collective national debt (at 1971 prices) stood at 685 thousand million pounds; it was to multiply fivefold in the next eighteen years.

Deferred payment had to be at the heart of the consumer revolution, since increased discretionary spending power was too small to enable large cash purchases. This increase did, however, allow for small changes in the way households proportioned their expenditure. More was spent on housing and transport, less on food; more on alcohol, less on tobacco; while expenditure on clothing, consumer goods and general services remained proportionately steady.

Nevertheless, the change was experienced as dramatic. Real disposable income doubled from 1951 to 1972, and, crucially, was not outstripped by price increases. This income was spent in ways oriented to the needs of the family, itself undergoing demographic change. Trends towards earlier marriage and childrearing did not, despite the 'baby boom' of the early 1960s, prevent the expansion of the (largely part-time) employment of married women, especially since new contraceptive techniques enabled control over the number and timing of child births. Much of the increase in 'family income' was attributable to this factor.

Private lives

The interaction of technological and economic change appeared to transform cultural patterns. Preference for a family based life style, in which time and money were spent on family entertainment, affected those forms of leisure which took place outside the home, e.g., the supplanting of cinema going by the television. Equally vulnerable were leisure activities appealing exclusively to men, such as football matches. Such male-dominated froms of leisure had previously been an escape from physical conditions or social obligations perceived as similar to those of work. Men now appeared to see home, not pub or club, as the basis of non-work. The basic division of domestic labour, between the roles of husband/father and wife/mother, may have remained immutable in its fundamentals. But, at the same time, men became more involved with their children, undertook many of their leisure activities with the family as a group, put more energy into work-in-leisure activities like improving the internal and external appearance of the house, made extensions of family life into their hobbies, such as looking after the garden or the car. The expansion of home-centredness seems to have involved the creation of an array of 'male' tasks on top of the day-to-day domestic labour which remained 'woman's work'.

Such changes are difficult to quantify, much less interpret. There were counter-trends, especially an increased level of participation in organised sport by young men. Sociologists differed as to whether these changes represented a 'normative convergence' between middle-class and working-class life styles or whether they were merely an adaptation of previously suppressed but still quintessentially working-class aspirations. 'Affluence' and 'privatisation' became the key concepts used to analyse such trends, beneath which there lurked, as image or hypothesis, the classless society. One central piece of evidence, used by some to argue the classlessness position, others to emphasise the enduring presence of class, was the emergence of 'youth culture'.

Talking 'bout my generation

Youth, more particularly male youth, has a long history as a problem for agencies of socialisation. That a new word – 'teenager' – was imported to emphasise the uniqueness of a particular stage of life, does not of itself indicate real social change. Yet it was certainly felt that young people were visible as never before; and there were some genuine changes in their cultural position. The roots, yet again, were economic. In a labour-hungry economy, entrants to work could command relatively high wages. Families had less need for their money and more liberal attitudes were taken towards control over their leisure. Teenagers' exploration of this new found freedom was not about to be ignored by a market geared to leisure consumption.

The key elements in youth culture were in many ways not new at all. Music and dance, fads and fashions, clothing and hairstyles, soft and alcoholic drinks, coffee bars and dance halls, were hardly revolutionary foci for the leisure of young people. And much of it remained in its accustomed place: on the street corner. But from the late 1950s the scale, style and visibility of youth culture changed: it pervaded the society. The scale was that of mass marketing: new technologies of record production enabled the production of cheaper records; synthetic fibres did the same for clothes. Small-scale entrepreneurs opened dance halls and cafés; guitars could be bought on hire purchase. Stylistically, youth culture placed a premium on display: the emotionality of pop concerts, the physicality of individually expressive dances, the overt sexuality of musical rhythms and lyrics, the ownership and exposure of the latest fashions. Even the BBC was affected. The suppression of the highly successful pirate radio stations in the mid-1960s provoked the reorganisation of its radio services. Radio One began broadcasting in 1967. Scale and style combined to make this youth culture visible in schools, on the streets in shops and on the air waves: the sounds and sights of the swinging sixties.

The 1960s established the paradoxes of youth culture: it was the most transparently commercialised form of leisure yet the least predictable (with supply often chasing demand); homogeneous yet fragmented; public in many of its venues, private in its pattern of consumption. Perhaps most paradoxical of all, otherwise disparate and segmented artefacts and activities were fused into coherent wholes. Configurations of music, dance, clothing and conduct coalesced into youth styles.

From the late 1950s had come the Teddy Boys (Edwardian suits, rock and roll, juke boxes in cafés). In the early 1960s there was a – sporadically violent – polarisation between the Mods (scooters, sharp suits, rhythm and blues, amphetamines) and the Rockers (motor bikes, zip-up leather jackets, rock and roll, beer). By the late 1960s the most visible style was a parody of the traditional worker: the macho skinhead (cropped hair, braces, football, Doc

Marten boots and, incongruous though it now seems, reggae music). There was little doubt that these styles came out of the male working class, a fact made more obvious by the contrast, and occasionally the conflict, between them and the more specifically middle class countercultural style of the hippies (long hair, soft drugs, heavy rock, hedonistic and anti-work).

To read youth culture in the 1960s through such forms may be to take the most symbolically articulate and integrated forms as if they stood for the whole. Most teenagers did not adopt such forms wholesale even if they could afford them retail. But equally, few were completely untouched by them.

There might at first seem to be little in common between the privatised leisure of the relatively affluent nuclear family of the 1960s and the largely peer group and public based leisure of young people. Yet, despite much agonising over the 'generation gap', most young people continued to be part of such families, which they would only leave to start one of their own. Despite its apparent flaunting of adult values of domesticity, responsibility and personal restraint, youth culture was potentially compatible with the adult world of leisure. This is attributable to three factors in particular.

First, youth culture operated *within* the dominant distinction between work and leisure. Occasional conflict with employers or teachers over personal appearance did not disguise the overall acceptance that stylistic expression was reserved for the sanctioned area of leisure. Only the hippies questioned the value, and could circumvent the necessity, of work. Secondly, youth culture could not and did not operate outside the established commercial framework and in fact made a massive contribution to its expansion. Where innovations came from the young themselves, they were soon incorporated into the commercial framework. No one could predict where the latest successful pop group might come from, but if its music was to find a mass audience it had to do so in the forms, at the times and on the stages provided by enthusiastic private enterprise. Thirdly, the values or ideals espoused by youth culture were often conformist, if at one remove. Nowhere was this clearer than in the area of sexual relationships. Mods, Teds and skinheads had their girl members but they were few in number and there on sufferance, positioned in relation to male sexual definitions and fantasies. Romantic love, with the girl as passive partner, remained a key theme of song lyrics. The control exercised over girls' leisure and the way their role was defined ensured that their participation in youth culture was on far from equal terms.

The recurrent discrepancy between the promise of leisure and women's real social experience is highlighted by the relationship of girls to youth culture. There is no doubt that they were actively sought as consumers by commercial institutions, but 'style' throughout the 1960s produced new versions of femininity which were compatible with more familiar female roles (e.g. free entry to discos on quiet nights was offered in the hope that their presence would attract paying male customers). But, here as elsewhere women's leisure took shape in the more private worlds – the bedroom at home, the cloakrooms at school and in the disco – exploiting those spaces where women can be 'on their own ground'. The temporary freedoms of adolescence were systematically more constrained for girls than for boys, and remained powerfully tied to their 'career' trajectory from daughter to wife.

If not in any simple sense conservative, youth culture in the 1960s was far from revolutionary or even radical. If it represented an exploration of some kinds of freedom these were stylistic rather than ideological, superficial rather than essential. If neither capital nor the state was ever wholly in control of the tastes and activities of young people, they did establish and patrol the boundaries of this apparently foreign land.

Young, gifted and black

Cultural diversity of a different kind began to appear following the inducements offered by employers from the mid-1950s to immigrants from the West Indies and the Asian sub-continent. There were perhaps three ways in which the shameful history of immigration and race relations in the 1960s affected the development of leisure. One was to introduce ethnic segregation into leisure. Even if white pubs and clubs had not tried to keep the 'coloureds' out, some sort of ethnically distinctive leisure enclaves would probably have emerged. Racist practices made their development a necessity. Otherwise very different groups of immigrants shared similarities in their cultural patterns, especially that leisure had a much less clear-cut status than that prevailing in white society. However different the Sikh Temple might have been from the West Indian evangelical church, or extended Asian family networks from the matrifocal structure of the West Indian family, there was a common emphasis on religious and familial relationships in shaping leisure. White society resented such commitment to a sense of community, especially when its own was dying. But even overt hostility could not prevent the creation and maintenance by immigrant groups of their own leisure spaces. Cafés became more than eating places, emerging as focal points for the male members of immigrant groups. Asians bought up cinemas for their own use and West Indians started up their own night clubs. The paralysis of the state, the hostility of white indigenous institutions and the indifference of commerce threw them back on their own considerable resources. From the late 1960s, certainly, no portrait of 'British' leisure was complete without including the leisure definitions and habits of those who came to live in the inner regions of Britain's larger towns and cities.

The second effect was more long term and visible in the city centre. This was immigrant entrepreneurship moving out into the white communities, especially in the form of restaurants. Experimentation in eating out was a by-product of affluence and a growing veneer of 'cosmopolitanism' in leisure. Immigrant entrepreneurs benefited from the irony that increasing numbers of British people, so antagonistic to the presence of 'coloureds', were eager to eat their food.

Thirdly, and more difficult to establish, was an element of cultural diffusion of immigrant cultures and styles into the host society. Black British sporting heroes and musicians were not to become visible until the 1970s but in the 1960s some diffusion was evident, notably between Afro-Caribbean influences and white youth culture. As white British musicians imitated black American rhythm and blues singers, West Indians were importing 'ska' records, the precursor of the reggae style which was later, in a suitably toned down form, to find acceptance by white record buyers.

Profit and loss

Thus, while affluence and privatisation appeared to make leisure more homogeneous, both youth and immigrant cultures seemed to exert an influence the other way, towards greater heterogeneity. Yet a single interpretation of these trends as cultural pluralism underestimates the extent to which different leisure cultures reflected and reproduced material and cultural inequalities. Some groups remained marginal in this new land of leisure opportunity. For women of whatever class age or ethnic group, leisure probably expanded in the 1960s, at least in so far as the emphasis on the family included them. But their defined role in the family left little room to explore leisure outside the home. One exception which proved the rule was bingo. The enormous popularity of bingo following its legalisation in 1960 reflected its status as one of the very few activities allowed to working class women by themselves, their husbands and their family responsibilities. In its function as a sexually 'safe' activity, and its location in converted picture palaces, it directly replaced the cinema.

Women were not alone in their exclusion. Those who were poor – as a result of sickness, unemployment or old age – were 'rediscovered' by social investigators of the 1960s. From material poverty, there flowed, in a consumer society, a poverty of leisure. The absence of communal leisure left such groups even more isolated. Generally the worst housed, clothed and fed, their domesticity was bare and enforced.

The response to pressure for state action to combat deprivation was piecemeal and fragmented, often discharged under the auspices of the welfare arm of the state, and occasionally producing some small-scale provision for leisure. In a more general sense, a leisure policy had become an expected function of an interventionist Welfare State. The Arts Council formed in 1946, had grown in status and budget; in 1964 a Sports Council was instituted on similar lines. Local government was given progressively more discretion in the use of the local rate to provide leisure activity, though as yet there were few specialist centres, and local authority provision remained largely confined to the traditional forms of parks, swimming pools libraries and museums. Some impetus was given to voluntary activity, though often to that of the middle class, with the power to organise lobbies to promote its own needs.

Substantial in some respects, not least in the sums of money involved, the State's role was still residual and enabling. It was, for example, responsible for legalising gambling through the Betting and Gaming Act of 1960, thus releasing to private enterprise the potential profit from betting shops, gaming houses and bingo halls. The State was also active in maintaining the media duopoly which had come into being with the introduction of commercial television in 1956, by granting a second channel to the BBC and suppressing the pirate radio stations.

Despite, and in some instances because of, such State activity, leisure was becoming one of the growth areas of private investment. Already evident in the 1960s were trends in economic organisation which were to dominate the economy of the 1970s and beyond. The expanding 'leisure industry' included such contrasting leisure commodities as bingo halls, motorway cafés, paper-back books and television stations. There were few surveys of ownership and control of the fast-growing leisure conglomerates, but of their economic power there could be little doubt. In 1965, for example, EMI and Decca shared 58 per cent of the records produced, Philips and Pye a further 16 per cent between them; 90 per cent of the Top Ten hits were produced by these four companies. Between 1960 and 1972 the proportion of all public houses owned by the 'big six' breweries (Ind Coope, Charrington, Courage, Scottish and Newcastle, Watneys, Whitbread) more than doubled, from just over a quarter to well over a half. Whatever else leisure was in the 1960s, it was highly profitable.

The good old days?

There can be little doubt that in the self-image of Britain in the 1960s, leisure occupied a central place. There seemed to be a lot more of it, whether measured in time, money or opportunity. It was not welcomed by all. For those of more conservative bent, large-scale hedonism threatened the Protestant ethic held to be the basis of civilisation. The activity of the young, in particular, seemed lacking in all restraint: bizarre appearance, sexual promiscuity, experimentation with drugs, seemed part and parcel of what could be shown statistically to be the increasingly delinquent behaviour of the young. While there was no objection to family-centredness, there was moral indignation about the sex, violence and bad language which television programmes brought in to the family living room. Affluence became coterminous with permissiveness as legal restrictions on abortion, adult homosexual activity and divorce were eased. Reservations of a different kind were expressed by some radicals who saw the success of consumer capitalism leading the working class to sacrifice its traditional values of altruism and community in favour of a calculated self interest.

Such interpretations did no more than scratch the surface of the deeply contradictory appearance of leisure in the 1960s. Apparently equal evidence could be adduced to support radically different analyses. Thus interpretative stress could be placed on the homogeneity of leisure evident in the pattern of 'privatised affluence'; on the equality of leisure opportunity produced by the removal of economic constraint; on the responsiveness of private and public institutions to the public's expressed leisure needs; on the lifting of legal controls such as those on gambling and sexual activity. Such an interpretation would see leisure in the 1960s as maturing, in line with a democratic, consumer-based, increasingly egalitarian society.

But there is also room for the opposite interpretation. Here stress would be on the heterogeneity of leisure styles as demonstrated by youth and ethnic cultures; on the continued exclusion of large groups (women, the old, the poor) from leisure opportunity; on the indifference of the providers to unexpressed needs of groups who were neither economically nor politically profitable; on the continued legal prohibition of soft drug taking. If there is development here it is uneven and contradictory, reflections of a society fundamentally undemocratic, materialist and unequal.

The truth may not lie somewhere between these versions but in them both. For the 1960s demonstrated once again that leisure could be both freedom and compulsion, both the active creation of cultural meaning and the passive consumption of received spectacle, both an exploration of the possibility of a different kind of life and confirmation of that which exists. Leisure as a category of experience was inherited from the period of capitalist industrialisation. Its segmented, specialised and institutionalised forms developed in ways appropriate to the economic and political organisation of a mature capitalist society. These economic and cultural forms – and the contradictions which they contain – are our inheritance from Britain's social and economic development.

Further reading

Some of the most innovative historical analysis of leisure has first appeared in journals, especially *The Journal of Social History*, *Past and Present*, and *History Workshop*. Two edited collections of recent social history articles deserve to be mentioned: Eileen and Stephen Yeo (eds), *Popular Culture and Class Conflict, 1590–1914* (Harvester, 1981) and A. J. P. Donajgrodski (ed.), *Social Control in Nineteenth Century Britain* (Croom Helm, 1977). Although less directly connected to the theme of leisure, a collection of History Workshop conference papers edited by Ralph Samuel, *People's History and Socialist Theory* (Routledge & Kegan Paul, 1981), deals with some of the central problems of social history.

A straightforward introduction to the history of leisure is J. Walvin's *Leisure and Society 1830 – 1950* (Longman, 1978), which could usefully be read alongside what remains one of the best economic and social histories covering the last two hundred years, Eric Hobsbawm's *Industry and Empire* (Penguin, 1969).

R. W. Malcolmson, *Popular Recreations in English Society, 1700–1850* (Cambridge University Press, 1973) details the decline of traditional popular recreations, while a more politicised interpretation of social change in this period is made in E. P. Thompson's brilliant *The Making of the English Working Class* (Penguin, 1968). He argues against the interpretation of the early nineteenth century suggested by the title of J. L. and B. Hammond's, *The Bleak Age* (Penguin, 1947). This portrait is also disputed by Hugh Cunningham in *Leisure and the Industrial Revolution* (Croom Helm, 1980), and by Peter Bailey in *Leisure and Class in Victorian England* (Routledge & Kegan Paul, 1978). Eric Dunning and Ken Sheard's *Barbarians, Gentlemen and Players* (Martin Robertson, 1979) provides one of the best accounts of the changing social ethos and organisation of sport – in this case, rugby.

Interesting contemporary accounts of late nineteenth century working class leisure can be found collected in *Charles Booth's London* edited by Albert Fried and Richard Elman (Penguin, 1971), and can be contrasted with the more theoretical discussion of the changing pattern of working class culture offered by Garath Steadman-Jones in his *Languages of Class* (Cambridge University Press, 1984).

The paucity of studies of early twentieth century leisure is emphasised by A. Howkins and J. Lowerson in *Trends in Leisure 1919–1939* (Sports Council, 1979). The social context is described in John Stevenson, *British Society 1914–1945* (Penguin, 1984), and the same historian has edited a collection of extracts from contemporary social investigators: *Social Conditions in Britain Between the Wars* (Penguin, 1977). The society of the 1930s is discussed by Noreen Branson and Margot Heinemann in *Britain in the Nineteen Thirties* (Panther, 1973), while Paul Thompson's excellent *The Edwardians* (Granada, 1977) deals with the turn of the century. Mass Observation's surveys provided distinctive contemporary observations of pre-war and war time Britain's social habits. Most relevant here is Mass Observation, *The Pub and the People* (Gollancz, 1943).

There are hardly any social histories of post-war Britain, much less ones dealing specifically with leisure. Arthur Marwick's British *Society since 1945* (Penguin, 1982) offers a descriptive review. More generally relevant to the whole argument of this book is the Open University course *Popular Culture* (Open University Educational Enterprises, 1981), and the course units dealing with 'The historical development of popular culture' are especially pertinent to this chapter.

With a few notable exceptions, the above references deal exclusively with the world of male leisure. The recent growth of women's history promises to remedy some of these absences. Sheila Rowbotham's *Hidden from History* (Pluto Press, 1973) remains a cogent argument about the invisibility of women in most historical studies. Steps in new directions are represented by the following. S. Burman (ed.), *Fit Work for Women* (Croom Helm, 1979) includes papers on the experience and ideologies of 'women's work' in the nineteenth century, as does M. Vicinus (ed.), *Suffer and be Still: Women in the Victorian Age* (Routledge & Kegan Paul, 1973). Jill Liddington and Jill Norris, *One Hand Tied Behind Us* (Virago, 1978) examine the role of working class women in the women's suffrage movement and other struggles over women's rights. Barbara Taylor's brilliant *Eve and the New Jerusalem* (Virago, 1983) examines the relationship between feminism and socialism in the early nineteenth century, and the ways in which that relationship was broken. Finally, one of the very few post-war social histories is Elizabeth Wilson's *Only Halfway to Paradise* (Tavistock, 1980) which examines the changing social position of, and ideologies about, women.

End of Part I: a pause for reflection

In the first part of this book, our concern has been to establish how a critical – and more adequate – approach to the study of leisure can be constructed. We set about this, on the one hand, through a critical encounter with existing sociological theories of leisure, and, on the other, through providing a history attentive to some of the major structural and cultural conflicts through which leisure has been created. Our intention here is to pull together the themes which have emerged from these two routes, and in doing so, to establish more sharply the essential elements of our own approach to the study of leisure. The general conclusions which can be drawn from our theoretical and historical arguments in Part I provide the preconditions for our analysis of leisure in contemporary Britain which takes up the remainder of this book.

One conclusion drawn from our discussion of theories of leisure was that the conception of contemporary leisure as the product of a history of steady growth was untenable. In Chapter 3, we attempted to show how 'leisure' has been the outcome of complex historical conflicts. These conflicts are concealed by the ideology of history as a smooth progression. Instead, we have seen that the existence of leisure as a 'separate sphere' of social life is dependent on the major reorganisation of *work* which took place in the period of capitalist industrialisation. This separation of leisure had to be enforced – the nineteenth century experienced a variety of efforts to inculcate good work habits and to eradicate irrational leisure patterns which threatened the development of an orderly workforce.

Nor can the boundaries of this separation of employment and leisure be viewed as the natural outcome of 'progress'. The length of the working day, week and year were, and have remained, focal points of conflict between employers and workers' organisations – even though they are now less dramatically visible than conflicts over pay and working conditions. One of the principal successes of capitalism in conflicts over leisure is not the establishment of any *particular* leisure behaviour, but the establishment of this de-marcation between work (employment) and leisure. The accept-ance of this distinction as 'natural' and 'inevitable' necessarily produces a splitting of needs, desires and expectations about life. The identification of leisure as the sphere in which needs are satisfied and pleasures found simultaneously makes work *less* susceptible to criticism as unsatisfactory and *more* salient as that which has to be tolerated to 'earn' the freedom of leisure. Instrumentalism about work is built into this enforced separation: 'leisure' is the prize to be won.

However, as we argued in Chapter 2, the identification of leisure with freedom, choice and satisfied needs is also misleading. While the demarcation of leisure from employment has been a focal point of conflict, so has the content of that 'free time'. The suppression of immoral, irrational and generally 'dangerous' activities; the permanent 'policing' of public space; the control of 'standards' in family life; and the provision of 'improving' alternatives, have all been elements in the struggle to control the uses of free time.

But the 'cultural politics' of leisure are not only contained in these efforts to *control*, they must also include the active attempts to make concessions to the needs and interests of subordinate groups. It is important to recognise that provision, through both commercial and state forms, is not simply a direct imposition. Provision attempts to meet the demands of social groups. As we saw with the case of music hall at the end of the nineteenth century, the aim is to meet the needs of social groups, to take account of their interests, and to turn that concession to economic or political advantage. Again, we must emphasise that these processes of economic and political *concession* are less concerned about the specific activities being provided than with ensuring that the *form* in which they are provided is regulated. If the working class wants alcohol and music, it shall have them – but only to be consumed under certain conditions.

While the demarcation of employment and leisure was capitalism's first achievement, the establishment of leisure – as – consumption, the limiting of the *forms* of leisure organisation, has also been of considerable significance.

One of the most striking features of the historical development traced in Chapter 3 is the increasing equation which is drawn between leisure and consumption, and in particular, the increasing dominance of commercial provision. This has affected not only the *logic* of provision (is servicing this need likely to be *profitable*?) it has also affected the sorts of social relationships which characterise leisure.

We want to suggest that it is possible to think of three possible sorts of relationship between a citizen and a cultural institution:

those of member, customer and consumer. The *member* has an active commitment to the institution, which is run on his or her behalf, and over which the membership exercises collective control. The *customer*'s stake is that of habit. Mutual expectations aise, and a contract of sorts is evolved, which both sides are reluctant to abandon. The *consumer*, however, has neither the commitment of the member, nor the informal contract of the customer. His or her expectations are altogether more specific: the maximisation of immediate satisfaction. If goods or services are not provided in the manner or at the price required, then the consumer will go elsewhere.

If we take an activity like shopping – each of these three relationships is *possible*: member of the Co-op, customer of the cornershop, consumer at the supermarket. But the dominant tendency has been towards the last of these, forced on by the economic logic of profitability for which the ties of membership or custom are 'irrational' barriers to rational economic organisation. So, for example, in the pressure of competition from large scale commercial retailing organisations, the Co-op has moved closer to consumer relationships, reducing the significance of membership to stamps and divi-books. Cornershops – and their specific local relationships – have also been squeezed by the power of economic concentration in the retailing business. Even where the rhetoric of 'membership' is revived (from sports centres to video-clubs), the desired relationship is that of the consumer: membership in these circumstances carries only market advantage (cheaper prices) rather than any active involvement in decision making and control.

For the economist (and particularly the monetarist), this growth of the consumer relationship represents a substantial gain. The market allows the exercise of rationally calculated choice on the part of the citizen, and 'consumer sovereignty' ensures that needs will be met through the supply of appropriate goods and services. For cultural critics, this apparent gain involves a qualitative loss – the disappearance of the potential for other kinds of relationships. The much vaunted democracy of the market-place (where rational individuals exercise their free choices) rests on the rather less democratic foundations of the profoundly unequal distribution of wealth and income. Even where the necessary membership card for the market society is obtained, the powers involved in consumer sovereignty are of a specific kind. The sanctions possessed by the consumer are entirely *negative* (we can choose not to buy), and depend for their existence on viable alternative sources of supply. And these 'alternatives' are increasingly to be found only in the form of other major companies engaged in the leisure business.

We have argued that one other central feature of the development of leisure is the sharp distinction that is constructed between employment and leisure. This separation is organised along a number of social axes. First, it involves a distinction in the sorts of relationships which characterise these two spheres – the difference between employee, subject to occupational constraints, and the variety of social roles which may be performed outside the place of employment. This distinction is commonplace to studies of leisure, but the attention it receives can distract attention from two other dimensions of this separation – those of time and space.

The distinction between employment and leisure creates two relatively distinct sets of time – on the one hand, that part surrendered to an employer in exchange for earnings; on the other, that reserved to oneself (and the others with whom one chooses to pass it). This pattern of weekdays *versus* evenings and weekends has come to be expected as the natural pattern of demarcation, although, as we saw in Chapter 3, it, too, is the outcome of conflicts over the allocation of time to employment.

The development of capitalism also produced a geographical segregation of employment and leisure, such that paid work mostly takes place away from the home. This separation of production from the household has been intensified by subsequent developments in the planning of residential, office and industrial building, with an increasing tendency to segregate residential districts away from city centres and industrial areas.

Nevertheless, as we argued in Chapter 2, this pattern of segregation (of roles, of time and of space) only holds good for the dichotomy between paid work and employment. It leaves out of account the sexual division of labour and the way that division affects domestic work. For women in the home, roles, time and space are not demarcated by this separation. Women's familial roles contain personal dimensions (wife, mother, lover) which are inseparable from their implications of domestic duties (cook, washer, nurse, child minder). Similarly, time 'at home' carries no definitive demarcations: no factory hooter, school bell or office

mark the end of the working day; and equally, no factory
office door to walk through to enter the different time and
place of leisure. This private work of reproduction is the hidden or
reverse side of the public world of capitalist production – shaped
by it, but not subject to its 'natural' demarcations of role, time and
place.

Ideals of a 'woman's place' have this precise *spatial* confinement
in mind – the woman bound by ties of love, obligation, obedience
and duty to the home. But no more than any of the other
demarcations that we have encountered, is this boundary fixed,
natural or inevitable. The past century has seen numerous
attempts to enforce or cajole women to occupy a woman's place,
usually supported by efforts to educate women as to their biological imperatives. At other times, the bounds of this biology have
been loosened in the face of the demands for productive labour. In
both world wars, the recruitment of women as wage labour was
supported by expanded provision of collective child-care, state
laundries, and restaurants, which promised, temporarily, alternatives to the privatised pattern of domestic labour. Over this
boundary, too, there have been conflicts ranging from the struggles to impose the idea of most paid work as male in the early
nineteenth century, through to contemporary campaigns around
state facilities, such as crèches and nurseries.

Between the places of paid work and domesticity, lies the
contested ground of public space. Since the enclosure of common
lands, there have been conflicts over the availability and use of
parks, footpaths, streets and the countryside. It is here that the
state has played its most active role in organising leisure. At one
point, it clears the streets of 'nuisances'; at another, it provides
public spaces for the purposes of rational recreation. It defines and
adjudicates the 'rights' to public space, and polices the uses to
which that space is put. The history of that adjudication and
policing has been one in which the formal rights inscribed in law
have always taken precedence over the informal and 'customary'
rights of popular culture. Yet, for those subordinate groups who
own little 'private space', streets, paths and open spaces have been
essential ingredients of leisure practices. 'Gossiping', 'doing nothing', 'hanging about' may not be clearly expressed 'leisure
needs', but they have remained strikingly stable uses which
popular cultures have made of public space.

Through these points, it is possible to understand why leisure is persistently ambiguous. It is the site of a number of conflicts – over time and space; over control of resources; over the character of social relationships; over the boundary between public and private; and over the tension between control and autonomy. What we now experience as 'leisure' is the current outcome of these historical struggles between contending social interests.

Discussions of the Leisure Society and the Future of Work, which are so visible in the 1980s, indicate that these conflicts are not yet over. But all too often, the structures within which leisure takes shape – the nature of work, its social distribution, the inequalities of wealth, power and other resources associated with it in the system of capitalism – are left to one side in these discussions. Leisure is yet again identified as the necessary consequence of economic growth and technological change. At the same time, leisure as the site of cultural conflict – of competing demands, definitions and ideologies of what is and should be – is also left out of account. The best, it seems, that can be offered is a wider range of market choice, and the servicing of 'deprived' minorities by the state.

Just as our account of the history of leisure paid attention to how social conflicts dictated the pattern which did emerge (and therefore what other possibilities were excluded), so our understanding of the contemporary trends and patterns of leisure must try to question the current assumptions of benign progress. In what follows, we shall be reviving our interest in the structural organisation of, and cultural conflicts over, leisure in contemporary Britain.

4

We sell everything – the mixed economy of leisure

There's a great industry in other people's pleasure. (Margaret Thatcher, interviewed in *The Director*, August 1983.)
Maggie's Mickie Mouse jobs plans. Daily Mirror headline accompanying report of the same interview (26 August 1983).

In Chapter 3, we argued that one of the most striking features of the history of leisure was the tendency for leisure to become *institutionalised* in the mixed economy of market and state provision. We also suggested that the private or commercial sector played the leading role in this leisure economy, with the state sector playing a more residual and supplementary part. Most studies of leisure recognise the existence of this leisure economy, but they neither explain it nor explore it. They treat it instead as the framework of opportunity within which individuals make choices in attempting to satisfy their leisure needs. Attention is focused on what individuals and groups choose to do with their leisure time within this framework of what is available. We believe that this treatment of the leisure economy as the passive background for studies of leisure activities is erroneous. Between them, the market and the state play an active role in constructing leisure. They determine what is available as leisure, controlling the supply of most goods and services among which leisure 'consumers' can choose.

This means that the considerable emphasis on 'choice' in studies of leisure refers to a very specific form of decision-making –

consumer choice. For most people in Britain, access to leisure is a matter of hard cash. Leisure is something which is purchased: attending sporting or cultural events; betting, drinking or eating; buying the equipment for hobbies and sports, or simply watching television. We have become accustomed to this pattern, so that it seems perfectly 'natural' that leisure needs should be satisfied in this way. But our encounter with history indicates that leisure-as-consumption is not perfectly natural, but the product of social processes, particularly the search of British capital for domestic markets for consumer goods during the interwar years.

In this chapter we shall be examining the contemporary results of these processes in the organisation of the leisure economy, and trying to asses the cultural consequences of the two major leisure structures – the market and the state.

Market well

Leisure is now 'big business' in a variety of ways. It accounts for over 25 per cent of consumer spending – over £23 000 000 in 1977–8, and this total has been steadily increasing. Clearly, servicing Britain's leisure needs is a potentially profitable form of investment. The leisure sector is also 'big business' when viewed as a sector of employment. Between 1960 and 1980, employment in leisure services increased by 36 per cent, while the proportion of all employment accounted for by this sector grew from 2.2 per cent in 1960 to 5.9 per cent in 1980. This expansion only contains those employed in leisure services, and does not include those employed in the manufacture of leisure *goods*. Small wonder, then, that in the midst of mass unemployment, Mrs Thatcher spoke of the leisure industry as one of the key sources of future employment:

> There's a great industry in other people's pleasure. We must expect that a lot more of our jobs will come from the service industries – from the MacDonald's and Wimpy's, which employ a lot of people, and from the kind of Disneyland they are starting in Corby. Leisure is a big industry. (quoted in *The Daily Mirror* 26 August 1983.)

Indeed it is, and it shares many of the characteristics of capitalist industrial development visible in other sectors of the economy. In particular, the leisure industry is highly concentrated, with the bulk of goods and services being produced by a small number of large companies. This concentration of ownership and production creates one of the paradoxes of the leisure business. The leisure consumer does not see a market dominated by a handful of monopolies, but a market of diversity – a profusion of possible choices. The leisure market offers a dazzling array of ways to spend our leisure – from discos to jogging gear, from bingo to roller skates, from squash courts to home videos, and from Butlins to the Costa del Sol.

The pattern of business organisation and share ownership in the 'leisure industries' follows that of the economy as a whole in the post-war period. The main tendencies are outwards *concentration* of ownership, with a few large companies ultimately owning or controlling the key enterprises in the leisure sector; the *interrelationship* of such large corporations both within Europe and across the world to non-communist Asia's 'newly industrialising countries', such as Taiwan and South Korea; and *diversification*, where corporations, or the individual firms which act as their trading 'fronts', seek to spread their interest across several different types of products and services. This 'political economy' of leisure would repay careful sociological attention. The effects of this political economy are, however, of some significance. What appears to the consumer as a multiplicity of choice between activities, services, and competing brands of leisure goods, looks from another perspective like the control of the leisure market by a few very large corporations.

For example, the Rank Organisation had its roots in the film industry, and this field of operations is still retained by the company as one of its fields of activity, but it has now grown far beyond these boundaries. It bought into 'home entertainment' through acquiring a number of subsidiaries manufacturing radios, hi-fi and televisions (Bush, Murphy, Wharfedale and Dansette, for example) and became the major holder in Southern Television. It offered alternative 'public leisure' to cinemas in the form of dancing, bowling and bingo (Top Rank), and, if you needed to get away from it all, Rank could help there too, owning hotels, marinas and holiday camps (including Butlins). But this represents only the specifically 'leisure' interests of Rank, since its full range of economic activity extends much wider than this. It is part of the

Rank-Hovis-MacDougall food combine, and a subsidiary of the American based multinational Xerox Corporation.

These broader connections of Rank should warn us against taking too narrow a view of the 'leisure industry'. Many of the major enterprises active within it have little or nothing to do with 'leisure' provision as their main focus of economic concern. They enter the leisure market (often absorbing smaller 'leisure' enterprises) as a means of discovering new sources of profitability. For example, Rediffusion and Thames Television are subsidiaries within the giant British Electrical Traction Company (itself the product of mergers and takeovers within the electrical engineering field). Drink Whyte and MacKay's whiskey, or buy a Pace postcard on holiday and you touch the fringes of the Lonrho multinational – to say nothing of reading the *Observer*.

It may not seem to matter much who 'owns' leisure. After all, 'they' own everything else, so why not leisure as well? And, besides, as the pluralists in particular would argue, consumer choices, when added together to create 'market trends', greatly affect how such corporations behave in supplying the leisure market. Power resides with us, the consumers, and the suppliers ignore our wishes at their financial peril. In our view, this greatly underestimates the power of business to persuade consumers, through advertising in particular, to make the right choices. The consumer demand argument also plays down the ability of the leisure industry to determine what is available for us to choose from. It is the industry which innovates, creates new products and services, and then attempts to create the markets for them (toy and fashion 'crazes' are the most obvious examples). However, it is not only their control of the range and form of leisure goods and services which constitutes the power of the leisure corporations. They can, and do, attempt to change the 'qualities' of leisure if they believe it is in their economic interest to do so. The recent history of the public house is a case in point.

'Last orders please': diversity and concentration among the breweries

One of the leisure fields in which the process of economic concentration has been most dramatically illustrated is in brewing. Before the Second World War, the industry was economically diverse, consisting of many small breweries primarily organised on a local or regional basis, with little attempt to organise a 'national market'. Since the middle 1950s, the industry has undergone a major transformation, involving the creation of national market almost completely dominated by six major companies. Various reasons have been suggested for this turn around – the development of pasteurised beers having a longer 'shelf-life' enabling national distribution; the threat of competition from 'foreign' brewers especially in the provision of lagers; and the interest of non-brewing property companies in the property assets of the breweries (hotels and pubs).

Whatever the weighting of these different factors may have been, what transpired was a massive process of mergers, take-overs and 'alliances' within the breweries involving the absorption of smaller regional breweries into national chains, leaving both brewing and distribution in the control of the 'big six': Watney-Mann, Bass Charrington, Allied Breweries, Scottish and Newcastle, Whitbread and Courage. This concentration of ownership resulted in 'rationalisation' of the brewing and distribution of beer in three main ways. Each of the companies found itself with a 'surplus' of small breweries, many of which were closed since production could be more efficiently organised in a smaller number of modernised enterprises. Secondly, the breweries also set out to rationalise their rental outlets, finding that the absorption of small breweries had left them with too many public houses. By 1969, for example, Watney-Mann alone were closing pubs at the rate of 120 per year. At the same time, the breweries were also attempting to change over the running of their 'outlets' from the tenant system (in which the tenant leased the premises from the brewery) to a system of salaried managers – creating a structure of tighter control over the running of the pub. Thirdly, the reorganisation of the brewing structure also had the effect of reducing the numbers of beers available, and the substitution of nationally marketed 'keg' beers for locally produced varieties – often accompanied by the removal of the original brewery titles from both beers and pubs.

However, the process of reorganisation of the brewing industry went beyond these economic rationalisations. The breweries also set out to change the character of the pub itself, in line with what they perceived to be the changing character and tastes of their clientele. The décor and interior layout were 'modernised' (often in Victorian or Edwardian 'style'); facilities for traditional games, such as darts and cards, were withdrawn, since they were held to be less popular and less profitable than fruit machines and video games; and music was made compulsory through the introduction of jukeboxes. While it can be argued that the spittoon and sawdust image of the 'public' had become outdated, the changes introduced aimed at promoting a new clientele for the pub – younger and more affluent. It was no coincidence that each of the innovations developed by the breweries was designed to yield additional profits, both from the new entertainments provided and from the increased drink sales which the new customers would provide.

This reduction of choice about what to drink, and about the context in which to drink it, produced one of the few collective consumer revolts in the leisure market. As with many other products, individual irritations with many aspects of the new model pub abounded. But the Campaign for Real Ale moved consumer irritation from an individual level to a collective organised campaign against the big breweries. The campaign focused on efforts to 'educate' public taste about the quality of beers, and ran a concerted attack against the 'gassy' keg beers being supplied by the major breweries, contrasting them unfavourably with the traditional products of the independent breweries. Enough consumers resisted the rationalisation of brewing that a substantial sector of the market moved towards the 'independent' breweries, and ensured their survival in the face of the overwhelming economic competition from the monopolies.

This reaction has led to the monopolies rethinking their marketing strategy, and reintroducing 'real' as opposed to pasteurised beers to compete with the independents. Accompanying this had been a reintroduction of the old brewery and beer titles to move away from the national image, and reconstruct 'local' segments of the market. For example, there has been a recent TV advertising campaign stressing the East London associations of The Romford Brewery, which avoids mentioning its status as a subsidiary of Allied Breweries. Diversity has once again reappeared in the market-place.

In many other respects, the brewing industry has reflected the broader patterns of economic concentration and diversification of the leisure industry. The expansion of the major brewers also involved their absorption of related market sectors, such as soft drinks, or wines and spirits. Subsidiaries of Allied Breweries include Britvic, Coates, Gaymers and Whiteways, Victoria Wine and William Teacher. Similar patterns appear in the rest of the 'big six'. This integration of other sectors of the drink market is accompanied by a diversification into other leisure sectors. Allied owns Lyons-Tetley; Bass-Charrington owns the extensive Coral Leisure Group (hotels, bingo, casinos, betting shops and Pontins). Others have themselves been absorbed as part of bigger enterprises: Courage is part of the Imperial Group – including Imperial Tobacco and The Ross organisations. Watney-Mann was taken over by the Grand Metropolitan Group, a multinational which includes among its activities hotels, inns (Berni, Chef and Brewer, Schooner), the Mecca range of leisure enterprises, wines and spirits (Gilbeys, International Distillers and Vintners) and food (Express dairies).

This monopoly structure is the dominant economic form of 'leisure capital'. As in many other sectors, diversity provides the appearance of consumer choice behind which stands a massive concentration of economic power. And this power extends to even the apparently most 'protected' place: the home.

'A fine and private place?' Leisure and the home

Most recent surveys of leisure have identified 'home based' or 'family centred' leisure as the dominant trend in leisure use in Britain. Data from the 1982 government publication *Social Trends* suggests that for men around 70 per cent of leisure activities are home based, while for women this figure is nearer 80 per cent. In the sociological literature, this had been described as a trend towards 'privatisation' – a removal from social activity based on networks outside the home in favour of increasingly family centred activity. However, this pattern may not be either as novel or as straightforward as this characterisation implies.

First, much historical work suggests that the pattern of 'family centred' leisure was already well established by the end of the nineteenth century. At least among the bourgeoisie, middle class and 'respectable' strata of the working class, the ideal of the home as a male haven provided a powerful structure in the organisation of free time. The power of this Victorian ideal of domestic life suggests that 'privatisation' may be less closely connected with the advent of post-war affluence than some sociologists have argued. The tendency to formalise a distinction between the traditional and the modern (between history and sociology) can have the effect of disguising powerful continuities in social patterns.

Secondly, the pattern of home-centred leisure brings us sharply up against the problem we have already encountered about the relationship between the work/leisure dichotomy and the pattern of domestic labour. Time in the home is differently distributed for men and women, and the attempt to establish the allocation of time in the home is fraught with difficulties. One major survey by the BBC (in 1974), used 'time diaries' to establish how different groups spent their time. The results can be seen in Figure 4.1.

The explanations of what these different categories of time mean highlight some problems about the distinction between work and leisure in the home. Although the 'leisure' category includes watching television, more recent surveys suggest that (for women in particular) television is often watched in conjunction with other activities, such as cooking, cleaning and sewing. Thus, one 'leisure' activity may well conceal time being spent on domestic work. In a different way, the category of 'sleep' is also confusing, since it includes time spent on 'meals' and 'personal care'. Meals, however, have to be prepared before they can be eaten, and we might have expected this part of meal-associated-time to be allocated within the category of house work.

In a different way, these problems can also be seen in the counting of other home based activities as leisure. For example, the General Household Survey (1977) records 'needlework/knitting' as one of the most frequent 'social and cultural activities' for women (51 per cent). This seems to us to be a classic example of how the work/leisure categorisation is inapplicable to much domestic activity. Needlework/knitting may be undertaken as a source of creative satisfaction or relaxation, but it is also an expected part of 'women's work', subsidising family clothing costs by making and mending. A similar dilemma is visible in the more culturally male tasks of home maintenance and DIY (51 per cent of men, 22 per cent of women). Here, too, the distinction between unpaid work to subsidise the family economy and 'leisure' is an uneasy one.

We have spent some time labouring this point because it is

108

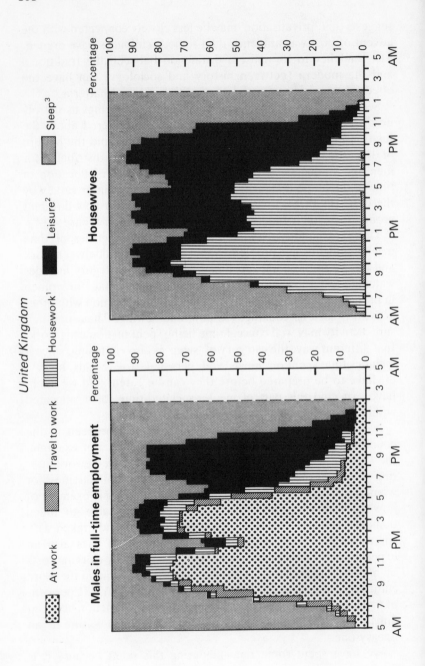

United Kingdom

At work   Travel to work   Housework[1]   Leisure[2]   Sleep[3]

Males in full-time employment

Housewives

109

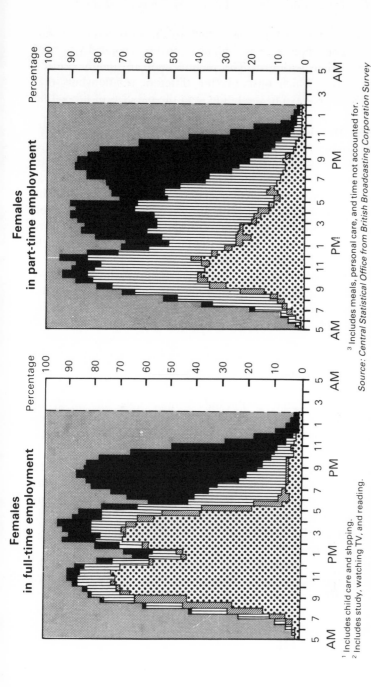

SOURCE *Social Trends 1980* (HMSO) p. 225.

FIGURE 4.1 *Use of time, summer 1974*

¹ Includes child care and shpping.
² Includes study, watching TV, and reading.
³ Includes meals, personal care, and time not accounted for.
Source: Central Statistical Office from British Broadcasting Corporation Survey

essential to establish how unsatisfactory the work/leisure dichotomy is when applied to the home, and the sexual division of labour and time within it. The identification of 'family centred leisure' is one which obscures the different relationships that family members have to the home, and the patterns of life within it.

Finally, the characterisation of home-centred leisure as a process of 'privatisation' – a retreat from outside social relationships into the domestic sphere – only captures a part of the patterns of interrelationship between the family and the wider society. Privatisation describes the reduction in social interaction outside the family, but does not deal with the way the family has been reshaped by closer and more powerful ties with the leisure industry. The 'private sphere' of the family has been increasingly penetrated by economic processes.

Let us take one form of home-based leisure, which is usually cited in discussions of this trend – the growth of 'do-it-yourself'. DIY rests on the interconnection between the family and the economy, and on the interests and ideas which bind them together.

First (and perhaps most obviously), its expansion is linked to the relation between families and building societies. The mortgage is an economic investment without which the psychological investment in 'a home of one's own' would be impossible. The expansion of the 'property owning democracy' (more accurately the expansion of mortgage debt) provides both the economic and ideological basis from which 'home improvement' has developed.

This potential market of home improvers has been serviced by the sorts of monopoly organisations which we came across earlier in other leisure spheres. Home improvements? Why not put up some Crown wallpaper, using Polycell, and some Walpamur paint. Throw in a new Sanderson carpet – and all your transactions have been taken care of by Reed International.

Perhaps your tastes in home improvement run more into the direction of new consumer durables. A Main Tricity, Moffat, or Parkinson Cowan appliance? A new Kenwood mixer? A television by Baird or Ferguson? Hifi – a Goodmans stereo? Buy them from Rumbelows, and your transactions will all crop up in the balance sheets of Thorn-EMI.

The home has been systematically reorganised through market

initiatives in almost all of its aspects, and in most of these changes the home has been brought into direct intersection with the monopolies. Interior decoration, domestic appliances, home furnishing (the MFI and Texas Homecare chains), food and shopping (the retail chains), reading (publishing houses have been absorbed into larger conglomerates such as Reed, Associated Newspapers, and Granada and the retail outlets are dominated by Smiths and John Menzies). But the dominant element of the privatisation of leisure has been television, the focal point of most people's leisure use.

Social Trends (1982) reports that TV watching accounts for almost 45 per cent of people's evening leisure time. In 1979, the BBC estimated that the average weekly viewing time for each individual (aged over five) was around 20 hours. The number of TV licences issued increased from around 2 million in 1951 to almost 20 million by 1978. (This, incidentally is an almost direct inversion of weekly cinema attendances which have declined from around 26 million in 1951 to 2 million in 1980.) The paradox is that it is in this pinnacle of the trend towards home-centred leisure that the leisure consumer most sharply encounters monopoly forms of organisation.

The content of television programming is in the hands of licensed monopolies (regional commercial organisation in the case of ITV and a state monopoly in the BBC). But behind the monopolies on our screen appear more complex connections with other elements of leisure capital. This may appear in the form of production subsidiaries owned by the TV companies (Thames Television and Euston Films, for example). More significantly it appears in the links between ownership of the commercial channel monopolies and economic interests in the manufacture of televisions. For example, Thorn/EMI have an interest in Thames Television, manufacture sets under Baird and Ferguson titles, and also rent them through DER, Multi-Broadcast, and Radio Rentals. British Electrical Traction, through their Rediffusion subsidiary hold the majority share in Thames, and, of course, rent sets through Rediffusion.

Even in the new rush of 'competition' accompanying the arrival of cable television, some of the old and familiar names seemed destined to reappear. Among the companies included in various consortia bidding for the new cable franchises are: Television

South, Telefusion, Whitbreads, Thorn EMI, Bass, Pontin-Coral; and the Ladbroke Group. Rediffusion have developed one of the new cable systems which may be used in the new networks, while they, along with Thorn-EMI, Rank-Trident, Visionhire, Ladbroke, and D. C. Thomson, are among the enterprises preparing programming for the new system.

This sort of interpenetration of different companies and different sectors is typical of the organisation of commercial television, but the BBC does not stand wholly outside the market structure of broadcasting. Although it does not have to engage in the competition for advertising revenue (the ITV companies' primary source of income), it is nevertheless involved in competition against the ITV companies. This competition is for audience ratings. And it is the quest for ratings which organises the BBC's programming policy as much as any of the strictures of the Corporation's charter. Audience share has become one of the significant criteria on which the BBC bids for increased revenue (in the form of higher licence fees). This quantification of 'success' is a necessary consequence of the dominance of the market model and its emphasis of 'competition': brand loyalty has to be established. The BBC has also had an eye on diversification, both in marketing (programmes overseas, records, books and videos at home), and in production, where 'co-production deals' (joint financing) are now much sought after for big budget programme making.

We have spent some time with these criticisms of the privatisation thesis not because we think it is wholly inaccurate. There is indeed evidence that more time is spent in the home, and more activities have the family as their focal point. To this extent, 'privatisation' captures a growing withdrawal from sociability outside of family relationships for those who live in families. But it seems to us that the idea of 'family centredness' underestimates the complexity of the *internal* relations of family life, and of the *external* connections between the family and the leisure economy.

Subsidising pleasure: capital and sponsorship

There is one final aspect of the relation between business and leisure which deserves to be mentioned. In the last fifteen years, businesses have been taking an increasingly active role in sponsorship of leisure activities. Of course, this is not an absolute novelty. Many companies have long been aware of the importance of 'recreation', particularly in relation to their own employees. Companies have provided sports and recreation facilities for their workforces (ranging from sports clubs to brass bands), and commercial philanthropy often emerged in the form of providing municipal libraries, galleries and museums through which cultural 'improvement' could be made available.

Two major differences stand out in the recent development of sponsorship of leisure which distinguish it from these more established forms. One is the *scale* of investment in sport and the arts, and the second is that it tends to be attached to national and professional forms of provision (both in sport and the arts) rather than to primarily local and/or amateur activities. In the last few years banks and businesses have become increasingly involved in sponsoring performances of 'cultural' events – in the theatre, the opera, concerts, and so on. Such investment tends to follow the 'prestige' companies and organisations providing conventional 'high culture' – the National Theatre, the Royal Shakespeare Company, the Royal Opera and Royal Ballet Companies, etc. As such, this direction of flow of the sponsorship tends to follow the same circuits as government subsidies through the Arts Council. In 1979, over one-third of Arts Council money in England went to the major national companies.

Two points are worth making about such sponsorship. First, that it provides the organisations involved with a discreet and prestigious form of advertising. (Discreet by comparison with some other forms of sponsorship – we have not yet been treated to the 'Barclays Bank Hamlet' ...) The organisations gain prestige through their association with and promotion of cultural 'good things'. More particularly, such sponsorship helps to maintain the links between economic capital and 'cultural capital', by helping to maintain uneconomic forms of 'minority high culture' which would otherwise not be competitive in the 'leisure market'. There is, of course, more than a slight irony here, since most of the organisations would have a very different orientation to the economics of the products which they sponsor, were they one of their corporate subsidiaries. That is to say, they would close them as economically unviable. It is the 'tradition' and 'prestige' which is associated with high culture which makes such sponsorship a valued association for business.

This discreet sponsorship of the arts contrasts very strikingly with the other major field of commercial sponsorship – in sports. Here the emphasis is self-consciously upon the advertising of company names and products which sporting events allow. Both in the activities sponsored and in the audiences involved with them (particularly through televised sport), sponsorship here has a 'mass' or 'popular' target rather than the 'élite' associations of high culture. Sponsorship in sport takes a variety of forms, ranging from the donation of the match ball at particular football matches up to the sponsoring of national and international events (Coca Cola athletics, the Prudential Trophy for one day cricket, the Embassy snooker championships). Sponsors may operate through individual competitors or teams (John Player and Lotus; Wrangler and Nottingham Forest FC) or through sponsoring particular competitions (John Player trophies in rugby league and cricket; the Nat. West trophy for cricket, The Milk Marketing Board's recent acquisition of the Football League Cup and so on).

One key element in this sponsorship is to find access to television audiences for company advertising, and so the focus for sponsors tends to be on televised sports, and on versions of sports which are televised (one day rather than three day cricket, for example). There is a tendency for sponsorship to follow televisual values about sport (identifying the dramatic and spectacular events which make 'good television') because it is here that mass audiences will be found. Commercial sponsorship of sport allows the escape from two main constraints on television advertising. Generally, it allows the presence of company names despite the BBC's non-advertising rule; and more particularly it has allowed the tobacco companies to evade the ban on television advertising of cigarettes (John Player, Embassy and Benson and Hedges are among the most prolific sports sponsors).

It might have been expected that contradictions would emerge between the interests of commercial sponsors and the ideals of those who run sport, but the opposite has been the result. Those who argue, for example, for keeping 'political' interests out of sport have been only too willing to let commercial interests in. The recent Howell Report on sports sponsorship, while critical of the manipulative activities of some commercial interests, reserves its most stringent criticisms for the 'amateurish' managements of sports bodies who have failed to take advantage of the open-handed generosity of multinational corporations.

The effects of commercial sponsorship may not be a matter of grave concern for the mass of the public, who receive in exchange large amounts of televised high-class sport. But quite apart from the moral debates about the 'integrity' of sport, the process of increasing commercialisation threatens to undermine one of the crucial strengths of sport's popular appeal. Sport appears to be outside of the everyday economic and political life of our society – subject to its own rules and involving distinctively different values. Current trends in the linking of sport and commerce threaten to make sport subservient to those everyday economic values that we know so well. To put it simply, sport is becoming an adjunct of the advertising industry. Those who measure how people spend their leisure time may soon have to change their categories, since those periods of time currently labelled 'watching sports' should perhaps more accurately be 'window shopping'. Market researchers are, as usual, way ahead, such as in developing a 'matchmarker rating analysis' which evaluates the success of the television exposure of brand names through perimeter board displays at sporting events.

The independence of sport and the arts from the rest of social life may always have been an illusion, but the current expansion of commercial interests threatens to undermine the basis on which that illusion was maintained. Spiralling costs, rewards, sponsorship, and growing involvement of accountants, the Inland Revenue and auditors, and the threat of the bankruptcy court, make it difficult to 'suspend disbelief' and share in the collective illusion that sport is 'different'. In one sense, leisure never has been the opposite of work. It has been different in the sense that consumption is the obverse of production. But current trends highlight the way in which leisure is being subjected more visibly to the power and control of the economic organisations which shape the reality of our working lives.

Making a mass of things

The expansion of the leisure market, and particularly the rapid growth of mass communications during the 1950s and 1960s, gave rise to an analysis of the growth of 'mass society' and 'mass culture'. This form of analysis argued that the expansion of mass media gave rise to an increasingly uniform pattern of culture which systematically reduced or excluded cultural diversity. While it is true that mass production and consumption are powerful tendencies in the organisation of the leisure industries, and the tendency to social and political 'consensus' building is powerful within the mass media, the organisation of the leisure market cannot be understood through this one principle alone. While mass production guarantees certain economic advantages (economies of scale in production and distribution), it runs counter to two other significant aspects of the leisure market. One of these is the consumer's orientation to 'choice' and 'freedom' in leisure, which, as we saw in the case of the brewing industry, may run counter to the economic logic of the producers. We do not mean that 'consumer resistance' can prevent the logic of economic interests from prevailing, but it can be an obstruction, around which a way has to be found. If attempts to manipulate the market go too far, too soon, then the public may exercise its consumer 'sovereignty' and take its custom elsewhere. But it must be emphasised that the power of the consumer is essentially a negative one. The consumer can refuse to buy, but cannot control what is produced.

But secondly, producers have a more active interest in creating not a mass market, but a range of markets – a diversity of groups of consumers, with *different needs*. In part this diversity of markets recognised real social differences – differences of class, gender, ethnicity, region and so on – which manifest themselves in different needs and demands for leisure. The fact that the producers do not see this as a 'mass' is reflected in their extensive investment on market research and surveying, using elaborate social classifications, to test out the responsiveness of these different social sectors to goods and services being offered. But this differentiation also reflects the constant *innovation* in the leisure business – the attempt to construct new markets with new needs which will create new sources of profitability. 'Tastes' have to be endlessly promoted by the leisure enterprises to avoid stagnation. For example, the attempt by the breweries to reconstruct services available in pubs (and their social image) involved a relatively self-conscious attempt to reconstruct the consumer's relation to the pub;

It is high time that Andy Capp was given a new suit and a car and took his wife out to one of the many popular north east pubs where he can still enjoy his pint of beer and Florrie can have a glass of sauterne with her scampi and chips. (Brewery executive, quoted in C. Hutt, *The Death of the English Pub*, Arrow, 1973, p. 128).

The leisure industries, then, always face a tension between diversity of products and markets (for example, companies in the 'holiday' business may own holiday camps, marinas, tour operators and 'prestige' international hotels) and 'generalisation' – the attempt to create as large a market for a particular service as possible.

The leisure market tends to be segmented in a number of ways, although probably the most potent of these differentiating mechanisms is purchasing power – disposable income. The innovation of new markets in the post-war period shows this tendency of leisure capital to 'go where the money is'. The increase in the 1950s of disposable incomes (supplemented by the expansion of hire purchase) underpinned the growth of leisure industries, and the most dynamic sectors were associated with the group which had the highest rise in disposable income – adolescents. The pool of spending power constitued the economic base for the creation and rapid expansion of the 'youth market': clothes, records, cosmetics, magazines, coffee bars, discos, and so on.

More recently, the target for the focus of leisure innovation has moved up the age range to the 20–30 group, not least because of the removal of the economic basis for the youth market in conditions of massive youth unemployment. The new consumer comes from the generation which is possessed of a youth cultural history, perhaps more precisely 'post-hippie', since the focus is on the young middle class with a 'cosmopolitan' culture, entering the consumer market of home ownership, but still socially active. The leisure culture which has developed in this market reflects something of this group's material position in the expansion of the 'human relations industries' (both state and private) since the 1960s. They are the taste leaders in a market of 'ethnicity' (foreign food, foreign travel, wine, etc.) and 'creativity' (most distinctively reflected in the rise of enterprises such as Habitat). Perhaps the increasing 'maturity' of this market sector was expressed in the moment when Conran (Habitat) took over Mothercare. It is also the group which has brought 'health' into being as a market force, rather than being the domain of the state, ranging from health foods to the dramatic increase in middle class athleticism, under-pinning the massive commerical booms in squash, dance and jogging.

Nevertheless, perceiving this leisure market as segmented rather than a mass market should not lead us into the opposite error. This is to see the market as the operation of groups of consumers – a plurality of groups differentiated by their 'tastes' or market choices. This plurality approach to leisure use is one which recapitulates the errors of economic theories of the rational, freely choosing, consumer, and treats the existence of the market as the condition of 'freedom'. But this 'freely choosing' rational consum-er is a myth – choice in market societies is structured by a whole series of powerful determination. *First*, economic constraints in the form of spending power operates as a powerful determinant of what choices are available in the market to any group. *Second*, there is the social constraint of time available for leisure – less for those who 'choose' to work overtime, or for those women whose 'domestic responsibilities' cut heavily into 'free time'. *Thirdly*, there are cultural determinations which link these social and economic positions to traditions and practices which shape what is acceptable and desirable in leisure. *Finally*, there are the economic determinants of what is produced for sale in the leisure market. As we have seen, this decision making power is highly concentrated in the large corporations which dominate the leisure industry. What is made available is dependent on financial and managerial calcula-tions of the market potential of particular goods and services, and this logic serves to ensure that the absence of a viable market means the non-production of a particular service.

A clear example can be found in the 'range' of national newspapers available for us to choose between. As determined by the finances of advertising, there are only two possible kinds of newspaper, based on two very different kinds of markets. One is a relatively small group of affluent people, at whom specific sorts of (usually classified or business-to-business) advertising can be directed. The second is made up by a much larger number of people from the middle or lower income groups, who make up a market big enough for display adverts for mass produced consumer goods, as well as providing a large enough readership for a profit to be made on the cover price of the newspaper. There are no other viable models of national newspaper publishing. Our 'choice' of newspaper has to be made within this very restricted – if highly polarised – range.

Nevertheless, this ideology of choice and the consumer has very real consequences. The procedures in the leisure industry do recognise differentiation within their markets and make attempts to accommodate these differently constituted groups (so long as they are 'worth' addressing). Newspaper producers address their particular audiences in different ways – they attempt to identify the appropriate 'voice' for their readership, News International, for example, which bestrides both 'quality' and 'popular' press, addresses its *Sun* readers in tones and words different from *The Times* audience – though not necessarily with divergent political views. Differences are *mobilised* in the leisure market as a means of producing consumer identification – and produce what appear to be different groups of consumers. The leisure public, then, appears as differently oriented groups of 'tastes' – opera goers, football fans, *Sun* readers, Crossroads watchers, first class train or air passengers. Because of the 'free market' ideology, these differences appear as choices. In reality they depend on very different processes – the very real divisions of class, gender, race and age which structure choice. But these divisions are represented through the leisure market as differences in taste. Differences in class appear in the form of quality and tabloid newspapers, differences in gender as choices between football and knitting, and so on. The way in which market research (and too much of sociology) 'understands' these differences is to represent social divisions as if they were personal preferences, matters of taste and choice, located in the individual's characteristics.

The celebration of diversity and choice in the leisure marketplace is a misleading one, emphasising choice at the expense of understanding the structures which constrain these decisions. On the one hand, the attention to choice conceals the social structure and ideologies which position individuals in relation to the market. On the other, the attention to diversity conceals the structure of economic power in the leisure industry. To focus on the varieties of washing powder available in the supermarket is an inexcusable error if it leads one to forget that this commodity involves on the one side, the domestic worker doing the family wash, and on the other, the two-headed monopoly of Proctor and Gamble, and Unilever. It is, however, regrettably true that many studies of leisure have been unable to tear their gaze away from the glittering display of the leisure market.

'Going too far': problems with the ideal consumer

We argued earlier that leisure often appears publicly as 'the leisure problem'. This emerges most strongly when particular groups of consumers are seen as using leisure improperly, producing various sorts of psychological or social deviance, endangering life and property, or outraging social convention. The list of these infractions is a potentially long one: the cinema was originally accused of inflaming youthful passions; gambling leads to neurotic obsessions; drinking leads to alcoholism; television may induce either passivity or violence; Bank holidays have suffered from excesses of Mods and Rockers; football fans have a propensity to turn into mindless hooligans; skateboarding threatened a danger to the public on the streets; and Space Invaders undermine young people's proper commitments to school and family.

Two things recur in the complaints about these dangers of leisure. One is the theme of 'excess' – either in the sense of over-indulgence (the alcoholic or the compulsive gambler) or in the sense of excessive commitment – taking one's pleasures too seriously (football hooligans who do not recognise that 'it's only a game', for example). The other theme is that of 'mis-use' – using the facilities, goods or services provided for something other than their intended purpose (of which the sharpest example may be 'glue-sniffing'). These problems have their basis in the relation between producers, the product and consumers.

Ideally, this relationship should be a straightforward one. Consumers have a need which producers recognise. They produce commodities which will satisfy that need. The commodity thus has a clearly defined purpose or use. But, unfortunately, consumers are not moulded in this simple and rational way. Culturally, they may have very different orientations to the commodities supplied in the leisure market – they may appropriate the commodity for some very different use. And once the cash transaction has taken place, the buyer possesses the commodity to make of it what he or she will. The ideology of the free market and of leisure as free choice conspire together to produce a 'permissiveness' in this realm of commodities, economically underpinned by the logic of profitability in the leisure industry, since it is the sale not the use of the commodity which is significant. Allied Breweries make the same profit whether one person buys seven drinks or seven people buy one drink, whether they are drunk in the pub or at home, in moderation or to excess.

This economic freedom creates a degree of cultural freedom in the appropriation and use of commodities in the leisure market. The ideal of the rational consumer allows the possibility of 'irrationality'. However, this relation between the logic of profitability and the uses of commodities is too starkly put – because, in different ways, some groups of producers do attempt to 'police' or circumscribe the uses to which their goods or services are put. Dance halls and discos use regulations on dress to attempt to ensure that only 'desirable' users of their facilities will be allowed in, and use bouncers to 'police' events within the building. The management of pubs and restaurants 'reserve the right' to refuse to serve. The record industry is currently trying to find ways of preventing the 'mis-use' of home taping equipment for the copying of records. In other instances, it is assumed that social conventions and 'educated' consumers ensure that proper behaviour is maintained (at museums, the theatre and so on). Elsewhere, the presence of the less educated may require the buying in of private or public police services (at football grounds, for example). However, it should be noted that such attempts to police or regulate the use of goods or services is not always an act of economic self-sacrifice on the part of producers. In many instances, their introduction of strategies of control is on the grounds that the particular 'mis-use' is 'bad for business'. One recurrent strand in the football business' concern about football hooliganism is that it has caused falling attendances by frightening off 'respectable' fans.

Nevertheless, this persistent tension between economic freedom and the irrationality of the consumer (leading to private and public disorder) is a field which has historically required more than the exercise of control on the part of producers. It is one of the aspects of leisure in which the market meets the state.

The state of play

In most studies of leisure, the state appears as a provider of leisure facilities (ranging from art galleries to sports fields). But this view tends to hide the other field of the state's practice in relation to leisure – that of regulation and control of free time and its uses. As we saw in Chapter 3, the suppression and control of different leisure activities has often involved the exercise of state power. In this chapter, we shall be examing the state's intervention in leisure around these two, connected, poles of regulation and provision.

In doing so, we shall be offering a variant of what Roberts called class domination theory. He is right to argue that in its most simple or vulgar form, this theory can produce a very mechanical model of the capitalist state. Beginning from Marx and Engels' famous observation that 'the executive of the modern state is nothing but a committee for managing the affairs of the ruling class', it is a short and tempting step to the assumption that this is all the state is and can be. It is, alas, not so straightforward. In this vulgar version, almost any action by the state can be regarded as 'social control'. Building an all-weather football pitch in any inner city area is a form of social control – but so is not building it and sending in the Special Patrol Group instead. Such an analysis simply will not do. While at a very general level, an all weather football pitch may be no more of a satisfactory solution to the structural problems of youth unemployment than the Special Patrol Group, these two policies nevertheless have very different social consequences. A class analysis of the state must at least distinguish between different sorts of state policies, and examine the different political processes which inform those policies.

While we share Roberts's scepticism about the simple version of class domination theory, we do not think it is necessary to go to the opposite extreme and accept that state policy is essentially benevolent, the product of muddling through with good intentions. In what follows we wish to draw attention to the power which the state possesses to control the form and content of leisure, and examine what that power consists of. This analysis of state power and policy in relation to leisure may help to reveal the ways in which both vulgar Marxist and liberal pluralist approaches are misleading.

Just as we have argued that the analysis of leisure needs to begin from a consideration of the socially structured divisions between work and leisure, so our discussion of the state's role must examine the part which it plays in the maintenance of these distinctions. Some of the separations between work and leisure are enshrined in legislation, and are supervised by the state. In particular, legislation exists which regulates issues such as working hours, public holidays and working conditions. Alongside these are statutes which determine who can be employed in different forms of work, affecting, for example, the employment of children and women. The state is also entrusted with ensuring (in very restricted ways) the maintenance of equal employment opportunities and equal pay for comparable employment.

These legal powers of the state for the regulation of employment (and by implication the boundaries of work and leisure) highlight the contradictory nature of the state's role in British capitalism. It works both to maintain the normal conditions of a capitalist economy (the character of employment itself), but also intervenes to make concessions demanded by subordinate social groups for their protection (e.g. over working hours and conditions, and equal opportunities). It is the framing of these concessions and political compromises within the broad logic of capitalist economic relations and requirements that makes sense of the description of the state as a capitalist state. As we shall see, time and time again, the state places restrictions and limits on the economic power of capitalist enterprises, while at the same time trying to maintain the 'normal' working of 'market forces'. Like Roberts, we would agree that the state is not simply a tool of capitalist interests, but we also need to be aware that concessions and compromises have taken place within the 'taken-for-granted' structure of a capitalist society.

Licensed leisure: the state and the market

One very clear example of this policy of both maintaining 'market forces' and restricting their 'excesses' is provided in the relationship between the state and the commercial provision of leisure. As we argued in Chapter 3, commercial organisations have increasingly come to dominate the supply of leisure goods and services, with state provision acting as a supplementary source of leisure services. But the state plays a particular role in relation to commercial provision – that of controlling the market through licensing.

Through its licensing powers, the state controls some aspects of what sorts of goods and services can be supplied in the leisure market. For example, through the British Board of Film Censors it monitors the supply of cinema provision, and is likely to acquire similar powers of inspection and control over commercial video distribution. Similarly, through the systems of public health inspection and trading standards officers, it can inspect and control the supply of meals in restaurants, cafés and takeaways.

Secondly, the state has licensing powers which allow it to regulate the conditions under which leisure goods and services are produced and consumed. It licenses places of public entertainment, establishing that they meet requirements of health and safety (e.g. fire precautions in places such as cinemas, dance halls and discos). Through such means, the state is empowered to ensure that pleasures can be achieved safely and in an orderly fashion.

Thirdly, the state's licensing powers also allow it to intervene in questions of who can produce and consume various leisure goods and services. For example, there are powers to ensure that the owners and managers of pubs, wine bars, betting shops and casinos are not 'undesirable' and thus likely to exploit the potential of such enterprises in a criminal or dangerous manner. On the other hand, the state's licensing powers are also used to protect 'vulnerable' groups of consumers, usually the young, who are thought unable to resist the power of commercial pressures for themselves (e.g. age restrictions on such matters as buying alcohol, certain sorts of entertainment and hire purchase agreements).

One main theme stands out in these licensing powers: state intervention in commercial leisure provision exists to prevent possible 'excesses' of unregulated market forces in their search for profitability. These 'excesses' may take various forms: the adulteration of food and drink; crowding more entry-paying customers into an entertainment venue than is safe, or offences against moral taste and social standards – but each marks the boundary between normal commercial enterprise and 'unreasonable' exploitation. The public – the mass of consumers – is placed in centre stage by these powers of the state. It is our interests as consumers that are being protected against exploitation. What is less visible is the way these licensing powers work to protect 'legitimate' commercial interests. Gross exploitation of the leisure market by 'cowboys' and 'pirates' threatens to spoil the game for the rest in a number of ways. The 'short cuts' of the cowboy operators (e.g., video pirating) threaten the profitability of the legitimate enterprises, and also by 'short changing' the consumer threaten to bring the *whole* business into disrepute. Licensing, then, while providing some degree of consumer protection also works to protect legitimate commercial interests. 'We' are preserved from gross forms of commercial exploitation in order that we will be available for its normal forms.

Disorderly conduct: the state and public space

The second major area of the state's regulation of leisure is the control of public space and the uses to which it may be put. The central role here is taken by the law's definition of public order and its interpretation and enactment by the police. But there are other official agencies who are also involved in the policing of public space. For example, the use of public parks is heavily circumscribed by municipal bye-laws mostly conceived in the nineteenth century, when the parks were created as an institution of 'rational recreation' to direct the working classes from their 'disorderly' leisure pursuits. The shout, common to many working class childhoods, of 'the parkie's coming' testifies to the vigilance with which disorderly conduct has been regulated in the parks, as does the introduction of 'parks police' by many local authorities in the 1960s and 1970s. The tension between non-organised and informal leisure patterns, and the 'proper' use of public space forms a central and unbroken thread in the history of the public parks, and this same theme recurs in the policing of other public spaces.

The crime prevention and detection role of the British police has always coexisted with the requirement that they 'maintain public order'. The task of keeping the streets safe for decent people has always combined these two functions in an uncomfortable mixture. 'Street crime' (robbery and theft) has always attracted the most visibility in this area of policing – producing moral panics about garrotting (1860s) through to 'mugging' in the 1970s and 1980s. Nevertheless, the policing of public space has more often had 'victimless' crimes as its main forms of attention. While robbery on the streets grabs the headlines, the mundane reality of public policing concerns offences against public order – the playing of games prohibited by local bye-laws; trespass; loitering with intent; being drunk and disorderly; causing a breach of the peace; and being a suspected person. Unlike robbery and theft, these offences against public order depend heavily upon police discretion, and their interpretation of social behaviour. By the early 1980s, the policing of public space in Britain's inner cities had become one of the most explosive 'leisure' conflicts. The use of the (now repealed) 'sus' law, and stop-and-search powers, produced recurrent confrontations between the police and working class (particularly black) youth on the streets, which were to play a major part in triggering the riots of 1981.

While all the evidence suggests that such laws dealing with public order offences have been applied in a discriminatory manner (targeting young, working class, black, males), the legal control of public space involves a more general level of discrimination. Given the inequality of access to *private* space in our society (available more to the wealthy than to the poor, to older rather than younger), those groups who have to resort to public space for their leisure time are automatically more vulnerable to policing. When this visibility coincides with police definitions of them as a 'threat' to public order or as suspicious persons, then they are subjected to a process of double discrimination at law.

Home and away: the state and family life

When on the surface it appears to be doing other things, such as maintaining public order on the streets, the state is actually imposing a particular ideal of acceptable leisure activity. There are other areas where the activity of the state has spin-offs for leisure. This is especially so for those policies and personnel designed to promote welfare to ensure that the public order of the streets is complemented by the private order of the home.

Just as the state regulates the working of the market, so too it possesses powers to regulate families to ensure that 'normal' life is maintained. Central aspects of private life are embedded in a network of laws: matrimonial law, the law relating to children and their protection from poor parenting, etc. Through a variety of agencies – social workers, probation officers, health visitors – the state supervises and attempts to promote 'good' family behaviour. But, in addition to these regulatory powers, welfare agencies of the state are also involved in forms of leisure provision.

Think for example of the role of outings and holidays – the provision of rational organised leisure – for groups variously described as deprived or 'at risk': problem families, inner city residents, the actually or potentially delinquent, the isolated or handicapped. Often no more is involved here than the genuine altruism of giving people opportunities for leisure activities they would not otherwise have. The coach outing for the old people's clubs, the subsidised group holiday for one-parent families are obvious examples. The attempt is to give groups outside the consumer market access to goods and services which others habitually enjoy.

But there are other instances where leisure is consciously used as an instrument of rehabilitation. Such an example is the strategy of intermediate treatment, which as the term implies involves an intervention between the alternatives of having teenagers 'at risk' to their own devices and removing them altogether into approved institutions. Directed mainly, though not exclusively, at boys, intermediate treatment involves a whole gamut of activities: regular group meetings, more 'therapeutic' versions of specialised youth clubs, involvement in good deeds for the old and the handicapped, weekend camps, often with an emphasis on outward bound activities. A number of objectives are held by IT workers: to let those involved let off steam, to develop social skills within their peer group, to relate positively to adults.

Implicit in this whole enterprise is what might be called a spill-over theory: that if proper habits and attitudes can be inculcated during leisure time, these will be carried over as the basis for a general code of conduct at home, in school or workplace. This is only a more intense form of a whole range of activities which have their rightful place in the work of social services and their voluntary ancillaries: playgroups, playgrounds and adventure holiday centres for the young; social clubs for the elderly and handicapped. We do not wish to denigrate such activities or to impugn the integrity of those involved in providing them. We know from first-hand experience and observation that they are often made to materialise from the thinnest of resources and are positively valued by those who benefit from them. Rather we want to emphasise how these examples need to be understood as a state intervention in the sphere of leisure. That they come under the 'welfare' category should not mean that they are simply ignored by leisure analysis. They are not marginal but integral to the state's attempts to compensate for the deficiencies of the leisure market and to convert leisure, that private haven of consumer choice by the individual, into the provision of public services for group enjoyment. They represent thus a contradiction: from one angle they are a continuation of state paternalism in leisure, the attempt to provide the 'right' trend of recreation for the otherwise deprived; from another angle, they offer a model, however limited, of leisure provision which does not depend on commercial consumption.

Broadly speaking, the state's leisure provision is shaped by its secondary role in relation to commercial provision. State provision aims at providing compensation for the deficiencies of market forces in a number of ways. The state subsidises some forms of leisure which are, by virtue of their limited audience, unprofitable but are nevertheless thought to be socially desirable (e.g. the arts). The state provides some forms of 'compensatory' provision for social groups whose lack of economic power makes them an unattractive market for commercial providers (e.g. the elderly poor). Finally, the state provides some of the infra-structure for leisure whose scale is too large or too uneconomic for single commercial enterprises to take on (e.g. lakes and waterways, parks and leisure centres). Such provision nevertheless provides the setting in which commercially provided leisure goods can be used for leisure activities (e.g. boats, sports kit and equipment), and thus forms an important basis for some of the leisure industries. Perhaps most importantly, however, the state intervenes to provide a population 'ready' for leisure through mass education.

Learning to enjoy ourselves: education and leisure

One central part of the state's role in providing leisure is in the provision of education. For children and young people, education includes elements of education *for* leisure, teaching them the personal skills identified as valuable for leading a full and rewarding social life. Schooling, for example, promotes sport both for its intrinsic educational purposes and as producing skills and attitudes which can be transferred to constructive leisure outside the school. The traditional 'arts' education (particularly in the guise of English Literature) aims to develop the civilising faculties of sensitivity and appreciation which will enable the young person to take advantage of Britain's rich (if rather narrowly defined) cultural heritage. More recently (and especially since the raising of the school leaving age), educational concern has been focused on the 'non-academic' pupils in secondary education. While 'academic' streams are assumed to acquire social adjustment through their academic education, the 'non-academic' seem to require a different sort of preparation for life outside the school. The 1970s and 1980s have seen a whole variety of schemes concerned with 'relevant' education for the non-academic. These have focused on 'vocational' training, coinciding precisely with the collapse of the youth labour market. But they have also aimed at the development of 'social and life skills' and at 'education for leisure'.

As always, the leisure of the working class young appears as a potential problem, and education for leisure aims to 'broaden the minds' of young people by introducing them to the opportunities for constructive leisure, and by providing the social skills necessary to take advantage of the possibilities that exist. Leisure preparation may range from attempts to popularise 'high' cultural institutions (visits to museums and art galleries) to efforts to introduce aspects of youth culture into the school curriculum (music appreciation based on pop rather than classical music). While some of these attempts do provide teachers with the possibility of developing critical skills and attitudes, the institutional motivation for them has been rather different. 'Relevance' emerged as an attempted solution to problems of classroom management – what to do with bored and intractable pupils who found no relevance in conventional academic curricula.

The state provides more than education for leisure, it also supplies education-as-leisure. For adolescents, the youth service emerged as an adjunct to the school system, providing 'constructive' leisure for some of the hours when the young were free from the confines of the school. More recently, youth work has been supplanted by the more selective provision of 'Intermediate Treatment' schemes for working class adolescents. IT, introduced by the 1969 Children and Young Persons Act as a means of diverting young offenders from institutional punishment has, in fact, been used to provide 'leisure' for 'pre-delinquents' who are identified as being 'at risk' of offending by social service departments.

Education-as-leisure has, however, been most developed for adults. The success of the Workers' Educational Association in providing part time evening education for adults led to financial support from local authorities, and the reproduction of those successes by local educational institutions, opening schools, colleges and universities to part-time study by adults seeking either education-as-pleasure or more instrumental academic or vocational study. This process of providing education-as-leisure has involved the state taking up, sponsoring and developing a successful *popular* initiative whose origins lie outside the state. However, in the current political climate of hostility to 'wasteful' public spending, this widespread pattern of adult education is endangered. Where it does not fall within government priorities about vocationalism and retraining, such educational provision is at risk of being designated a luxury. As a financial squeeze is put on local authority budgets, so educational priorities become those of trying to maintain statutory commitments (to primary and secondary schooling) rather than the 'extras' like adult education classes.

The same processes are visible in the one national institution which aimed to provide adult education at university level – the Open University. Although its patterns of student recruitment suggest that it has extensively serviced middle class interests in 'topping up' other educational qualifications and some professional retraining, its commitment to openness and broad-based conceptions of adult education are currently endangered by the cutting of financial support and pressure to become more 'vocationally' oriented.

'Healthy minds': the state and culture

We saw earlier that state initiatives in welfare often began from philanthropic roots, a similar pattern is visible in the state's contribution to the 'cultural life' in the nation. The state is now the main provider of 'culture' – through its network of museums, galleries and libraries and, indirectly, through its subsidies of the arts. Many of these responsibilities have been taken over from nineteenth century philanthropic attempts to provide 'improving' experiences for the lower orders. But it is now the state which is the guardian and guarantor of the 'national heritage' in its varied forms.

The preservation of this heritage involves a representation of 'our' history as a succession of cultural achievements. Although a majority of the nation will not have encountered them outside the classrooms or school visits, Shakespeare, Constable, and the 'stately home', are indissolubly 'ours' – part of the 'greatness' of the Great Britain. The preservation of this culture involves a profound social tension: a tension between élite tradition and the democratisation of culture. As Raymond Williams has argued, the creation of a 'tradition' in cultural forms is a process of selection, and in Britain this transformation of elements of culture into 'Culture' has always been dominated by élite values. Culture is the selectively constructed culture of particular social groups. In spite of this, the state's preservation of it is represented as a *national*, rather than a class culture. It is represented as 'our heritage', even though it is the 'heritage' of a particular class. Not surprisingly, it is the members of that class (and those who seek to emulate them) who express their 'appreciation' of it, and dominate the use of galleries, museums and theatres. It is not the nation which consumes 'Culture' but overwhelmingly the middle classes. The role of the working class in this selective process is to subsidise the maintenance of the 'national' heritage.

However, the 'nationalisation' of culture exists not solely for this subsidisation of middle class taste, but because of a continuing belief in a crude psychology of 'civilising influences'. Art is presumed to be intrinsically civilising, and exposure to it will be an improving experience. More improving still is the development of a sensibility of 'appreciation' – the creation of a ground of common values from which we can speak to each other. The state's education system, and the founding values of the BBC, testify to the strength of this attempt to civilise by trying to democratise access to dominant values. It has been a failure. The mass of the public seems neither to understand nor appreciate art, and express little interest in learning how to. They remain resolutely 'uncultured' – at least in the sense of 'culture' as the prerogative of the educated middle and upper classes.

The historical failure of this attempt to bring about social integration through a democratised access to a national and nationalised culture has, more recently, led to state initiatives in rather different directions. These revolve around, not the democratisation of access, but a limited democratisation of what counts as 'culture', with a stress on participation. State funding (though on a much smaller scale than for established institutions of high culture) has been supplied to promote community-based cultural activities, community theatre, writers-in-residence, street festivals, and so on. The commitment here is to promote *local* cultural life through sponsoring 'grass roots' activities, and encouraging the formation of 'community spirit'. These initiatives form the cultural 'wing' of a much wider array of state attempts to integrate 'deviant' localities back into the mainstream of British political life – for example, through Community Development Projects, Community Centres, the Urban Aid programme, Inner City Partnership, and so on. In addition to fostering grass roots activities, such initiatives have also involved efforts to 'de-institutionalise' existing provisions – travelling exhibitions, mobile libraries, street theatre – which again reflect patterns of de-institutionalised practice in other fields of state intervention (detached youth work, 'outreach' probation work, 'patch' systems in social work, etc.)

We shall return to some of these issues about integration through culture in state policy in the conclusion to this chapter, but for the moment we must consider another aspect of state provision: around sport and recreation.

'Healthy bodies': the state and sport

Once again, the origins of state policy are marked by a range of voluntary and philanthropic initiatives in the late nineteenth century – in particular by the focus of public school ideologies and 'muscular Christians' on the social value of organised sports. The resonance of 'Englishness' and sport tends to be associated with the zealous spread of the civilising influence of sport through cultural colonisation, but the same missionary fervour also identified sport as a harmonising influence in intervention in the 'dark continent' of working class Britain. Organised sport was valued as a means of promoting cross class contact, providing healthy and 'constructive' recreation, and an exposure to the improving sentiments of the 'sporting code'. From the late nineteenth century, the state has been increasingly involved in supporting and subsidising this centrality of sport – first through education, and the provision of recreation grounds and playing fields, swimming baths and latterly, the importance of sports centres in recreation provision.

The harmonisation of classes follows a very different trajectory here from that of the provision of 'Culture'. Where the latter has historically been ignored, sport has had a very different response – at least from the male working class. In part, this stems from the fact that sport represents a very different cultural process from that of the arts. While 'culture' was an élite tradition imposed from the 'top downwards', sport involved a more complex cultural alliance. As Chapter 3 recounted, the provision of organised sport often took the form of a remodelling and codification of already existing popular practices. The accomplishment of the 'public school tradition' was not to *create* popular recreations, but to provide structures of organisation, codes and patterns for existing (though often 'disorganised') pursuits within which subordinate classes could still recognise themselves. Sport was not simply an attempt to impose a model of culture on the lower classes, but a compromise created between 'educated' and 'popular' patterns of recreation.

The state's long history of involvement in recreational provision is marked by a concern for 'substitution' – the provision of 'rational' alternatives to disorderly patterns of leisure on the part of the working class. The creation of parks, for example, by municipal authorities involved conceptions of providing orderly and supervised areas of diversion from disorderly social, moral and *political* activities in city streets. It needs to be stressed again that public parks are not simply 'space', but a regulated and supervised space.

As with the general issue of sport, however, this concern for diversion sometimes encounters demands from sectors of the subordinate classes for facilities and access. The mass trespasses of the 1930s, for example, involved struggles over access to the countryside for working class walkers and ramblers; and at local levels, the state's concern for order could encounter working class demands for recreational facilities, through the provision of playing fields. The tension in this compromise is persistently one between organisation and supervision on the one hand, and 'authority' on the other. The creation of facilities is always coupled with the requirement that they be used in a 'proper' manner, subject to regulations, scrutiny and control.

To a large extent, this has biased access to facilities and resources in favour of 'responsible' groups who have formal and recognisable organisational structures (e.g. leagues and clubs with members and officials). But not all groups fit this pattern of conventional organisation – and nor do they all wish to. Informal, spontaneous and unorganised leisure activities persist on the fringes of the more visible organised forms. Street football, and the use of parks pitches when the park keeper's not looking, remain the 'popular' basis of football in Britain.

This antagonism between provision and autonomy has always surfaced most sharply around male working class youth. From the inception of youth clubs and youth organisations in the 1880s, the efforts to provide supervised leisure have always run up against the 'unclubbables', leading to constant innovation aimed at reaching this group. Since the Second World War, such innovations included the 'modernisation' of youth work (following the Albemarle Report) in an attempt to compete against the seductive attractions of commercial youth culture. Subsequently, the priority became 'detached' youth work, intended to encounter the young in their natural habitat of the street to win their trust. The 1960s also saw the development of the adventure playground movement, adopted by many local authorities, aimed at providing more innovatory (and supervised) forms of play in working class neighbourhoods, particularly in the new 'high-rise' districts.

In spite of the different arguments which have influenced these innovations, their adoption by the state has involved a constant repetition of the litany association with the 'problem' of working class youth. One: 'off the street'; two: 'under supervision'; three: 'something constructive to do'. The motivating forces have remained strikingly similar in spite of the diversity of forms of provision.

The new 'people's palace'? Leisure centres and leisure management

One effect of the major reorganisation of local government following the Redcliffe Maud Report, was the creation of leisure or recreation departments within most local authorities. These took over functions from the old 'parks departments' but were expanded to deal with a wide variety of leisure provision. By 1981, local authorities were spending an estimated £630 million on leisure and recreation. While the bulk of this expenditure remained connected to parks and open spaces, over a tenth was devoted to the new jewel in sporting provision: the leisure centres. From the 1960s, the Sports Council had been urging the development of multi-facility sports and recreation centres as an integral part of leisure planning, and to good effect. Between 1972 and 1981, over 400 new sports centres were built. These centres have supplemented the old 'playing fields' focus of the Parks Departments by providing for indoor sports: typically swimming, squash, badminton and gymnasium based activities. In many cases, they provide tuition as well as facilities, and also include social facilities such as cafés and bars.

Such centres were intended to widen access to sports which had been relatively 'closed' because of the expense of equipment and special facilities. To some extent, this widening has been successful (e.g. among the skilled working class), but the leisure centres appear to have been equally successful in subsidising the sporting activities of professional and managerial groups. Sports Council surveys have identified the 'non-participants' as housewives, the semi-skilled and unskilled, the non-car owner, the lower income groups.

It might, uncharitably, be thought that this list should come as no surprise. Even if the desire to use the facilities exists, the patterns of inequality surrounding leisure which we have already considered suggest that time, money and transport are likely to be effective barriers. But the question of desire is also significant. If the participants are predominantly male and middle class, this may confirm non-participants in their non-participatory reaction. A glance at the list of the Sports Council's ten most funded sports suggests that, with a few exceptions, the suspicions of non-participants about class and male bias provision may be correct:

1	Squash	6	Tennis
2	Swimming	7	Golf
3	Athletics	8	Shooting
4	Sailing	9	Cricket
5	Rowing	10	Canoeing

The problem is that in the Sports Council's vision, neither sport in general nor particular sports are seen as embodying distinctive class and gender values. Instead they are treated as having universal appeal: 'sport for all'. Hence the surprise when 'take-up' is not representative of the local population. The associations of class and gender carried by sports may be historical 'accidents', but they will not vanish overnight. Not only the associations, but the definition of sport may need to be challenged. A Sports Centre is not a flexible community resource for the use of young and old, men and women, working class and middle class alike. It is 'for' sport, and hence will be used by those for whom sport is a conventional and attractive cultural choice.

This blindness to what sport means permeates the forecasting and management of demand in leisure. Surveys of demand and exhortations to participate are likely to elicit the demands and responses of precisely those groups who have clearly defined leisure purposes, and will result in provision which follows those demands. This does not mean that the pattern of provision is deliberately restricted, but it will tend to follow clearly identified 'needs' with other, less clearly voiced or even unspoken, needs coming lower in the list of priorities. That the articulation of clearly defined needs should reflect patterns of class and gender inequality in other areas of life should not, we repeat, come as a great surprise.

However, this market or consumer model of leisure planning is not the only means through which policy is formulated. 'Consumer demand' has to compete with a different model of leisure policy – that of 'leisure-as-compensation'. Here, leisure provision is aimed at those with 'unspoken needs'. It is created as a compensation for those who suffer disadvantage, deprivation and other associated social evils. To some extent, it is hoped, satisfaction in leisure may make up for dissatisfaction in other spheres of life. Sometimes leisure provision is explicitly charged as the responsibility of the welfare 'arm' of the state, and its voluntary ancillaries. Clubs for pensioners or mothers-and-toddlers, adventure playgrounds and youth centres may be sponsored by education or social services, departments, or with charitable assistance. But more self-consciously leisure oriented provision may be produced to help with pressing social problems. Leisure initiatives in the inner cities of Britain, or in Belfast, where in 1984 there will soon be eight leisure and sports centres, are obvious examples of leisure as compensation.

The political insult which is contained in this policy of leisure as compensation should, we hope, need little discussion. What is more significant is the continuing belief in leisure as a force for social *integration*. Confronted with groups who are structurally disadvantaged and potentially disaffected or alienated, we see a state policy which reviews 'rational recreation' as a means of promoting social cohesion. And sport, as in the nineteenth century, is in the vanguard of this search to create harmony out of division. This search for integration through leisure, although particularly sharply revealed in policies directed at the unemployed and inner-city populations, is in fact the key to understanding the organisation of state policy and leisure.

The nation at play

The various activities of the state which we have discussed in this chapter are shaped by this quest for integration. The state aims to absorb all social groups into the life of the nation – to make us all participating citizens. The failure to participate – in the approved forms – raises suspicions. In relation to both body and mind, the state has pushed policies aimed at drawing subordinate social groups into 'rational recreation' in order to curb the potential dangers of free time. In the development of state policies for leisure, we can identify one major change of strategy, which can be best described as a change from 'assimilation' to 'multiculturalism'.

The strategy of *assimilation* rested on the belief that there existed a single national culture into which all social groups could be drawn, by exposing them to 'improving influences'. By bringing the arts and sport to the masses, they could be 'civilised' (or 'rescued') and turned into responsible citizens. The persistent refusal of subordinate groups to be improved in this way lies at the heart of the change in state policy. In the last twenty years, the state's leisure policy has increasingly come to recognise the existence of different cultures and the diversity of leisure needs.

Multi-culturalism, by contrast speaks of 'minorities', different 'communities' and the problem of 'access'. It seeks to identify the needs and interests of different social groups, and to discover ways of addressing those different interests. The list of 'minorities' is sizeable. The Sports Council's plan for *The Next Ten Years* (1982) identifies six major 'target' groups: teenagers; school leavers; parents with young children; low income households; ethnic minorities; older and retired people. While the overlap between these 'different' groups raises some questions about the Sports Council's analytic grasp of the British social structure, it also indicates something of the scope of this policy of integration-through-leisure-participation. In one sense, this policy values the *fact* of participation above the nature of the particular activities in which people take part. This changing strategy is also visible in other cultural institutions, for example, in television. The BBC has accepted the 'need' to broaden its content from its original Reithian ambitions of cultural improvement and enlightenment, first to 'popular' programming aimed at competing with ITV for mass audience, and then subsequently to the sponsorship of 'minority' voices through access slots on BBC2. Similarly, the second commercial channel (Channel 4) was established to provide programming for 'minorities' not served by the main channels of both companies. With awful predictability, it had no sooner begun broadcasting, than it was subjected to intense public criticism for giving over air time to undesirable and unrepresentative 'minorities'. Not everyone is fully committed to a multi-cultural policy of integration.

This concern to increase participation may seem to contradict our own arguments about the relationship between a capitalist state and leisure. Surely, this pattern of provision directed at minorities and their diverse needs is, in fact, more in line with Roberts' argument about leisure pluralism? We remain unconvinced that this is the case for a number of reasons.

First, this attempt to widen the leisure 'franchise' is one which fails to engage with the *structural* inequalities of British society. It can only think of those who are 'left out' through a model of 'deprived' or 'disadvantaged' minorities. This model leaves us with a view of society in which the majority are happily at play, while – on the periphery – a few unfortunate groups are suffering. This view, while doubtless an advance on the older policy of cultural assimilation, nevertheless involves a profound misunderstanding of the ways in which class, gender, race and age are social structures which produce a systematically unequal distribution of all types of economic and social resources.

Secondly, the policy of multi-culturalism also misunderstands the nature of cultural difference. As with Roberts' pluralism, it can only see a diversity of needs. It cannot grasp that these are related to structural patterns, or that they involve relationships of cultural power. 'Minorities' are, by definition, marginal to the assumed mainstream or majority culture. For example, the creation of 'minority' television for black audiences means that the mainstream broadcasting can continue as a white wonderland with all its racist assumptions untouched.

Thirdly, this policy of multi-culturalism involves a very powerful notion of *sponsored* access. The emphasis is on provision *for* minorities as an act of professionalised patronage. The aim is to 'invite them in' through more sophisticated planning and management techniques. As the Sports Council put it:

> Although participation is made *possible* by facility provision, it is made *actual* only by sensitive management, inspiring leadership and energetic promotion. (*The Next Ten Years*, 1982, p. 31.)

We feel that this enthusiasm for entrepreneurial zeal among recreation managers involves a misunderstanding of the social processes by which people come to participate. It remains, for all its rhetoric about participation and identifying different needs, a 'top down' model of provision. It is structured and shaped by *professional* definitions of interests and needs, and of the ways in which such needs *should* be met.

Fourthly, the model of the 'participating citizen' which this policy aims to produce is part of the dream of social integration. Leisure-as-compensation has the ambition of drawing the nation together through play. This ideal of integration assumes two things: one, that the existing structure of society is *basically* stable and continuing; and two, that conflicts, alienation and non-participation are aberrations from this basic stability. By treating the results of social divisions as if they were only differences of interest, multi-culturalism believes that (given enough resources) they can be comfortably accommodated.

Finally, the development of this policy of 'multi-culturalism' demonstrates the strength rather than the weakness of a Marxist analysis of state policy. It indicates the centrality of the state's commitment to promoting social integration through the sponsorship of rational recreation, even though the *content* of that recreation may have changed. The failure of cultural 'assimilation' was based on the refusal of subordinate groups to surrender their own culture in favour of a state sponsored 'national culture'. The policy of integration through difference recognises this failure and attempts to substitute a recognition of diversity for an assumption of uniformity.

Multi-culturalism, then, recognises different interests and needs among subordinate social groups. It recognises them in a rather distorted fashion, and maintains a paternalistic view of the importance of professional control and sponsorship of provision and access. Most importantly, that recognition of diversity is born out of very familiar concerns of the state about maintaining social integration and harmony in the face of an unequal and conflictual society.

On the one hand, this concern to promote social integration makes the state responsive to demands expressed by subordinate groups, and the state can make concessions to those expressed interests. These concessions do not necessarily meet the needs expressed by such groups in any exact way (e.g. mother and baby groups are not the same as meeting the expressed need for more nursery provision, since they require the mother's presence), but they do involve the state in activity trying to 'take account' of such pressures.

On the other hand, the concern for integration also means that the state may intervene to make provision for those groups who appear to be in danger of becoming dis-integrated, and may pose a threat to social order. Such groups may not express any leisure demands at all, but state policy is likely to identify them as a priority. The 1980s spotlighting of the 'need' for leisure provision for the young unemployed and inner city populations provides an example of this pressure for integrative leisure provision.

Rolling back the state: conservatism and municipal socialism

Since 1979, some very sharp distinctions between possible directions for state policy have emerged, most clearly in the conflict between central and local government. At a national level, the political success of a Conservative party committed to 'Rolling back the state' and allowing the free play of market forces has resulted in reduced government spending, including spending which affects leisure. The effects of public spending cuts are visible in a number of the areas of state policy which we have discussed. In terms of state regulation, there have been reductions in the number of civil servants involved in various state licensing activities such as the Health and Safety Executive. More strikingly, almost all the areas of state provision have been cut – education, arts subsidies, sports funding. The 'public' is increasingly exhorted to stand on its own two feet, assert its independence and make its own consumer choices.

However, this is not the complete story. The new Conservatism is not opposed to all public spending. In particular, it has increased funding for some forms of state regulation and control – those associated with law and order. The police – have been the most visible beneficiaries of this – in the form of increased personnel, increased wages and proposals for increased powers.

Those powers and agencies which contribute to producing a tougher and more disciplined social order have been excluded from the assault on public spending. Less fortunate have been authorities, particularly Labour controlled ones, who stand accused of wasting the tax payers' and the ratepayers' money. The new Conservatives have increased the control of central government over local authority spending and, as we write this book, are passing through Parliament proposals to abolish a whole sector of local government – the Metropolitan Counties and the Greater London Council.

While the government aims to cut back many of the welfare and social activities, some of these Labour controlled local authorities have also been making efforts to change the relationship between the state and the local population, although in a rather different way. We would want to emphasise two aspects of these local initiatives. First, they have been exploring ways of making local state provision responsive to locally expressed needs through the decentralisation of provision, and creating channels for local state decision making to be more accountable to the particular communities receiving services. One aim of these innovations – most visible in the reorganisation of housing and welfare services – is to change the modes of professionalised 'patronage' which we discussed earlier, where state 'clients' are expected to be the passive recipients of professionally sponsored and delivered service. By contrast, some local authorities are seeking to create greater client involvement in the organisation of state services, as well as expanding the availability of public facilities, public space and, not least, public transport.

In a similar way, local authorities are trying to go beyond the philosophy of 'multi-culturalism' to a policy of positive discrimination, through which the resources of the local state can be used to redress some of the structural inequalities of class, race, gender and age. Clearly, the level of resources which the local state can command cannot 'compensate' for the whole of social inequality. Nevertheless, policies which aim to promote the interests of the most disadvantaged and simultaneously try to combat the patterns of racism and sexism in the 'mainstream culture' of British life represent an important step beyond the pluralism of multi-culturalism. The GLC, for example, has supported black, Asian and women's cultural organisations as well as organising anti-racist events, education and policy.

We are under no illusions that these policies represent anything other than small and difficult steps in new political directions. We are also very aware of the political odds that are stacked against them, especially in terms of the current policy of central government. Nevertheless, these efforts to break longstanding traditions of state paternalism, however fragile, do point to important possibilities for the development of political action and organisations.

In this chapter, we have focused attention on those institutions – the leisure industry and the state – which together command the provision of leisure. In our analysis of this 'mixed economy', three themes in particular stand out. The first is the dominance of the commercial model in the leisure economy, and its accompanying identification of the leisure-person as a consumer. Even in the state sector, we have seen that this consumer model of leisure choice plays a significant role in shaping leisure policy. These shared assumptions about the leisure consumer are only one of the many ways in which the commercial and state sectors are linked together.

Secondly, we have seen how, in both these sectors, power and control is concentrated within major institutions – the commercial enterprises and the state agencies. In the commercial sector, we observed how the diversity of goods and services on offer in the leisure market, and the rhetoric of consumer sovereignty, worked to conceal the massive concentration of economic power in the corporations of the leisure industry. In the state sector, we argued that, with rare exceptions, the formation of leisure related policy is dominated by the objective of social integration. This policy has been increasingly administered through professional patronage – the leisure experts who assess 'needs' and define how they should be met. As with commercial consumers, beneficiaries of state provision are expected to choose and participate – but only within the range of what is provided.

Thirdly, and perhaps most importantly, we have recurrently drawn attention to the ways in which this economy of leisure does not work according to the intentions of those who control it. 'Irrational' consumers who do not choose to consume in the proper manner, the resistance of some groups to becoming cultured, the resistance of others to being designated as 'minority interests', the insistence of still others on more, better or different sorts of leisure, and finally political attempts to promote more democratic control and institute policies of positive discrimination – all indicate that the wheels of the leisure economy do not turn smoothly.

Because in this chapter our attention has been directed to the institutions of leisure, these social irrationalities, refusals and alternatives have appeared at the margin of our analysis. In the following chapter, we intend to move them to the centre of the stage by examining the ways in which the structural and cultural patterns of our society are combined in the making of leisure in contemporary Britain.

Further reading

Most of the information about patterns of ownership in the 'leisure industries' in this chapter was derived from *Who Owns Whom?* (published annually by Dun and Bradstreet) and from the Independent Broadcasting Authority's *Annual Reports*. Christopher Hutt's, *The Death of the English Pub* (Arrow, 1973) provides a lively account of changes in the brewing industry and their consequences for the public house, while M. Baran and

P. Sweezy, *Monopoly Capital* (Penguin, 1968) remains a powerful though more abstract account of the tendencies of concentration in Western capitalism. A leisurely walk down a high street or through a shopping centre will suffice to confirm the diversity of the market-place.

A. S. Travis, *The Role of Central Government in the Provision of Leisure Services in England and Wales* (C.U.R.S., University of Birmingham, 1981) provides an empirical survey of the various leisure functions performed by central and local government and 'quangos', which contrasts with the more theoretical position taken by O. Newman in *Corporatism, Leisure and Collective Consumption* (Centre for Leisure Studies, University of Salford, 1981). The Sports Council's *The Next Ten Years* (Sports Council, 1982) is one of the clearest examples of the practice of recreation research and policy planning. A very different approach can be found in Garry Whannel's *Blowing the Whistle: the Politics of Sport* (Pluto Press, 1983), which provides a critical analysis of the history, organisation and ideology of sport. The articles collected in Jennifer Hargreaves (ed.), *Sport, Culture and Ideology* (Routledge & Kegan Paul, 1982) explore a similar set of issues.

In this chapter we have dealt with leisure institutions primarily in terms of their structures of ownership and control rather than the cultural meanings of the commodities and services which they provide. This is not because we attach no importance to such cultural and ideological meanings, but because these issues have already been extensively explored elsewhere. The Open University Course *Popular Culture* (Open University, 1981) contains studies of a wide range of popular 'entertainments' ranging from the rituals of Christmas to television drama. There exists a substantial 'media studies' literature dealing with televisual products rangranging from news to situation comedies. Among these studies are: R. Dyer *et al.*, *Coronation Street* (British Film Institute, 1981); The Glasgow Media Group, *Really Bad News* (Readers and Writers, 1982); BFI, *Television Sitcom* (British Film Institute, Dossier 17, 1982). Stuart Hall. *Reproducing Ideologies* (Macmillan, forthcoming) deals with the relationship between the media and social and political ideologies.

5

Divided we play: leisure and social divisions

no mode of production and therefore no dominant social order and therefore no dominant culture ever in reality includes or exhausts all human practice, human energy and human intention. (Raymond Williams, *Marxism and Literature*, Oxford University Press, 1977, p. 125.)

Throughout this work on leisure, we have been arguing for a more sophisticated understanding of leisure than any of those currently available in mainstream leisure studies. In this chapter we want to argue that the explanation of leisure activity patterns as the outcome of untrammelled individual choice is deficient. We wish instead to substitute a model of leisure as constituted by a number of subcultures rooted in what particular social groupings have succeeded in claiming for themselves as legitimate and appropriate leisure activity. In particular we wish to extend the point we have initially established that class, race, age and gender are not tangential and incidental but central and fundamental influences on leisure 'choice'.

In the previous chapter we explained why the nature of leisure 'choice' posited by the consumer model is in large measure illusory. The kinds of leisure goods and services made available and the institutions owning and controlling such provision are in reality highly restricted. The leisure market is neither as comprehensive in scope nor as competitive in ethos as is often assumed. If what can be chosen from is limited, so is who can do the choosing. Consumers are not just the hypothetical figures of market projections. They are also social beings, members of a particular society and of structurally located and culturally defined social groups within it.

This matters for understanding leisure in a way the consumer model cannot begin to encompass. Such a model has to present leisure choice as beyond the influence of group relationships and identities. Potential markets are often targeted through indices of gender and socioeconomic status, but the essential model is one of random individual choice. It is this assumption we are challenging.

Leisure may reflect social divisions less directly or transparently than other areas of social life. In education, for example, the model that educational attainment depends on individual effort and application simply collapses under the onslaught of data demonstrating how membership of gender, class and racial groups directly affects educational opportunity. We wish to suggest that leisure opportunity is also predetermined by such factors.

Inequality of leisure opportunity has both a material and a cultural aspect. The material aspect inludes access to key resources, essentially those of time and money. The cultural aspect includes the perception of what is appropriate leisure behaviour for a member of a particular social group. Such perceptions may be variously held by the group itself and by those outside it but in a position to enforce their expectations. It is the ability to negotiate a favourable settlement of such definitions which indicates leisure privilege. Such definitions and expectations abound, distinguishing men from women, middle from working class, white from black, young from old. They may be inconsistent in their application or shift over time but they remain powerful influences on what is culturally sanctioned leisure behaviour.

We see little point in arguing which factor – class, gender or race – is the primary influence on leisure, especially as in practice they intersect. The particular influence of one factor, say age, will depend on the particular combination of other factors present, on the gender and class and race of the person or group involved. It might be possible to erect a sliding scale to measure leisure opportunity, on which we can compare whether, for example, a white, middle-class, female, thirty-years-old will have more or less access to leisure than a black, working-class, male, teenager. We doubt the feasibility and desirability of such a comparison. We are in any case at the much more preliminary stage of attempting to demonstrate how leisure is less a matter of individual choice than a concomitant of social position, less a means by which society is unified through a leisure-consuming democracy than divided by material and cultural inequality.

The argument needs restating if only because others have attempted to suppress or supersede it. As we saw in Chapter 2, a common form of argument is to play these different social divisions off against each other. The undeniable influence of gender, for example, has been used to discredit the factor of class. We therefore begin our discussion of social divisions with what seems an assertion of decreasing credibility; that contemporary leisure can usefully be understood in terms of class.

In a class of its own

In social science the 'class factor' is generally taken to mean the problem of whether a working class exists and if so, what it is like. Leisure analysis is no exception. The question about class and leisure is thus whether there is a distinctively working-class style of leisure. With the possible exception of Stanley Parker, the writers we examined portrayed leisure as relatively immune from the influence of class. In so far as it did exist it operated at one remove, more a question of occupational category or car ownership than simple class membership. We by no means agree but first it may be useful to extend the discussion to a model of all social classes, not just the working-class.

Let us begin by suggesting that there are three classes rather than just two. The upper class, who have or are in the process of acquiring wealth and the power which goes with it, may be numerically small but their influence is large. If we ask whether class affects leisure, perhaps we should start with this group for they, more than almost any other, provide a positive case. It is difficult to think about this group at all without recognising the centrality of leisure to their and others' sense of who they are. The networks and institutions which sustain the upper class may be more economic and political than cultural but leisure is symbolically crucial. From exclusive gentlemen's clubs in the West End to royal garden parties, from patronage of leading national charities to local acts of minor benevolence, from foxhunting to wildlife preservation, from Ascot and Henley to St Moritz, upper-class

leisure centres on people, places and pastimes which are prescribed for members of the class. Leisure style and social status
become indistinguishable.

The 'middle' classes are altogether more problematic: no one is
quite sure who they are. The Registrar-General's classification
which lumps together a 'professional and managerial' group at the
apex of the occupational hierarchy is a statistical necessity without
a theoretical justification. The boundaries of the middle class are
not absolute but relative. The boundary between it and the upper
class may be marked by the inheritance and accumulation of
wealth. At the other end the mdidle class have in common with the
working class the fact that they sell their labour in the employment
market but do so under marginally or significantly better conditions. This blurring of boundaries also applies to leisure. Upper
middle class interests and life styles may be versions of upper class
life writ small; lower middle class people work and live in ways
which are less distinguishable than they might like from lower
grade clerical or skilled manual workers. This group's leisure
activity profile differs in paradoxical ways from other classes. They
participate more in the 'private' leisure activities of gardening and
house maintenance, yet also appear more frequently at the 'public'
venues of theatres and restaurants. Seemingly more individualistic, they are prominent in voluntary and charitable work.

Reflected here are the greater material resources of the middle
class compared with the working class. Persistent differences in
income and fringe benefits do allow them more open access to the
leisure market. And in leisure, no less than in education and
health, this group who cannot afford to 'go private' make the
fullest use of public services. These material differences do show
through the leisure statistics, despite the crudity of measurement
and categorisation. But there are also cultural inequalities, subtle
differences of status, disguised by conventional statistics. Three
aspects are worth mentioning: differences in kind between superficially similar forms, differences in the meanings attributed to
particular activities, differences in the total leisure context in
which individual activities are placed: 'It ain't what you do but the
way that you do it'.

First, differences in kind occur where leisure statistics do not
and perhaps cannot differentiate within categories of leisure
activity. Thus 'going out for a meal' may be a leisure activity

common across all social classes but hidden from view are crucial differences in the sorts of food, restaurants and groupings involved.

Secondly, differences in meaning attribution occur when apparently similar activities have an altered significance dependent on the social class involved. For instance, it may be true of the upper and some middle class groups that leisure is caught up in status considerations, often with practical pay-offs. Membership of a private golf club carries a different set of meanings from belonging to a pub football team – though both might be categorised as 'playing sport' or 'club membership'.

Thirdly, and as a result of the first two, there is a sense in which the whole pattern of leisure activities is as important as individual components. Class may less affect the 'choice' of this or that leisure activity than the interrelationship between a set of leisure activities. Community studies of middle and working class neighbourhoods frequently stress the coherence of a leisure culture. It is also all around us. One of the present authors lives in a suburb where a distinctive middle/lower middle class leisure culture is apparent. Local churches for example are important focal points. In addition to formal worship, they are the location of Sunday Schools, wives groups. Brownies and Cubs, mothers and toddlers and play groups, dramatic and musical societies, appeals to support charitable work. Some of these are directly sponsored by the church, some have no more involvement with religion than is implied by their use of church premises, some fall in between these two extremes. What is important is that the addition of other more specialist institutions – pubs, sports clubs, evening classes – they constitute a network of leisure activities. The same people will be met in different contexts, even though individuals may only mobilise part of the whole network. The common assumptions and interests reflected and sustained by such a network – and underwritten by the class segregation inherent in suburbia – do amount to a segment of a class culture.

It may be thought that there are working class equivalents. At least for young people, the statistics show as much interest in music and sport. But the forms, meanings and networks of such activities are quite different. Music and sport are internally divided along class lines: the working-class club will be less well resourced and hence more improvised than its middle-cass counterpart: the lesser geographical mobility of the working class is almost bound to produce a more enduring sense of neighbourhood. These differences are perhaps more subtle than the model which sees middle-class culture as essentially individualistic and working-class culture as collectivist. Rather each contains a different conception of the relationship between individual and collective interests. The point, however, remains that if we are to identify class leisure cultures, it is to the subtleties of kind, meaning and context that we must look, not simply at statistical aggregates of stated participation in individual categories of leisure.

'Will the real working class please stand up for itself?'

The denial of the importance of class for understanding leisure has in part been achieved through this way of computing leisure behaviour. Equally important has been the argument or assertion that the relative affluence of the post-war period (or more accurately the twenty or so years after about 1956) has released the working class from material hardship and the life styles it brought about. Analysts of various political persuasions – conservative, liberal, radical – have argued that the working class has been as a result, successfully incorporated into the political, economic and cultural ideals of contemporary capitalism. The life styles peculiar to a distinctive working class culture have decayed and with them have gone the alternative ideas of social relationships they embodied.

This has become The Debate About The Working Class. In one way it is a limited debate because it has been restricted to the internal cultural dynamics of working-class life rather than to external structural changes in relation to other – especially the 'new' middle – classes. In another way the debate is extremely wide-ranging, covering the distribution of income and wealth, patterns of consumer expenditure, the changing composition (not to mention shrinkage) of the workforce, the effects on the ecology of the city of redevelopment and trends in housing tenure, shifting political affiliations and trade union membership, the rise of the nuclear family at the expense of the extended form, not to mention ownership of consumer durables and the revolution in leisure brought about by extended ownership of cars and televisions. The list is (almost) endless, perhaps because what is actually being analysed is the whole rate and nature of social change in contemporary Britain.

A book on leisure is no place to contribute to this debate though we have made, albeit oblique, incursions elsewhere. The problem is less to establish the fact that working-class life has been changing than to understand the causes and effect of such a change. The working class has been recomposed from the outside and as a result recomposed itself from the inside. Its traditional jobs have declined, its neighbourhoods been redeveloped. Since these were the key factors shaping 'traditional' working-class culture it too has been attenuated. The working class is not what it was nor could it be. It has become less identifiable as an occupational grouping or as a presence on the streets. It may also have been partially converted to the idea that its interests are individual rather than collective and as such synonymous with those of capitalism.

But the picture can be overdrawn. There remain large disparities of income and wealth, exacerbated by structural unemployment. Changes in culture are, as for the working class they have to be, adaptations to circumstance rather than choices from freely available options. Ideologically the position is much what it has always been, only worse: a susceptibility to appeals to the British way and strong leadership, to concerted campaigns to scapegoat extremists, scroungers and foreigners.

In all this, the daily routines of non-work life, whether defined broadly as culture or more narrowly as leisure, have been asked to carry too much significance. The popularity of watching Coronation Street or reading the *Sun* newspaper cannot be set off against declining attendances at football matches or less drinking in pubs, to 'read' the shifts in working-class consciousness. Nor can the preference for do-it-yourself, car maintenance and gardening be usefully contrasted with the closure of working-men's clubs or corner shops. There is a 'class politics' of leisure but this does not mean that leisure as a whole has direct ideological meaning.

Knowing your place

There are, however, some areas where leisure does retain elements of identifiable class conflict. One of these is the continued struggle over definitions of space. As we saw earlier, there has historically been a disjunction between the ideal of public space advocated by the state and the conceptions of public space embedded in working-class culture. The latter is essentially informal, involving the appropriation for communal purposes of space nominally administered by commerce or government. Thus the idea of the street as a thoroughfare has been continually undermined by an alternative version of its functions as an area of social interaction. Doorstep banter and gossip, children playing and teenagers hanging about, the maintenance of cars and the parading of BMX bikes – all represent thrusts to define the space of the street in a particular direction. These have not generally found favour with public authorities and planners, whose activities have been expressly designed to curtail such activities. The suppositions behind the location and design of tower blocks, housing estates, shopping precincts, sports and leisure centres, have, with notorious consistency, failed to understand the existing and potential meanings of space within a locality.

Thus if the working class has accepted an increasingly 'privatised' notion of space, that may be as a result of the undermining of an alternative definition of public space. The physical and psychological security of the home has come to be contrasted with the insecurity and strangeness of the streets. With one or two exceptions, such as the local 'rec', what is provided as public space is alien – museums, botanical gardens, sports centres. And access to private space is conditional upon the ability to pay. The shopping centre, patrolled by a private police force moving on those who do not show the proper propensity to consume, points up the unequal struggle over leisure space and the potential ugliness of its outcomes.

In this last example, as in all our generalisations and illustrations, it is obvious that not all members of the working class would see their interests in the way we have defined them. The working class is not a homogeneous whole. It is and always has been internally divided by such factors as levels of income and types of housing tenure, conditions of work and patterns of family life, regional economies and cultures, perceptions of 'rough' and 'respectable' elements.

Not the least of these social divisions within the working class is that of race. Differences of culture between the white working class and black immigrants and their descendants have been a marked source of racial antagonism. The religious observances, culinary habits and customs of dress brought halfway round the world have provoked a defensive response by a white working-class culture, eaten away by its own prejudices. We do not know whether leisure surveys have samples large enough, or questions specific enough, to identify ethnic differences in leisure. What we can state with some confidence is that leisure activities superficially similar to those of the white population are contextualised quite differently in Afro-Caribbean and Asian cultures. The roles of family life, religious institutions and musical traditions, the attitudes towards drinking, smoking and sexual relations, are not uniform as between white and black or brown members of society. To talk here of equal access to leisure goods and services, of individual consumer preference, of the democracy of the market-place, is to be blind to the material inequalities and cultural tensions produced by the complex racial mix of contemporary Britain.

Hopes that for the young the 'race problem' will evaporate have not been fulfilled. Identities of race and class are too deeply structured to be dispelled by the common experience of youth or any other 'stage of life'. Yet age, too, is an important social division with implications for leisure. Like those of class, they are not always what they at first seem.

Leisure through the ages

At first glance, it seems reasonable that age should be found to have a considerable effect on the kinds and rates of leisure activity. The biology and psychology of the ageing process seem likely to involve different physical abilities and personal interests at its various stages. That much is not disputed. More controversial is the attempt to assess how far such stages of life and the leisure activities perceived as appropriate to them are constructed by society. To the extent that they are, the effects of age on leisure are not natural and inevitable but socially imposed and open to change.

We begin with the final stage of the ageing process: old age. Three things need to be noted about this category. First, it is demarcated by retirement. Life may begin at forty but old age definitely begins at sixty or sixty-five. The old are by definition those who have ceased employment or whose partner has. This is not a biological or psychological boundary but an economic one. Secondly, old people are predominantly female and the older the age band considered the more this female predominance occurs. Women who marry are likely to eventually face a period of widowhood, lasting perhaps as long as a quarter of their life span. Thirdly, the conditions under which people enter old age vary considerably, especially by social class. Inequalities of income, housing and physical health are not distributed randomly amongst individuals but systematically between classes.

These are just some of the ways in which old age is socially constructed. We are not here denying as a biological fact the progressive decline of faculties which occurs in old age. These physical factors should not, however, be confused with social ones. In America, the study of old age has come to be dominated by theories of 'disengagement', referring to the psychological withdrawal from the network of social roles, in work, family and community, which have previously sustained identity. What such an approach disguises is that 'role-loss' is not intrinsic to old age. The elderly do not lose their social roles: they have them taken away. What the elderly have to adjust to is not only their physical decay or the prospect of dying but that their worth in the eyes of society has clearly been devalued.

Consistent with this status devaluation is the peripheral position of the elderly in relation to the leisure market. Since they no longer have the disposable income necessary to be part of a significant target population, no great effort is made to solicit their custom. When recognised at all, their leisure needs are to be met by councils and voluntary groups providing clubs and outings. For the most part, since ageing is presumed to involve increasing physical and mental passivity, they are quietly left alone.

They are also increasingly left alone and left behind as the consequences of other social processes. Their children may through choice or necessity have moved away. Though the evidence suggests that families do not in fact abandon their elderly members or become indifferent to their fate, the monitoring of their daily lives frequently becomes the exclusive responsibility of whichever relative happens to live nearby. Thus the old are doubly deprived. The limited interest shown by commerce and the state is compounded by decreasing access to the alternative of family-based leisure. The family is increasingly scattered and sooner or later the elderly married couple will become one elderly person living alone. This is 'privatisation' with a vengeance.

It is only when such factors are taken into account that the oft-noted ambiguity of free time for the elderly can be understood. The removal of the structure inherent in the clear demarcation between work and leisure may well be a problem for those who have been habitually in full-time employment, especially men. The domestic work of women does not diminish and in fact becomes more problematic. The budget is tighter, shops less accessible; cooking and washing clothes become more burdensome; the heavy work of cleaning may become impossible. The existence of the home help service demonstrates that it is not the absence of paid work which is a problem for the elderly so much as the continued presence of domestic work.

Thus the leisure problem of old age is not simply one of an excess of time and a deficiency of resources, real enough though those are. It is also one of enforced dependence on a home life progressively more difficult to manage and increasingly isolated from the context of extended family and community. Such problems are recognised by statutory and voluntary agencies who with the most meagre of resources do what they can to mitigate the effects of social isolation. The Sports Council, for example, has identified the over sixties as one of its target groups in its programme for 'The Next Ten Years'. But the economic and social structuring of old age, and the psychological consequences which follow, make it difficult to improve the access of the elderly to a meaningful range of leisure activities.

Such a generalisation needs to be qualified. There are many vigorous elderly people in society who do not appear to suffer from an excess of free time or crisis of identity. Some even experience old age as a period of liberation, at last providing the opportunity for forms of leisure impossible before. How typical and durable such achievements are is difficult to judge. They certainly receive little support from private or public initiatives.

Growing pains

'Too much time and too little to do' might well be the leisure lament of the elderly. It is a refrain whch finds a sympathetic echo at the other end of the age range, amongst those who have not yet reached adult status. Adolescents might justifiably perceive the interest of commerce in their needs as highly restricted and public provision unimaginative and under-resourced. It is not to such similarities but to differences between these age statuses that attention is normally directed. Old age is regarded as a period of physical, psychological and social decline, adolescence as a transitional period of growth. The transition is from childhood to adulthood, marked physically by puberty and its aftermath, psychologically by the exploration of identity, socially by the entry into work roles. These are undeniably experiences common to all adolescents in our society. There must, however, be two severe qualifications to this apparently universal portrait of adolescence. One is that adolescence, no less than old age, is socially structured; it is a social as much as a biological or psychological division. The second is that, again like old age, adolescence has divergent meanings for members of different classes and genders.

Adolescence is an historical creation peculiar, in the form we know it, to industrial society. As child labour was slowly eradicated from the industrial system in the nineteenth century, so compulsory State education was introduced to control the time and habits of the young. To appreciate the arbitrary nature of the defining limits of adolescence we need only recall the early experiences of those who are now old. For most of them, adult status was achieved by going to work at an age – thirteen or fourteen – we would now consider to be verging on childhood. As the boundary between the dependence of full-time education and the relative independence of work moves up the age scale, society protracts the transition to adult status. Adolescence is the label attached to this hiatus.

The anxiety of many working-class children to leave school is in part an attempt to claim some of the privileges of adult life, especially the freedom promised by having money to spend and lessening adult control. (Sometimes of course a prime motivation is pure hatred of school; but that is another story.) The middle class young are encouraged to defer this moment, and the gratifications which supposedly go with it, to improve their employment prospects with better educational qualifications. Thus they may still be at college when their working-class peers have been at work for some years and may even have married. In a number of ways – money and time, preferrred or available leisure activities, relationships with parents and other significant adults – adolescence has a class quality.

Gender is an even more powerful influence than class. The definition of what it means physically, psychologically and socially, to be female is present from birth but hardens considerably during adolescence. The leisure of adolescent girls is more controlled from within and without than that of boys. The premium placed upon sexual attractiveness and its implied subordination and vulnerability to boys makes leisure a tentative enterprise for girls. Their greater domestic responsibilities and the stricter supervision exercised by parents further narrow the potential scope and focus of leisure. Overcoming such restrictions is generally a private and frequently a vicarious matter. The culture of the bedroom and intense 'best-friend' relationships serve as protective devices against a public leisure world dominated by male expectations. Adolescence for girls is frequently hard work; leisure means going about their 'natural' business of finding, catching and keeping, a man.

The middle-class girl may have greater leisure opportunities than her working-class sister but they are differences of degree rather than kind. Both will have a necessarily circumspect approach to places of public entertainment: personal reputation and physical integrity are at risk. For good reasons they will be excluded and will exclude themselves from what is for boys a central, if not the central, leisure time activity: hanging about the streets.

Boys will be boys

This comparative freedom of boys' leisure has historically been a cause of concern to authority. Calls for 'something to be done about' the problem of young working-class men with enough time on their hands to get into mischief and worse have a long history but have escalated with increased public consciousness of adolescents as potentialy rebellious. In the affluence of post-war Britain, time and money were in abundance and spent on the display of clothes, objects and behaviour at odds with the values of adult society. The rise of youth subcultures and the way society has reacted to them (frequently through the hysteria of 'moral panics') has been the subject of a number of academic studies. Such subcultures have been found to centre on leisure. Weekends, evenings and holiday times have been the significant times for subcultural activity: the streets, clubs and holiday resorts the places where their behaviour has been most resented. So it is very much a 'leisure problem'. But it is not simply a 'youth' problem, since those involved have been mainly male and working-class. In Britain at any rate, it has proved impossible to validate the model of a generation gap, dividing adult society from a single youth culture common to all young people. Youth, like old age and all stations in between, does not override other forms of social division but overlaps them. Age, class and gender interact to stratify leisure, and the surface complexity need not disguise the fundamental inequalities on which they are based.

This has remained so despite the economic recession, the effects of which have been felt most heavily by the young, half of whom could expect to be unemployed in the early 1980s. Some have been able to find 'unofficial' employment in the fringe areas of the economy: a supplementary benefit of their own to add to that provided by the state. But such occasional and insecure work cannot compensate for the loss of spending power unemployment brings. It is worth repeating that what unemployment does before anything else is to make those who experience it poor. Excessive free time or a sense of uselessness may follow, but do not precede, such material hardship. There is a sleight of hand involved in the attempt to portray the economic problem of youth unemployment as a psychological problem of leisure disorientation.

One factor in such deceit is the fear that youth will become ungovernable and resort to the ultimate in deviant leisure, crime. The inner-city riots of 1981 heralded a climax of such fears, provoked by the threat to private property and public space they appeared to represent. The need to establish political order took precedence over any desire to restore economic order. Young people, especially the male, the working class, the black, required immediate supervision by the police on the streets, by job instructors in training centres, by parents in homes. In the absence of work, the discipline it would normally be expected to inculcate had to assume other forms. The youth leisure problem has here become subsumed under this massive effort of social control.

The relationship between leisure and the economic and political order could not be more starkly revealed. The case is exceptional only because it makes transparent what is normally opaque, that the age of youth is constructed, and if necessary can be rigorously disciplined, by political and economic forces.

Engendered leisure

Gender is the last but by no means the least of the social divisions within leisure. On any statistical measure, gender is a crucial determinant of leisure activity. Figures compiled by the government's Central Statistical Office show this clearly. Men report more leisure activity and of a particular kind. They dominate those activities which involve leaving the home unaccompanied, such as all forms of sport and going out for a meal or a drink. The only things for which women more frequently leave the house are to go to bingo, cinema or theatre. The main household leisure activity of media use shows few gender differences, but men are most involved in gardening and 'do-it-yourself'. Women's other home-based leisure consists of that interest in sewing and knitting 'exclusive' to their sex.

Other data show a few minor activities outside the home where women predominate, in visits to church, leisure classes, opera and ballet. These do little to alter the general picture. Women have less leisure time, participate less in most leisure activities and draw on a narrower range of leisure options than men. They also spend most of their leisure in and around home and family. These differences of form, time and place do not represent a more limited version of male leisure but a qualitatively as well as quantitatively distinct female leisure pattern. The only apparent anomaly is that women in fulltime employment have a leisure profile more similar to men than to other women.

This exception proves the rule: that for women having young children decreases access to work and leisure. The leisure allowed to young mothers is often used in ways which reflect and extend their domestic role. Sewing and knitting may be pleasurable in themselves but also provide useful additions to the household economy. Watching television and listening to the radio may occur while the real domestic work of cooking, child-care, cleaning and ironing, goes on. Some activities classified as leisure, such as visiting the park, may in reality be as much for the benefit of children as for 'mum'.

Thus the female forms of leisure are those most easily compatible with the primary domestic role of wife and mother. The contrast between 'compulsory' and 'freely chosen' activity becomes blurred when the times, places and nature of 'leisure' are indistinguishable from those of work. Unlike employment, housework does not have a definite and fixed allocation of time. It contracts and expands according to the needs and demands of the household. This ambiguous pattern means that it is hard to fix the working day with any precision. Children do not fall ill or require attention within the precise and convenient confines of an eight-hour day allocated to 'child-care'.

This timeless nature of domestic work has the apparent advantage of giving women some discretion in pacing their work, though night-time rarely goes according to plan. More fundamental is the experience of being permanently on call: 'a woman's work is never done' (especially by a man). As the time of work dictates the time of leisure, so the place of work dictates the place of leisure. For the woman with children, home may serve as both work and leisure place. (Occasional evenings out may be arranged, if a baby-sitter is available. Yet even in baby-sitting circles the women are the organisers. Though the couple benefit, it is the woman who is expected to reciprocate the service. Ironically some women welcome the chance to babysit: they can take little of their own domestic work into someone else's house, so it becomes one of the few occasions when they can genuinely relax.) There are severe restrictions on when and where women, especially if married, can spend leisure time outside the home: the potential social stigma and physical danger we saw to threaten teenage females does not disappear with age.

Gender as a social division in leisure does not simply produce the effect that women have less time than man and are less mobile; it redefines time and space for women as compared with men. Women are expected – and come themselves to expect – to participate in those leisure activities defined as appropriate for women, at those times and in those places compatible with established female roles. All these are severe enough limitations on the access to and enjoyment of leisure. But there is more. For the inferior status of women's leisure has as its obverse the superiority of men's interests within leisure.

Throughout our discussion, we have tended to show how leisure reflects social divisions ultimately rooted outside leisure itself. In so far as leisure is dependent on the social organisation of work and family life, this is a valid approach. Leisure, however, does more than simply reflect social divisions. It 'realises' them, becoming one of the powerful means by which social divisions receive expression and validation. This double relationship between leisure and social divisions is particularly evident in the case of gender. The quantitative and qualitative differences between male and female are first an extension of the sexual division of labour within society as a whole. They are also secondly ways in which the dominant definitions of what it means to be male or female are enforced and confirmed. Leisure 'celebrates' gender differences.

May the best man win

As an example we can take the case of sport. Primarily a physical activity directed towards a competitive goal, sport has a number of secondary characteristics, including emphases on victory, aggression, training and dedication and athletic skill. It does not require much examination of sport and society in the past and the present to appreciate that there is a close fit between the values expressed by sport and the conventional male role. The result is that women's participation in sport is conditional. For the most part, they compete with each other and not against men. Some sports, mainly those involving physical contact, prohibit female participation. The preferred sports for women are those which lay great stress on the sporting value most compatible with 'normal' femininity, that of aesthetic skill. Hence gymnastics and ice skating, with their emphasis on grace, balance and poise, fulfil rather than contradict ideals of 'womanhood'.

Restricting women's sport to a ghetto of this kind is not a viable strategy. Women are able and like to run and jump, hit balls and throw objects, ride bikes and drive cars, dive off boards and bounce on trampolines. A second set of conditions are therefore introduced to guarantee that such behaviour does not undermine conventional gender roles. These require the sportswoman to demonstrate that sport does not put her 'true' femininity at risk, that she retains a hold on conventional female interests. Much media coverage of women in sport is of this kind, seeking a set of assurances that the sportswoman does have a boyfriend, that he 'doesn't mind' her devotion to sport, that one day, yes, she will 'settle down', marry and have children. Such direct interrogation is reserved for those whose commitment and achievement (and thus potential gender deviance) is exceptional. Those physical activities which stop short of real sport and remain as recreations are perceived as less of a gender threat. Jogging, cycling and hiking are less likely to be challenged as legitimate female leisure. What amounts to a cultural 'sex-test', then, will be applied selectively, according to the nature and seriousness of the sport involved. There are also areas of resistance; female athletes can and do occasionally challenge the assumptions of others that their right to participate is conditional.

Yet for all the signs of change, sport remains largely an area where existing gender roles are reestablished and confirmed. Segregation is its ultimate form. With the exception of riding and driving, sport demonstrates that women are the weaker sex: they are neither as fast nor as strong as men. That the gap in achievement may be narrowing is not the major observation we would wish to make, nor even that a peculiar notion of average ability is involved, masking the fact that the 'best' women can and would beat all but the very best men. Rather we would simply wish to emphasise how sport at all levels converts physical differences into cultural definitions of superiority and inferiority, ensuring that women come off second best.

This subordination of the female to the male is also evident in other areas of leisure, where the emphasis is on the integration rather than segregation of the sexes. It is a commonplace (if often unarticulated) observation that much of leisure is 'about sex'. The promise of meeting someone of the opposite sex, or of confirming an existing relationship, is inherent in the structure of parties, discotheques, night-clubs, not to mention pubs, restaurants and cinemas. The specific leisure activity may be as much a means to an end as an end in itself.

For those not yet married, much of leisure will be charged with sexual promise. At its crudest (observable at any pub disco after 10.30 p.m.), it is a form of hunt, packs of males moving in predatory pursuit of female victims. At its subtlest, it is an elaborate game of ambiguous rules, high stakes and uncertain outcome. Ironically enough, since it is the one area of leisure to which it is least applied, the market model is appropriate. Wares are displayed, consumer choices made, sexuality bartered. The outcome of successful negotiations is a contract – that of marriage.

Sex – as pursuit, charade, exchange – underlies the most naive and innocent leisure activity. Commerce knows that the attractiveness of what it has to offer may depend on its perceived potential for romance. Reduced entry fees for women in clubs and dance halls are one of the more cynical recognitions of this fact. Advertising proceeds on the basis that almost anything can be sold through an association with sexual imagery. The media provide as leisure entertainment the playing out of gender roles; for situation comedy the man meets woman/husband relates to wife situation can draw on a common stock of knowledge about the rituals of relations between the sexes.

The best situation comedies recognise that the unspoken assumptions of sexual relationships can cause misunderstandings from which comic situations can be fabricated. In real life, the potentially hazardous nature of such relationships is more likely to lead to minor forms of tragedy than major comedy success. A misplaced word or gesture, a misinterpretation of a sexual cue, are that much more likely when so much artifice is required. The passive and reactive role of the women restricts her initiatives. The man, cast in the leading role, may live in fear of failure. With the temptation to achieve by foul means what cannot be attained by fair, the potential for sexual intimidation and worse is ever-present.

That gender relationships are so central to leisure can be confirmed by the strategies adopted by those prevented by circumstances or inclination from taking part in the normal course of events. Leisure clubs for those who are single, divorced or widowed, demonstrate that age and marital status can form an effective barrier to normal leisure pursuits for those who do not fit into the expected categories. Others find the presumption of heterosexuality a bar. Gay and lesbian subcultures seek to create networks of places and activities in leisure, where their own sexuality can find that open expression forbidden by the taboos of 'straight' society.

The social division of gender within leisure can, for many different kinds of groups and individuals, be a problem. It is always as well a promise, which finds its final expression in the marriage vow. With the birth of their own children, parents begin the whole cycle again. Teaching children appropriate sex roles is often presented as the 'work' of families; it is also an integral part of their leisure. Those analyses which see the modern family as the final solution to the leisure problem seem all the less credible to the extent that they virtually ignore its perception of unequal gender roles.

Coming home to roost

The family is the cornerstone of contemporary leisure analysis. All survey data show an accelerating trend towards home and family based leisure. The interpretation of this pattern has stressed the actual or potential cultural uniformity it induces. Different social classes appear to have a common aspiration towards a leisure style based round an ideal home and family. Other sources of division are similarly defused by the family. Age groupings exist mainly through the life cycle, which in turn largely depends on the stage of the family the individual has reached. The persistence of gender inequality may be only temporary as more egalitarian relationships filter down from the middle classes. Some rough edges remain, but the basic pattern is one of symmetry.

In arguing against this interpretation in Chapter 2, we suggested that it involved a blinkered perspective, seeing neither the connection of the family with other social institutions nor the complexities of its internal dynamics. It is now time to extend that argument.

The family, we suggested, has to be understood in its basic characteristics, of which there are at least three. It is a structure, reflecting and absorbing influences from the social context. It is an ideology, a set of ideals about what could or should be achieved. It is a culture, where individuals find their way through the family as a structure and ideology to create their version of family life. These are our starting points; to understand the family at leisure, we must first see it in its other guises.

The form of the family is not wholly determined by economic factors but it bears their imprint. As we saw in our history chapter, the ideal family for modern capitalism is one which is a mobile unit of consumption and cultural reproduction. The role of consumer unit follows from the historical tendency of the economy to depend on mass demand for goods and services. That demand can and does take forms other than the family but few markets are as durable or as predictable as that of the family: a guaranteed source of continuous demands for comfortable and labour-saving environments, accessible and novel entertainments. The more so, since the home base is continually being remade. Especially for the high-consuming middle classes, the family is constantly on the move, housed on estates no more than temporary settlement camps on the road of social mobility. The system of production, from which the family seems a retreat, here bears heavily on where and for how long a family shall dwell, for such decisions are at the behest of employers. For those unwilling to uproot themselves and their families and follow where employers beckon, economic and political leaders have harsh words: 'on your bike'.

The consumerism and mobility of the modern family are necessary complements to the system of economic production. There is another way in which the family, no longer a significant unit of economic production, contributes to the conditions necessary for such production to take place. The family reproduces not only a new generation of potential recruits for the process of production but also the habits and assumptions which legitimate such participation: the divisions of time and space between work and leisure, the divisions of responsibilities between breadwinner and home maker.

To achieve this, the family embraces a sexual division of labour if anything more exaggerated than that which prevails outside it. The evidence suggests that, despite some marginal changes, gender roles within the family remain mutually exclusive and unequal. Who goes out to what sort of work, who has the most interests outside the family, who performs which daily menial task around the house, who takes primarily responsibility for the care of children, are not allocated on the basis of ability or choice but on the basis of gender. That we may choose and feel most able to carry out those tasks appropriate to our gender, is not proof of biological programming but the successful education of our personalities into gender roles. Inevitably so, since they are learnt initially in and through the family. There we learn not only specific social roles ('that's what daddies do') but also sets of relationships ('that's how daddies talk to mummies'). Individuals and groups make innovations in these practices, otherwise there would be no social change, but such change is limited to those details which can be accommodated within existing social arrangements.

For the family is arranged, in ways we are too commonly unaware of. These arrangements become visible most clearly when the family ceases to function 'properly' and becomes dependent for its income on the state. The social security system is particularly notorious for the assumptions it makes about relationships of dependency which should prevail between the sexes inside and outside family life. Most obviously, the cohabitation rules for supplementary benefit still (despite cosmetic change) take as their premise the idea that a woman ought to exchange her sexual services for economic maintenance by a man. Like many norms of behaviour, these are implemented most harshly against the unsupported and the unemployed but even those in work will enounter a tax system operating a set of categories in which sex and marital status are the most important characteristics.

Thus the state – here subtle and indirect, there brutal and direct – enforces a set of regulations arranging family affairs. Such policies are the material consequences of ideas about the family. The family as a structure, a social institution, produces and is produced by an ideology of family life. The ideology has its apologists. A whole phalanx of pedagogues – politicians, sales directors, social workers, agony columnists – endorse the normal, average family as being what politics/selling/case work/real life are about. Ideologies work most effectively as common-sense images, in which the media trade. In advertisements, advice and exhortation, appeals to the common interest, the family, subcategorised as the family man or the housewife, is the natural reference point. And the point about these images, together with those about gender from which they are indivisible, is that they are conveyed during and about leisure activity. As the family, together or separately, relax and enjoy themselves they will soon encounter distortions of their own images, as others would like them to be, perhaps as they would themselves like to be, but rarely as they actually are.

But what is this thing that families actually are? We have been insisting on the need to understand the family as both social institution and moral ideal, since these aspects have been consistently underrated by leisure analysts. Yet these only provide the structural and ideological context in which the everyday culture of family life is lived. They furnish both frame and canvas, but do not of themselves define the outline or the texture of the finished portrait. Many have tried to enhance our appreciation of family life. Treatises have been written on the biology of sex, the psychology of love, the sociology of marriage. Handbooks are provided on how to find and keep a mate, achieve sexual satisfaction, avoid neuroses in your children. Yet for all the theorising and occasional empirical analysis devoted to it, the family remains an enigma. It is by definition (and perhaps fortunately) impenetrable to social science. It cannot be observed form the inside, except as autobiography. Observation from the outside is limited by the resistance of its members to revealing what they consider to be the most private and personal parts of their lives. How families live is something on which we are all individually expert and collectively ignorant.

Common-sense is, by and large, an obstruction to the kind of understanding we are advocating in this book but there are times when appeal to our common experiences can usefully serve as a bench-mark for theory and argument. We are all perhaps more familiar with the intensity and ambiguity of family life than is much of the literature. Relations between a wife and a husband can, as all married people know, be loving, fulfilling, mutually respecting; they can also be hateful, cramping, domineering. Children can, as all parents know, fuse a relationship, provide a common goal, be a continuous source of wonder and pleasure; they can also bitterly divide adults, be constantly tiresome and make unremitting demands. Our own experience of family life enables us to recognise such potentialities and the ways in which our particular families have managed to cope with these inherent contradictions of family life.

We must insist again that harmony and stability are not the natural outcomes of family life; they have to be worked at. One index of the difficulties involved may be found in the divorce statistics, evidence for the familiar projection that one in every three new marriages will end in a decree. If crisis may occur in individual families, there is no crisis in the institution of the family. Most of those divorced will eventually marry again (though being female and/or old decreases this probability). The project of marriage and family life retains its attractiveness. Even those who have had good cause to count the costs involved still assess them to be outweighed by the potential benefits.

Some kinds of costs are unequal in their distribution and permanent in their consequences, even within those families who stay together. Various measurements of depression, from the prescription of tranquillisers to mental hospital admissions, indicate that the most common victims are likely to be female, relatively young and with small children. As a result, it does not seem unreasonable to postulate some connection between the incidence of psychological stress and the dual role of wife and mother in the family. Depression is not randomly distributed amongst those who happen to have a predisposition towards it. The costs of family life, no less than its benefits, are socially patterned.

If our analysis is not be imbalanced, some attention needs to be paid to those benefits. There is no doubt that many of us look to the family as our major source of motivation and sense of purpose. The question therefore arises as to the kind of satisfactions to be derived from family life and the forms they take. Psychology offers some models to explore this: hierarchies of need, measurements of life-satisfaction, categorisations of motivation. Converting the otherwise inexpressible into a series of formulae is largely reductive: we cannot recognise ourselves there. In part this may be due to a narrow conception in which the 'science' suppresses the 'social'. More generally it may be further demonstration that social science is at its weakest when trying to explain the nature and sources of human pleasure. Misery, yes, we can analyse that, but happiness is best left to the philosophers. The presence of problems we can indicate; their absence merits no attention. Our own argument is no exception: division and inequality are easier to demonstrate than unity and reciprocity. But perhaps if we retrace our steps we can get at some of the compensations of family life through some of the difficulties.

We have emphasised how much of family life is in actual practice hard work. We work at our marriage partnerships, at bringing up children, at providing a safe and secure physical and psychological environment. Thus some members of the family undertake one kind of work, selling their labour on the open market, to provide the conditions and resources which make family work more viable. Some of this family work may have little or no inherent interest. Doing the washing, hoovering the floor, cleaning the windows, are jobs which simply have to be done: an endless cycle in which, even as the job is being finished, the need to do it again reappears.

Yet at least some family work has visible results and perceptive purpose. To use one psychological model we do find useful, such work is as much 'expressive' (providing some intrinsic satisfaction) as it is 'instrumental' (undertaken for extrinsic, normally financial, reward). A neatly dressed child, a carefully arranged garden, a rust-free car, cannot be achieved without hard work, some of it arduous. But these achievements may belong to us more closely and more permanently than anything we can produce outside the family. Thus the family restores a sense of meaningful endeavour, tasks which fit into an overall project we ourselves design, plan and execute. It may not be much but it is all our own work.

This gives point to our earlier scepticism about the usefulness of categorising such activities as 'satisfying physiological needs' and 'non-work obligations', or trying to place them on a continuum between the externally imposed and the freely chosen. In making families, we choose to enter into a set of mutual obligations, in which caring and being cared for are inextricably mixed.

Such obligations are built into the networks of which the individual family is part. The rituals of family life draw the 'whole family' together around key points in its cycle: birthdays, marriages, christenings, anniversaries, funerals. Such ceremonies integrate the nuclear family with its extended kin, symbolically reaffirming the unity of this one family and the universality of the family as a basic human institution.

There is work here too, before, during and after the event: invitations to be sent out, catering to be arranged, interactions to be managed. Who should sit next to who is a matter of some import in such a fragile enterprise, if potental disunity is to be kept in check. Each family has its own folklore of disasters, featuring at least one spectacular family row threatening and sometimes succeeding in ruining the whole occasion. If forgotten and thus not a possible source of future rows, their import fades with time. When the family next meets, to commemorate the birth or death, maturation or marriage, of one of its members, codes of behaviour will have been reestablished.

Both the work of family life and its rituals deserve, in at least some of their aspects, to be included in a review of leisure and the family. Their ambiguous and contradictory nature may remind us that the definition and model of human activity offered by 'leisure' has severe limitations. Family life is a complex mix of work and play, tension and relaxation, constraint and choice. To see the part called 'leisure', we must see the whole called 'family', if its core, the capacity to make us feel human when so much else does not, is not to remain elusive.

What we call family leisure is part of this total pattern but it has its own distinctive attributes. To explore these a little further we have chosen the instance of the family holiday.

Getting away from it all

Statistics show the holiday to be one of the most favoured areas of leisure expansion. Here surely the economic functions, sexual politics and psychological strains of family life are least evident: the family seems at its best. Well, it all depends, not least on the weather. They may not last long in the memory but some holidays are disastrous – sunburn, rain, illness, food poisoning, transport which does not arrive, hotels lacking basic facilities....

These are some of the known hazards of holidays which careful planning (and the necessary luck) can help avoid. This is one reason why the annual holiday is a major family project; it may only last two weeks but its influence pervades the whole year. Planning begins immediately after that other highpoint of the family calendar, Christmas. Prospect starts with retrospect. The family photograph album is retrieved and memories of people, places and activities from past holidays are recounted. Brochures are obtained and pored over, the costs and benefits of alternatives compared in detail. Some may wish to try something new, the experiment being part of the excitement. Others may prefer repetition – 'let's go there again' – which can eventually become a holiday tradition – 'we go there every year'. The decision to be made has to be negotiated: different family members have their own preferences. As children grow up, their wishes may be difficult to accommodate. It is perhaps one of the few decisions genuinely made by the whole family, even if some opinions carry more weight than others. Once the choice is made and the deposit (having been carefully protected from the ravages of Christmas) has been paid, the waiting and the saving begin. Eventually holiday time arrives. And it is a special sort of time. If not actually timeless, holidays replace the rhythms of paid and domestic work obligations with potential choice over the use of time. Some may choose to have others restructure their time for them, by opting for holiday camps or package tours – 'the coach will leave in twenty minutes'. Handing over control of your own time is not without its compensations – 'we didn't have to worry about a thing; it was all laid on for us'. Less highly organised holidays have the attraction of improvisation: 'what shall we do today?' Time does not cease to exist. Every holiday has its own schedules. But its meaning and its use are different: it is yours to dispose of as you wish.

Complementary to an altered sense of time is a different sort of place. It is not a real holiday to spend it at home; a change of environment is required. We must get away, above all out of town or city to the country or the seaside. This may sometimes be less of a difference than it appears: high street is merely exchanged for promenade, the crowds of the city centre for those on the beach. There may even be a loss of space, holiday accommodation rarely allowing the family to spread itself about. Still, exploring a new if temporary habit, of woods and fields or beaches and cliffs, even shops and restaurants, remains a source of pleasure. Perhaps the ideal is a balance between the known, familiar, relied on, and the novel, strange and untried. Holiday resorts abroad aim at this kind of balance: enough which is familiar to reassure visitors, enough which is exotic to convince them that they reall have 'seen Spain'.

Time and place: two of the constraints of everyday life from which the holiday offers relief. Another is self-restraint, replaced by self-indulgence. The pay-off for the saving of innumerable yesterdays is to spend as if there were no tomorrow. Food and drink are consumed to excess, known trivia purchased and treasured for their worthlessness. For a couple of weeks life is a funfair; being taken for a ride and not caring an essential part of the pleasure. Not only money can be wasted; so can time. Lying about, that primaeval Protestant sin, becomes on holiday a virtue. Time and money have been carefully hoarded to be carelessly squandered.

Holidays thus reverse, or at least modify, those influences which structure our everyday existence. Family relationships similarly undergo a partial transformation. The rigid roles which normally provide the base of family life become blurred. Men, for example, are more available to wives and children than at any other time of year. Depending on the type of holiday chosen, the woman may be relieved of her usual domestic duties (though some, like the washing, may simply be stored up for later). Child care is more shared and relaxed. Children experience a greater freedom in where they go, what they do, when they go to bed. The sharing of a holiday acts as confirmation that the members of the family exist for and through each other. Perhaps as a result, relationships with other families are easier. Friendships are made instantly by children and adults alike, sealed by the recognition of a common interest – 'we're all here to enjoy ourselves'.

High days and holidays

Holidays are lived fantasies. The elements of the fantasy have been described as the four S's: Sea, Sand, Sun and Sex. It is possible to interpret these features as the reclamation of a self in communion with nature, in direct contrast to the artificial self of civilised society. Our own preference is for a more low level explanation. One, and only one, way of understanding not just holidays but family leisure in general is through the concept of play. In our discussion of the spatial and temporal realignment of the holiday, its concentration on self-indulgence and self-confirmation through the family, we may have been talking about no more than how holidays provide playtimes, playgrounds, playthings and playmates.

We think of these terms and indeed of play itself as something confined to childhood. The process of achieving adult status is one of learning to forsake play, suppressing childish impulses and channelling those which remain into activities for which we have names other than play: sports, hobbies, leisure interests. The family disguises its retained forms of play under the heading of games: party games, board games, card games, video games – 'games for all the family'. It is no accident that these are often the first way to cope with bad weather on holiday. For the basic point about our sense of play, and why it fits so well with the general ethos of the holiday, is that it needs no rationale, no purpose other than its own intrinsic satisfaction. That sense is present in less intense and visible forms in a whole range of family leisure activities: watching television, visiting the park, having a day out. The incorporation of much of the new technology into family life, from computers to video-cassette recorders, depends upon its convertibility into items of and for play.

Play is a necessary illusion. It is necesary because our pleasures must appear to lie out of the reach of social and economic influences: in their very 'otherness' is their appeal. It is an illusion because play is not and cannot be beyond their reach. The interaction of child and adult around play of all kinds is, for example, a powerful instrument of socialisation. The acceptance of rule structures, the pitting of skill against chance, the ackowledgement that some must lose in order for others to win, are all ways of preparing the child through the unreality of play for the 'realities' of adult life. Adults, while teaching the child to play, may also indulge in that sense of anarchy – 'behaving like a child' – which maturity has untaught them.

The antithesis of work and leisure may, then, more usefully be understood as that of necessary labour and unnecessary play. Yet opposition is itself a kind of relationship. The positive is defined and structured by the negative, play and holiday by what they are not: labour and workaday. Society does more, however, than provide the context and thus the meanings for the significance we attach to the holiday experience. It also influences who gets access and under what conditions to which sort of holiday experience, a specific example of what we called 'at the beginning of the chapter' the distribution of leisure opportunity.

'You don't know what you're missing'

Acknowledgement of the political, economic and social shaping of access to, and enjoyment of, an annual holiday needs to be more than skin deep. In our history chapter we noted how paid holidays were an integral part of the claim to leisure made by working people and their families from the end of the nineteenth century. At the present time (at least until the onset of recession), there is a preference for any extra free time to take the form of longer paid holidays rather than a reduced working week. For the mass of the population, holidays away from home are a relatively recent innovation. As noted in Chapter 4, the leisure industries have responded by providing a range of holiday possibilities, differing in location, cost and appeal. Travel is a profitable if high risk business, backed by increasingly sophisticated marketing techniques, the mainstay of television advertising in the early part of the year. Holidays are thus political and economic in origin. The culture of the holiday, its otherness in time, place and activity, is not less bound to the prevailing social order and its routines of paid and domestic labour.

Even this does not exhaust the social influences upon this 'freest' of leisure activities, for the holiday reproduces all the social divisions we have been discussing in this chapter. First, that between social classes. In 1979, 40 per cent of the British population took no holiday away from home; an estimate three years earlier was that eight million had enjoyed no holiday away in the previous five years. The deepening recession will not have improved these figures. Containing as it must, the elderly, the sick and the poor, this group remains as deprived of holidays as it does of most other things. If this is leisure democracy, a substantial minority remain disenfranchised. Not for them the naked egalitarianism of the beach, since they cannot afford the price of admission.

Such egalitarianism is in any case misleading. There are different beaches in separate locations for particular social groups, defined as much by income and social status as by personal taste. Some resorts are reserved for the affluent (skiing in St Moritz). Other holidays, in guest house or chalet, cater for those who can only just afford the whole enterprise (a week in Scarborough). There are also different kinds of holiday, fitting into the overall leisure style of particular groups. Two weeks at Butlins and a month in a French villa might look like equally viable alternatives; in practice, they require different levels of resources and rest on contrasting cultural affiliations. For those whose class or social status is denoted by their colour, the holiday is paradoxically a chance to go home to visit friends and relatives left behind as a result of emigration. For them the end of the holiday means leaving home once again; for their children, possibly an increased uncertainty as to just where home is.

Age is no less an influence than class and colour. The leisure market has recognised and institutionalised its significance, the most obvious examples being holiday packages aimed exclusively at the under twenty-fives or over-sixties. Adolescence may be no less problematic here than elsewhere. Tussles over participation in family holidays or the attraction of going away unsupervised with friends are its minor manifestations; more major ones are evident in the sporadic confrontations between the police and male working-class youth, when and where else but on Bank Holidays and at seaside resorts. Meeting someone of the opposite sex for a holiday romance is not the least adolescent aspiration; it also underlies the holiday experience for a wide range of ages. In a more relaxed form, the gender relations dominant in leisure generally prevail on holiday too. Discos, bars, beaches and promenades hold the potential for sexual adventure, possibly without the complications and consequences normally attendant.

If that potential is primarily for exploration by the young and unattached, gender relationships on holiday do not cease to be of significance after marriage. The trend emergent amongst the middle classes to eschew fixed holiday accommodation for caravans and tents may suggest that some families want more autonomy and flexibility in their holiday schedules. Their designation as 'self-catering' may raise the question as to which 'self' does the catering. Facilities for cooking, cleaning and washing have to be part of the essential equipment carried by itinerant holiday-makers. Responsibility for these tasks has to be parcelled up too. The luggage of gender roles may not be declared at customs, labelled his and hers in hotel rooms, or insured against loss in transit, but it is as present as if it were strapped to the roof rack on the car.

The social division of leisure

In opening this chapter, we argued that we wanted to reformulate the terms in which the established consensus discussed the topic of social divisions within leisure. We particularly wanted to recast a model of individual choice from a mixed market of leisure orientated around common family needs, into one which revealed the social structuring and economic underpinning of access to a market of imbalanced provision, to which families no less than individuals had far from equal access. This we felt could be understood as the dimension of leisure opportunity.

The argument seems to us (and perhaps to the reader in retrospect) remarkably simple and obvious. If we substitute social patterns for individual choice and systematically interrelated social divisions for independent socio-demographic variables, some straightforward propositions emerge. Leisure has not expelled class from its influence. Superficially similar leisure activities are given differences of form, meaning and context which are class-based. Evident in neighbourhood culture and in conflicts over the definition of public space are class images of family, community and the links between them. The presence of ethnic minorities has complicated the class profile of contemporary Britain but does not obliterate its outline.

Age is another form of social division which affects leisure in more than simply physiological ways. Socially constructed age groups are placed in distinctive relationships to education, family and work, from which follows their economic and social access to leisure. Old and young differ in precisely where they are placed in relation to essentially the same processes. What matters is not how biologically old you are nor how psychologically young you feel but where you are in the systems of economic production and cultural reproduction.

The same basic pattern, although along a different axis, emerges for gender. Women's leisure is quantitatively less than men's and qualitatively dependent on a narrow definition of the female role, especially within the family. Men dominate leisure physically and culturally, of which sport is the most transparent example. Gender relations, in all their complex inequality, are further evident in the sexual rituals without much more public and private leisure cannot be understood.

The supposed capacity of the family to dissolve all forms of social division is not demonstrated in leisure. If anything, the family actively reproduces them in subtle and not so subtle forms: resources of time and income, relations between the generations, interactions between husband and wife. Even the holiday, that wilful attempt to escape the categorical imperatives of everyday life, can never entirely do so.

What we find in leisure, then, is a reflection and expression of the main social divisions of class, age and gender, which the family may modify only within limits. The measures we can take of the distribution of leisure opportunity – time and money, moral prohibition and control, commercial provision and state services – indicate a degree of inequality as profound as, if less immediately visible than, those evident elsewhere in society.

It could be suggested that the case has been overstated. Surely, there *are* convergent trends in the indices of leisure activity; the family *is* of increasing importance as the central place and motivation of leisure; the market *does* provide a range of possible choices which may be influenced but can never be manipulated. Further, even the major inequality of leisure, that between men and women, already shows some small signs of decrease which *may* accelerate as the movement for women's equality gathers pace.

There is enough accuracy in such a view for it to retain some credibility but it is a partial and selective truth. The nearest we can get to condoning it is to say that there are some striking parallels between the distribution of leisure opportunity and that of employment. Some (who manage to convince themselves and some others that it is the result of merit), actually prosper. Many more, perhaps the real majority, manage to get by, though not without an occasional anxious look over their shoulder. A minority, more sizeable than is generally recognised, suffers increasing material deprivation. The same groups often end up disadvantaged in both work and leisure; in the cruellest of ironies, those most deprived of work are consequentially unable to enjoy leisure.

The unequal distribution of work is frequently presented as an unfortunate by-product of economic change. The unequal distribution of leisure is recognised so infrequently (those without leisure not being required to register their availability for it), that no explanation is thought necessary. No doubt if it were recognised the same basic model would apply: 'there's not enough leisure to go round and won't be unless or until we all work a lot harder'. The perversity of such a position is perfectly compatible with its approval of market forces. Wherever they operate in relative freedom, market forces generate systematic inequalities; it's what they're designed (and despite claims to the contrary, they are designed) to do. There is no reason or indeed evidence to suppose that capitalism has produced within leisure that equality of opportunity which has eluded it in education, employment, housing or income distribution. No more than in those instances are 'compensatory' policies adequate. The sum of all the groups who, on one criterion or another, suffer from inequality of leisure opportunity, comes to rather more than an excluded minority for whom special provision can be made.

The genuine difficulty is that inequalities of leisure are often invisible and intangible. They are also, and this is not the first time we have encountered this problem, difficult to measure. It is not easy to construct statistical tables showing the proportions of the population who admit to being or feeling unable to go out as much as they would wish – though with careful interviewing it can be done. Spurious measures are used instead. For instance, to note that most of the population have access to a television set and can even on occasion be found watching the same programme, is no more a measure of equality than to say that most of the population enjoy free education until the age of sixteen and study the same subjects. The behaviour, what is being done, is not the same as the action, what it means. The meaning of leisure is another reason why inequality is so difficult to track down. We feel differently about leisure from the way we feel about much of the rest of our lives. Since we feel leisure to be more or less our own creation, more so than say our work, we feel less disposed to compare it unfavourably with that of others. We may even fail to resent the leisure privileged, of whose exotic and spectacular activities we are often willing spectators.

That leisure inequality is less recognised and recognisable than other kinds of inequality does not make it any the less real. It may be of less significance than some other inequalities, a point we discuss in our epilogue. Here we must reiterate that, muted and modified though it often is, leisure does ultimately express those social divisions and systematic inequalities inherent in the organisation of contemporary capitalism.

To have written those words ten, or more especially fifteen, years ago would have seemed more of a heresy than it does now. The recession has reopened the problem of inequality, especially around the condition of the unemployed. Such discussion has frequently served to fragment the groups affected into school leavers, the over-fifties, those unfortunate enough to live in certain areas of the north, Scotland, Wales or Northern Ireland, those previously employed in heavy industry – as if in the end, these are not fundamentally the same people. Thus we may fail to see that the brunt is being borne, as it always has been, by working-class men and women.

Our use of that term 'working class' throughout this book invites a very different line of criticism – that we are out of date. The times have changed, and we are still trying to analyse them using concepts invented for understanding an earlier sort of society, now passing into history.

There is now a substantial body of argument which claims that a 'class' model is no longer appropriate for analysing a society experiencing profound and permanent economic and social change. This argument does not have to rest on dubious assertions about the convergence of life styles and incomes around a democratic norm. Rather, it identifies deep-rooted changes in the economy and occupational structure, with potentially far-reaching implications for the experience of work and leisure, class and culture, family and community. Accounts of the nature, causes and effects of the changes now in train vary widely. At their most ambitious, they see society as on the brink of a change as radical as that instigated by the process of industrialisation. At their most modest, they see a fundamental change in the distribution, nature and place of employment. Virtually all such analyses, however, are agreed on the need to create a new theoretical framework to understand a new sort of society. The changing patterns of production and consumption, and the new possibilities they create for social and familial interaction, threaten to outrun our archaic theories. The consequences of these economic and social changes for leisure – for its forms, contexts, meanings and distribution – require that new understandings be created. Whether this new society will make our radical alternative to leisure studies redundant as a by-product of making so many other things obsolete is therefore the main consideration of the following chapter.

Further reading

One of the best discussions of class inequality in Britain (though without specific reference to leisure) remains J. Westergaard and H. Resler, *Class in Capitalist Society* (Penguin, 1975). On middle class leisure styles, see the relevant chapter in R. King and J. Raynor, *The Middle Class* (Longman, 1981), and aspects of working class culture are examined in J. Clarke, C. Critcher and R. Johnson (eds) *Working Class Culture* (Hutchinson, 1979). The upper classes are discussed in John Scott, *The Upper Classes* (Macmillan, 1982), and aspects of their leisure styles may be discovered in media coverage of Ascot and Henley, and in almost any programme by Alan Whicker.

For conventional views on the relationship between age and leisure, see the section on leisure and the life cycle in M. Smith, S. Parker and C. Smith, *Leisure and Society in Britain* (Allen Lane, 1973). Studies of the elderly tend to be dominated by the specific concerns of welfare policy, though some useful survey evidence can be found in S. Parker, *Work and Retirement* (Allen & Unwin, 1982). Kenneth Roberts has recently provided a pluralist account of youth in *Youth and Leisure* (Allen & Unwin, 1983). Alternative approaches to the study of youth and youth subcultures are usefully summarised in John Muncie, *The Touble with Kids Today* (Hutchinson, 1984). Chris Phillipson, *Capitalism and the Construction of Old Age* (Macmillan, 1982) presents a valuable alternative to the more conventional accounts of ageing.

Sara Delamont, *The Sociology of Women* (Allen & Unwin, 1980) provides a readable introduction to women's position in society, including a brief discussion of leisure. A more extended analysis of women and leisure can be found in Margaret Talbot, *Women and Leisure* (Sports Council, 1979). Interesting articles bearing on women's involvement in leisure and free time can be found in two collections: E. Gamarnikow *et al.* (eds), *The Public and the Private* (Heinemann, 1983) and J. Finch and D. Groves (eds), *A Labour of Love* (Routledge & Kegan Paul, 1983). The journal *Feminist Review* regularly deals with issues of direct relevance.

The analysis of sport is little more advanced than that of leisure, though the papers collected in J. Hargreaves (ed.), *Sport, Culture and Ideology* (Routledge & Kegan Paul, 1982) mark the development of new perspectives, including on the relationship between women and leisure. The Open University course *Popular Culture* (Open University, 1981) has a unit dealing with *Holidays* (Unit 11), and a complementary discussion of another family ritual in Units 1 and 2: *Christmas: a Case Study*.

Finally, Bea Campbell's retracing of George Orwell's steps in *Wigan Pier Revisited* (Virago, 1984) provides a readable and combative account of working class life in Thatcher's Britain.

6

Future imperfect: leisure and the post-industrial society

A new type of society is now being formed. (Opening sentence of Alain Touraine, *The Post-Industrial Society*, Wildwood House, 1974, p. 4.)

When the post-industrial thesis is broken down into specific assertions, examination dissolves it into the familiar story of plus ça change, plus c'est la même chose; or, the same, only more so. (Krishnan Kumar, *Prophecy and Progress*, Penguin, 1978, p. 237.)

Our argument in the previous chapter was that leisure remains entangled in the social divisions of British capitalism, and that these are continuous with the social processes which shaped the historical development of leisure in Britain. But this view does not command universal agreement. On the contrary, many academic, professional and political commentators have argued a very different case – that Britain, along with the other Western liberal democracies, is in the process of a dramatic economic and social transformation which will make our argument an anachronism.

In Chapter 1, we considered how ideas of a leisure society have been increasingly central to public discussions of Britain's future. These ideas of a leisure society take up the enhancement of leisure as the outcome of diverse economic and social changes: the advent of new technology, the rise in unemployment and the decline of the Protestant work ethic. In that chapter, we suggested that these ideas worked at the level of public prophecy rather than reasoned analysis. Nevertheless, they do have some significance for the study of leisure.

181

Each of the books which we examined in Chapter 2 as being central to the sociology of leisure takes up the theme of the leisure society and the future prospects of leisure. As before, they are not in direct agreement about these trends, and it is worth briefly considering their different evaluations of the future for leisure.

Kenneth Roberts foresees no dramatic discontinuity between the present and future of leisure. His argument that leisure, work and politics have become socially segregated means that changes outside leisure are unlikely to have effects on leisure itself. While leisure *time* has grown, this has not produced any major changes in the social significance of leisure itself. It has not taken a more dominant role in either the individual or collective psyche of our society. Nor has a leisure ethic spilled over into other areas of life. These areas of life have become distinct and will remain so.

Stanley Parker takes up the implications of new technology for changing patterns of work and leisure in a completely new chapter for the second edition of his book. He argues that much routine and semi-skilled employment in the manufacturing and service sectors of the economy could be replaced by computer based technology, possibly polarising the workforce into a technological élite and a mass of unskilled labour. He argues that this replacement is only likely to occur where the new technology is cheaper than existing labour. This is unlikely to be the case in those occupations where labour is cheap, plentiful and pliable, such as cleaning, catering and the distributive trades. For Parker, the main effect of the new technology is the creation of mass unemployment. In relation to leisure, while recognising that the new technology may provide new sources of entertainment, he argues that these do not produce any qualitative changes in the pattern and experience of leisure. He is sceptical about claims that the new technology will blur or change the boundaries between work and leisure. Because in his analysis work is the primary factor in shaping leisure patterns, he views the impact of the new technology as wholly negative. By destroying work, it negates the possibility of any relationship between work and leisure.

Parker's scepticism about the new technology is not shared by Young and Willmott, who view it as opening up new possibilities for the arrangement of work and leisure. They argue that the new technology has the potential to change the place, time and nature of work, allowing it to be adapted more closely to the interests and the needs of the family. It may also ease the burdens of domestic work, combining with the changing social attitudes promoted by feminism, to change the patterns of domestic roles inside the family. It will be clear from this that Young and Willmott remain committed to viewing the family as the major social institution shaping future social patterns.

Technology and changing social attitudes help to promote the interests of the family as the motivation for future change. These tendencies will operate through the principle of stratified diffusion. Society is becoming more middle class in its occupational structure, use of technology, family relationships and attitudes towards female roles. Logically it follows that changing leisure patterns will come to approximate to those currently enjoyed by the middle class. Their patterns of work and income, of consumer demands and life styles will diffuse downwards into the rest of the society.

This optimistic view of social change is shared by the Rapoports who suggest that new economic developments might combine with changes already visible in personal attitudes and life styles. They see the possibility of a new set of attitudes towards the self, social organisation and ecology which may reverse the individualistic, bureaucratic and wasteful trends of contemporary industrial society. They argue that those responsible for leisure planning have a unique opportunity to foster the growth of such ideals, especially because of the strategic role occupied by the family in relation to leisure. The family is already 'humanising' its roles and relationships, and this private endeavour could be turned into a public one by emphasising these ideals in the organisation of leisure.

Each of these assessments of the future of leisure – agnostic (Roberts), sceptical (Parker) and optimistic (Young and Willmott, the Rapoports) – tries to deal with the impact of other social changes on leisure. Each of them tries to take account of new economic and occupational developments. But they deal with them as secondary matters, as 'factors' which may or may not have an impact on the main focus of attention – leisure. Their discussions of the future of leisure are haunted by an invisible theory – the theory of 'post-industrial society'. Each of them knows it is there, most of them make fleeting reference to it, but – to mix our metaphors – the skeleton is never taken out of the closet and subjected to a thorough scrutiny.

We argued in Chapter 2 that the separation of leisure as an area of analysis for sociology had severe consequences for the analyses that were produced. This same separation, taking leisure as the primary focus and dealing with other aspects of society as factors whose effects can be weighed, is equally visible in these considerations of the future of leisure. It is striking that the extensive literature on social change and the development of 'post-industrial' society is relegated to glancing references and footnotes. In what follows, we hope to remedy this.

The development of 'post-industrial' theories has been one of the growth areas of the social sciences since the mid-1960s. Authors of varying political and theoretical persuasions have discussed the emergence of 'a new type of society', and in doing so have issued a diversity of judgements about the human and social consequences of this new order. We have no intention of surveying the whole of this post-industrial literature here. It has been subjected to extensive and critical reviewing elsewhere (see the *Further Reading* for this chapter). Our purpose here is altogether more modest. In the post-industrial arguments, there have emerged a number of common themes which have a very direct bearing on the analysis of leisure which we have been offering in the preceding chapters.

Our aim here is to consider those social changes identified by post-industrial theorists as marking the movement from one type of society to another, as they bear on our discussion of the relationship between labour in leisure in British society. Our attention will be directed to three aspects of social change in particular:

(a)   Changes taking place in the economic structure of Western societies, and their implications for the distribution of work.

(b)   Related changes taking place in the occupational and class structures of Western societies.

(c)   The impact of the new 'microtechnology' and its implications for work and leisure.

While post-industrial theorists are divided in their interpretation of these changes and the desirability of their social consequences, they are united in the belief that these changes are reshaping the structure of Western societies in a profound way, and are sufficiently far-reaching to justify claims that a qualitative transformation of these societies is taking place – from industrial to post-industrial. If this is so, then it could be argued that the analysis we have been presenting of the relationship between work and leisure within capitalism is, like other features of industrial society, redundant, and should gracefully bow out in favour of new analyses. Our intention, then, is to assess these social changes and their implications for the emergence of a new type of society in order to tell whether this retirement is perhaps a little premature.

Are we being served? The changing economy

Post-industrial theorists have identified the changing economic structure of Western societies as central evidence for the 'new' society's arrival. In particular, they have pointed to two trends in economic organisation: first, the declining significance of manufacturing industry (in terms of investment, contribution to the Gross National Product, and as a source of employment); and secondly, the simultaneous expansion of the 'tertiary' or 'service' sector of the economy, measured by the same criteria. This shift of economic activity is itself a central indicator of post-industrialism, since it marks a movement away from industrial production as the main focus of Western economies. However, the second element – the expansion of the service sector – has been viewed by post-industrial theorists as involving not merely a quantitative change in the distribution of employment, but as also involving a change in the quality of work in post-industrial society. Whereas industrial labour was characteristically intensive manual labour, the service sector centres on work that involves interpersonal contact and the manipulation of information. Such work – in scientific, professional or 'human relations' based occupations – offers the prospect of a job which, unlike the alienated drudgery of industrial labour, provides the worker with intrinsic job satisfactions, along with a better working environment and improved social status.

While we would not dissent from the description of much industrial labour as arduous drudgery, containing little intrinsic pleasure, we are more sceptical about whether the quality of jobs in the service sector is likely to promote a new ethos of work based on autonomy, creativity and interpersonal communication. There are, of course, 'service' occupations which carry with them a considerable degree of work autonomy, creativity and high levels of interpersonal contact in the delivery of their services – and we would, indeed, include our own jobs among them. However, academics and their equivalent are not the characteristic occupations of the service sector. The vast bulk of work in this sector is involved in delivering such services as secretarial and clerical duties; distributive tasks in shops, mail-order houses and transport; cleaning, and catering. To say the least, we are not convinced that such jobs are distinguished by their autonomy, creativity and interpersonal contact, nor by their intrinsic satisfaction. And since many of them are socially identified as 'women's work', they do not include high pay among their rewards.

This sectoral shift of employment in Western societies does not mark a revolution in the quality of our working lives. It is better understood as the spread of conditions of employment, previously familiar in industrial production, to new occupations. This shift of employment follows the movement of investment. As the profitability of manufacturing has declined, service delivery has proved to be an alternative source of returns on investment. Fast food, industrial cleaning and private health care are some of these expansionary 'services', and part of their attractiveness for investors lies in the low labour costs by comparison with industrial workers.

What lies at the heart of this sectoral change in economic activity is a redistribution of employment as capital investment finds new 'needs' to satisfy profitability. Employment has been redistributed in a number of ways: from unionised to non-unionised workforces; from experienced to 'green' workers who do not yet know the 'ropes' of collective organisation; and from full-time to part-time workers, who receive less protection under employment legislation. Each of these changes aims at lowering labour costs for employers, and each of them has contributed to an expansion of women's employment – since they are less unionised, less experienced and will more readily take part-time work to fit in with their other 'responsibilities' in the home.

So far, we have considered the growth of the service sector, but there are also reservations to be expressed about the decline of the manufacturing sector. The post-industrial theorists are strikingly ethnocentric in their assessment of economic change, for, although manufacturing has declined in the major Western economies, it has not shrunk on a world-wide basis. What is left out of the post-industrial account is the *global* redistribution of manufacturing; in particular, the way in which manufacturing processes are being relocated in the 'newly industrialising countries' of South America and the Far East. The search for cheaper labour and advantageous political conditions (tariff free zones, low tax rates and anti-union legislation, for example) has meant that large scale capital investment has increasingly become a trans-national process.

This transfer of industrial production to the 'developing' economies involves a geographical segregation of different stages of the capitalist economic process. Financial and managerial decision-making, and the processes of research and development remain located in the 'home' country, as does much of the marketing of the finished product. It has been mainly the labour intensive processes of production and assembly which have been 'exported'.

There is one very sharp irony in the way that the decline of manufacturing coincides with the growth of leisure in Western societies. Much of 'our' expanded leisure consumption is serviced by the products of manufacturing processes in the developing economies of this world market. 'Leisure-wear' is imported from Thailand; squash rackets from Pakistan; video games and computers from Taiwan and Hong Kong. The 'leisure explosion' is massively supported by this global redistribution of labour.

An endangered species? The vanishing working class

The decline of manufacturing is viewed by post-industrial theorists as having important consequences for the occupational and class structures of Western societies. The combination of its overall decline with the impact of new technologies in remaining production processes has had the effect of reducing the number of manual working class jobs, at the same time as there has been an expansion of non-manual or white collar work. The argument is most familiarly put in the description of an old occupational structure in the shape of pyramid (with a large manual working class base) changing to a diamond-shaped structure, in which non-manual, white collar occupations are the most numerous. This evidence has been used to revive, in a new form, the arguments about 'classlessness' current in the 1950s and early 1960s. At that time, classlessness (or, more accurately a social uniformity based on middle class life styles and aspirations) was supposed to result from the affluence delivered by post-war economic expansion. Increased incomes would allow the working class to participate more fully in the consumer society, and the distinctive patterns of working class community and culture would be eroded. Like affluence itself, this thesis rested on a rather shaky foundation and was relatively shortlived.

In the post-industrial version, however, the disappearance of class seems to have a firmer basis: not the result of rising incomes, but the consequence of real changes in the occupational structure itself. Post-industrial theories consider that this changing class structure is likely to have significant social and political consequences: as the working class declines, so should the patterns of collective organisation in trade union and political forms which have been historically associated with it. Freed from the pursuit of collective vested interests, post-industrial society might develop a more individualised pattern of life choice in work, leisure and politics which would correspond to a more middle class ethos.

Once again, we cannot disagree with the evidence about the changing occupational patterns on which the post-industrial theories are based. Manual working class jobs are declining in the Western economies. (Although we should once again remind ourselves that a manual working class is being expanded on a world scale through multi-national investment.) However, what is at stake here is not the evidence, but how this basic data about occupational patterns is to be interpreted. For us, the central difficulty arises from the too easy equation of occupational categories with social classes, so that manual work = working class, and white collar work = middle class. The growth of non-manual occupations cannot, in our view, simply be treated as the 'growth of the middle class'. The expansion of non-manual work in numerical terms conceals a number of contradictory social processes. First, many of these non-manual occupations share the same sorts of working conditions and authority relationships at work as manual occupations. That is to say, such jobs are highly routinised, highly controlled, of low status and low paid. The majority of 'white collar' workers are to be found in the clerical, secretarial, distributive and service trades, where perhaps *only* the colour of their collars distinguishes them from their 'blue collar' manual counterparts. There is a similar error of identification here to that which we observed in the service sector argument. There, we saw there was a tendency to take the experience of service profession-als as typical of service work. Here, white collar work is similarly typified by the 'élite' of white collar occupations – the professional and managerial middle class – rather than by the working condi-tions of the majority of non-manual workers.

The difficulties go further than this mis-identification. Many non-manual occupations are experiencing those changes in their jobs and working conditions which hasten the numerical decline of the manual working class. The processes of automation, rationa-lisation and the search for productivity which were once the experience of industrial workers are now making their presences felt in the world of white collar work. The computerised office supplants the secretary; the cash dispenser removes the need for the bank clerk, and so on. Kumar, in his review of post-industrial theories, provides a telling description of these trends which provides a sharp counter-weight to celebrations of white collar work:

> Taylorism, the principles of 'scientific management', having conquered the factory have moved into shop and office. Shop and office have been 'industrialised': that is to say, they have been subject to the same processes of increasing rationalisation, routinisation, division of labour, and mechanisation, as had the factory in an earlier period. Following the logic of 'economies of scale', units have increased in size and centralisation, thereby increasing the impersonality of the enterprise and dividing, segregating and fragmenting the workforce...
>
> ...On present trends, the computerised office of the future will resemble the automated factory in most important respects: a few highly trained systems analysts and programmers at the top, segregated in almost every conceivable way from the mass of 'proletarianised' office workers at the bottom...
>
> ...Setting off at different times, diverging on the way, factory and office at the end are united in a common space and a common condition. (Krishan Kumar, *Prophecy and Progress*, Penguin, 1978, pp. 209–211.)

Class, it may be said, stubbornly refuses to be buried. Each announcement of its death has, so far, been premature and the post-industrialist view of an expanding middle class swallowing the remnants of the working class is no exception. On the contrary, we would agree with Kumar that the expansion of non-manual occupations coincides with processes which 'proletarianise' them. The failure of this particular burial ceremony for the working class is not terribly surprising. Just as we argued that the post-industrial theory mistakes the decline of manufacturing industry for the end of capitalism, so, too, it mistakes the decline of manual occupations for the end of the working class. Just as capitalism is not essentially about industry, but about the ownership of capital and the search to accumulate profit, so the working class is not essentially defined by manual work, but by its exclusion from the ownership of capital and the need to sell its labour to survive. This inability to distinguish between the general processes of capitalism and the particular forms of investment and employment is as much a testimony to the optimism of social scientists, who would clearly like to consign capitalism to history, as it is a sad comment on their analytic abilities.

A terminal case? The new technology

Underlying some of the arguments of the post-industrial theorists are speculations about the effects of the latest technological revolution – the advent of the silicon chip and the computing and information systems to which it has given rise. Whereas the previous two themes we considered were based on economic and social trends visible from the mid-1960s, the relationship between this new technology and existing patterns of work and leisure is altogether more recent and more uncertain in its outcomes. This uncertainty has provided very fertile grounds for 'futuristic' speculation about how the microtechnology may revolutionise our whole social order. One further difference from the previous two themes is also worth noting. They were primarily concerned with changing economic and social patterns related to employment. In contrast, the new technology appears to have a more wide ranging impact, affecting work, leisure, the home and the relationship between them. We intend to begin with work.

So far, the most dramatic consequence of the new technology has been its impact on employment, particularly in relation to industrial processes. Automated production lines, computer controlled systems, manufacturing computer designed products are the industrial vanguard of this technological revolution. As we noted in the previous section, the 'labour saving' potential of the new technology is now being applied elsewhere – in offices, banks, shops and warehouses. Human labour, with all its irritating characteristics of tea breaks, holidays, personal problems and trade unions, offers a less efficient and less well integrated service. Even though the application of such technology is still in its infancy and relatively fragmentary, post-industrial theorists have made a number of prognostications about its future effects. One central argument is that post-industrial societies will become 'information centred' rather than 'labour centred'. As manifested in the new technology's uses, information will replace human labour as the key factor in the process of production. Scientific knowledge and expertise will take over the role of the 'hired hand' in making the business work. Similarly, the new communications processes which have been part of this technological revolution will allow more flexible, faster and more efficient means of interacting between individuals, businesses and, perhaps, nations.

The prospects for employment as a consequence of these innovations are complex. Two different trends have been identified. First, the 'labour saving' capacity of the new systems has been interpreted as making possible the abolition of work – at least in the mundane forms of factory and office drudgery. Secondly, however, the rapid development of interactive systems and new means of communication means that, for some sorts of workers (particularly those involved in the manipulation of information), their work will not need to be done *at* work. The home computer terminal means that they will be able to conduct their business without ever leaving the front door. For example, instead of writing this book through endless trips between Sheffield and Milton Keynes, posting archaically hand-written drafts back and forwards, we could (should?) have linked up our (non-existent) word processors through British Telecom and happily chattered away to one another without actually needing to meet. The point is that distance is of no significance to the new information systems, so that the physical boundaries of the factory and office become an outmoded convention.

The home is being invaded by the new technology in other ways. The new 'leisure goods' are the by-products of these technological and communication revolutions: home computers, video-games and recorders, the prospect of cable and satellite transmitted television. They threaten to make the home a hi-tech entertainment palace. These new goods create both new leisure activities and change the relationship between public and private entertainment. Video, cable and satellite contain the promise of never having to leave your home to attend the cinema, concert hall and sports arena. Public entertainment, it seems, is set to come in from the cold. The intense competition visible among potential producers and distributors for the new video and cable markets indicates a commercial belief in the ready availability of audiences for still more home centred leisure.

New technology has also affected the development of other consumer goods in the home. The tasks of domestic labour are now being 'eased' by a variety of appliances either containing innovations from, or at least claiming the magic aura of, the new technology: remote control televisions and hi-fis; microchip controlled toasters; 'turbo-power' vacuum cleaners and computer programmed washing machines. To use the Zanussi Corporation's words, 'the appliance of science' offers to take the drudgery out of housework.

At the experimental stage are further innovations using the new technology not merely as consumer goods, but as new *means* of consuming. The linking of telecommunication systems with home computers and banks and shops promises a whole new mode of home shopping. The mail order catalogue will be replaced by Teletext, and your computer will allow you to 'window shop', make purchases and have them charged to your account without leaving the terminal.

In these ways, it is the home computer terminal which most clearly represents the potential of the new technology to overturn all our existing ideas of work, leisure and the home. The one piece of technology contains the worlds of work, entertainment, shopping, household responsibilities (accounts), and, last but not least, education. The whole world can be at our fingertips.

We warned that microtechnology has given rise to some of the most speculative prophecies about its impact on social change. Some of these visions of the future highlight the decline of work, the terminal family, the information society, and the erosion of the social and geographical boundaries between work, leisure and the home. We think such prophecies should be approached with a degree of caution. In particular we think it is important to distinguish between the *potential* of the new technology, and the social arrangements under which the new technology is being put to work. Optimism seems to be an occupational hazard of social prediction, and, too often, predictions are made which have very little regard for the issues of power and control which will shape the social consequence of the new technology. Technology is neither invented nor put to use outside of the contemporary social, economic and political structures. With these reservations in mind, let us return to the relationship between technology and social change.

We do not doubt that micro-technology has the potential to abolish some forms of labour which are arduous and boring. Some of the tasks already replaced by technology would, in themselves, give little cause for sorrow at their passing. However, we must record two fairly obvious, but none the less significant, qualifications about this decline of work. First, as Stanley Parker rightly argues, the replacement of human labour by technology is subject to a very conventional economic calculation: does it reduce the cost of production? The criterion which governs the substitution of technology for jobs is not a social one (is it the sort of work no one should be asked to do?), but an economic one (will it increase profitability?). We would add a subsidiary 'managerial' criterion to Parker's economic one: that is to say, another consideration is whether the labour to be replaced is highly organised and disputatious. Organised labour has a tendency to limit the 'right of managers to manage'. Both non-organised workers and technology are less likely to dispute this authority.

Secondly, the consequences of these labour saving processes are also subject to conventional economic criteria rather than social ones. Which jobs are to disappear, and which workers disappear with them, are decisions which are left to the 'inevitability' of 'market forces' – or, more accurately, are left in the hands of the owners and managers of capital. The creation of 'free-time' by the introduction of new technology is not socially managed, with any assessment of how it should be distributed, and who should benefit from it. Instead, this free time is unequally distributed by class, age, race, gender and region. Its allocation lies in 'private' hands, and the acceptance of its benefits is ruthlessly enforced. The decline of work, in fact, appears in the all too familiar guise of mass unemployment: the expansion of what Marx called the 'reserve army of labour'. We have in this book tried to use quotations sparingly, but on this occasion, we think one particular quotation is particularly apposite:

> capital increases its supply of labour more quickly than its demand for workers. The over-work of the employed part of the working class swells the ranks of its reserve, while converse-ly, the greater pressure that the reserve by its competition exerts on the employed workers forces them to submit to the dictates of capital. The condemnation of one part of the working class to enforced idleness by the over-work of the other part, and *vice versa,* becomes a means of enriching the indi-vidual capitalist. (Karl Marx, *Capital, volume I*, p. 789, Penguin, 1976.)

This brief paragraph, we are sorry to say, is considerably more accurate than most of the contemporary speculations about the decline of work and the growth of leisure. The economic logic of social change is here made clear: not leisure but 'enforced idleness'; not more free time, but the creation of 'competition' between the employed and the unemployed; not the abolition of drudgery, but a 'means of enriching' capital.

The impact of the new technology on the home must also give cause for some qualifications. First, and equally obvious, access to these new leisure and consumer opportunities remains conditioned by spending power. Access is still obtained through the market-place of capitalism. Secondly, as we noted in Chapter 4, the control of the production and distribution of these new leisure possibilities remains firmly concentrated in the hands of the corporate leisure industries. Who is producing video recorders and video games, cable links and cable programming? Home enter-tainment is now the province (or colony) of those who dominated the previous entertainment 'revolutions' in film, music and broad-cast television.

Thirdly, the intensification of privatisation inherent in these trends is likely to exacerbate the conflicts over public space which we have already considered. As relative wealth brings both access to private space and the expanded means of consumption to enhance the home, so public space will become increasingly the last resort of the 'dispossessed' – those with less access to private space and less spending power to be entertained, educated and serviced at home. The progressive evacuation of the public domain means that those who are left using public space are likely to be increasingly defined (and policed) as dangerous. The pressure will intensify to 'sanitise' the public places of our society to keep them safe for the occasional excursions of the privatised.

Finally, we must consider the interrelationship between these questions of economic control and the development of 'interactive' communications systems. The introduction of these new technologies for 'home consumption' is not separate from economic issues, and the problems of control they contain. The development of 'home shopping' for example, depends upon market criteria both in terms of ownership of the necessary technology, and 'credit worthiness' for participation in such schemes. Further, the shopping 'services' offered are likely to be selective, aimed at 'affluent' market sectors. The 'interaction' in these systems is of a very particular and very familiar kind: 'active' consumer choice within the framework of possibilities established by the commercial provider. One striking example of this home based democratisation of access was provided by an American cable station which 'allowed' its viewers to choose which of three endings to a soap opera episode they preferred. Once again, we must emphasise that power resides primarily in the control of what can be chosen rather than in the act of choice within that framework. The new communications technology may enhance the means for making individual choices (for some individuals), but it shows no signs of democratising the pattern of control. On the contrary, much communications technology has been developed precisely to *enhance* the control of information by business and the state.

This does not mean that we cannot envisage socially useful possibilities for this new technology. Just as there is the potential to abolish forms of labour which are harmful, so, too, communications systems could bring with them social benefits. We could, for example, imagine that 'interactive information systems' could assist in the social circumstances of those who experience enforced 'privatisation' in the home – the housebound elderly and disabled, for example. However, while the applications of new technology are driven by the logic of market forces, rather than social value, such groups and uses emerge (as usual) as a low priority.

The picture we have painted is a bleak one. Unfortunately, it seems to us to be a more realistic one than those optimistic prophecies which concern themselves only with the *potential* of the new technology. Our pessimism derives not from disagreement about that potential, but from an assessment of the social and economic conditions in which the new technology is developed and put to work. The economic imperatives of capitalism seem to us to mean that such innovations will work to confirm the continuation of existing patterns of social organisation rather than to revolutionise them.

A sense of direction?

We began this chapter with two purposes in mind: to assess the argument that there are qualitative changes taking place in leisure; and to assess the argument that profound economic changes have reordered the very structure of the society. We stressed at the beginning that 'leisure society' or 'leisure explosion' arguments pay relatively little attention to economic patterns beyond gesturing to the 'decline' of work and the worth ethic. By contrast, theories of 'post-industrial' society concentrated on economic and work-based changes without developing detailed discussions of changes in leisure. Taken together, they speak of a transformed society featuring the decline of alienating labour, the expansion of a new work ethic based on 'service', the extension of leisure opportunities and a leisure ethic based on creativity and self-actualisation. Examined separately, their assessments of the pace and scale of social change seem to be somewhat unsatisfactory.

Our dissatisfaction with these analyses of change centre on three related points, which we think are (or should be) indispensable in sociological theorising. First, these arguments too readily mistake quantitative change for qualitative change. Whether these changes are greater leisure opportunities, the shrinking of manufacturing, or the replacement of labour by new technology, the factual *evidence* of such changes cannot be simply read as meaning that qualitative new patterns of economic and social life are the inevitable consequence. On the contrary, we have suggested that such evidence can be better understood as the continuation of familiar patterns and processes in capitalist society.

Secondly, this difference in interpretation rests, for us, on an argument about the potential consequences of social and economic changes. In many instances, we think that the prophets of the leisure society and post-industrialism are guilty of wish fulfilment in their theories. The *potential* consequences of social change are presented as if they were the *inevitable* consequences: new technology = the decline of work = the enhancement of leisure. Our own observations have been both more pessimistic and (we hope) more realistic. We do not doubt that some of these changes contain the possibility of a society which is more humane, more open, less oppressed by the unequal distribution of work and its rewards. Nevertheless, these possibilities are far from being inevitable outcomes. Indeed, the way those changes have been brought about within the structures of control and power of contemporary capitalism suggests to us that those possibilities are prevented from becoming real except where they coincide with the economic and political imperatives of the current social order.

This brings us to our third and final source of dissatisfaction. Too many of these pronouncements – of the end of the work ethic, of class, and of industrial capitalism – show an inability to identify the essential features of our society. As a consequence, they are able to claim that the changes they have spotted involve a qualitative transformation in the whole social structure. For example, post-industrialism mistakes manufacturing industry for the capitalist system of production. 'Manufacture' is not the essential feature of capitalism; the economic logic of profitability and the private ownership of capital are essential – and they are unchanged by the growth of the service sector or the export of industrial production to developing countries. Similarly, post-industrialism identifies the 'working class' with manual labour and so happily proclaims the end of class divisions. As we have seen, such a theory is blind to the 'proletarianisation' of other sorts of occupations. Manual or blue collar employment is not the essential feature of the working class – its exclusion from the ownership of capital and thus its subordination to the control of capital, in and out of work, are essential.

We could go on, but it should not be necessary. We continue to

live, work and play in a society which remains essentially capitalist. This does not mean it is unchanging: locked in some timeless
picture of the cigar-smoking boss, the dark and satanic mill and the
cloth-capped workers. Indeed, we would argue that one other
essential feature of capitalism is its dynamism; its endless (so far)
creation of change. The search for profit makes the idea of a stable
capitalist society an impossibility. Innovation – the search for new
producers, new materials, new methods of production – means
that capitalism is constantly changing. Nor are these changes
merely peripheral or inconsequential. The transformation of half
the world into new sources of labour and places for investment is
hardly an insignificant matter. Nor, closer to home, is the enforce-
ment of 'free time' on four million unemployed a peripheral issue.
Nor, yet again, is the expanding employment of women without its
consequences. Even the constant revitalisation of the leisure
market with new goods, services and promises of satisfaction has
its social effects.

But (and it is an enormous 'but') the speed and scale of these
chages should not mislead us into thinking that everything has
changed. The direction of those changes is guided by a social and
economic logic. The concentrations of power and interest which
control that direction survive to tell us that their way is the natural,
inevitable and only path to follow. There remains, however, the
suspicion that this inevitable path may yet turn out to be a dead
end.

Further reading

Daniel Bell's *The Coming of Post-industrial Society* (Basic Books, New
York, 1973) remains the clearest and most theorised account of the social
changes involved in post-industrialism, while the most speculative account
of the impact of changing technology on social relationships and attitudes
is provided by the futurologist Alvin Toffler in *Previews and Prophecies*
(Pan, 1984). Krishan Kumar's *Prophecy and Progress* (Penguin, 1978)
provides a very cogent review and critique of post-industrial theories, on
which our own account in this chapter has drawn heavily.

Andre Gorz's *Farewell to the Working Class* (Pluto Press, 1982) is a
controversial and stimulating attempt to use some aspects of post-
industrialism to challenge conventional Marxism and suggest the need to
redefine the project of socialism. A more sobering review and analysis of
contemporary trends in the 'decline of work' is to be found in Doreen
Massey's excellent *Spatial Divisions of Labour* (Macmillan, 1984).

End of Part II

We can identify two sets of tensions from the analysis we have presented in Part II, which we believe are the central contradictions of contemporary leisure. One is between the institutional control of leisure and the highly individualised model of leisure choice. Rather than choice being the outcome of control it becomes compensation for the absence of control. Choice has become the ideological validation of a system which in practice denies people the power to exercise control.

The second tension is between change and continuity. The major forms and definitions of leisure seem to be changing under the diverse pressures of economic recession and the transition to a post-industrial society. An adequate analysis needs to set the reality of such changes against deeper continuities in the basis structure of capitalism and the social conflicts which it produces. Here we want to clarify the separate meanings of these sets of tension and to consider the connections between them.

The concern with control was most evident in our chapter on the market and the state. The freedoms provided by the market are limited in range and kind. The production of marketable goods and services remains in private hands. The myth of consumer power disguises the extent of capital's power. Modern leisure corporations may follow consumer demand but they can also create it, and their ability to do so increases with their growing domination of leisure production. Specific markets may be difficult for individual corporations to control, but their collective control of the market system remains uncontested. The success of the market lies not only in its material domination of the production of leisure goods and services but in its cultural domination of ways of thinking about leisure as a set of commodities. Thus the market both produces goods and services and reproduces itself as a working model of society. Its most powerful image is that of the consumer. Apparently a universal role, in practice only those with the qualification of income at their disposal get to play the part. The historically specific processes of market production and mass consumption have become translated into the only valid model for economic, social and even political life. Thus leisure becomes a commodity like any other: we use it, and see ourselves using it, through the processes of exchange and consumption. The successful equation of the private interests of producers with the leisure preferences of consumers marginalises any attempt to conceive of the public interest in terms other than those of the market. The only control to which this economic and cultural power submits is that of the consumer electorate. All the candidates are on the same slate: vote in the market and you vote for it.

In the ideology of the market-place, consumer choice is allowed to substitute for leisure opportunity. Our ability to choose between what is on offer is stressed: our inability to decide what should be offered is conveniently ignored. The economic, political and cultural constraints within which choice is exercised appear as supposedly free-floating preferences for leisure life styles. Choices about the future shape of leisure become projected changes in market 'taste'.

The consequences of the control of leisure by diversified corporations is that consumer choice is always more limited than it appears or is felt to be. Presented and packaged differently, the goods and services supplied by the market are similar in kind, the multiplicity of brand names traceable back to a few corporate sources. The whole marketing enterprise is designed to persuade us to exercise consumer choice in particular ways. But its most potent effect is less on the specific choices we make, than on our attitude to the process of choosing. The market does have difficulty structuring and predicting particular choices. Consumers will weigh the costs and benefits of a particular choice in ways which the producer is unable to influence. Leisure products are used in distinctive ways, assembled around perceived needs and meanings which have sources other than the colour supplements. They may even be used, especially by the young, in ways never intended or understood by the manufacturer.

In such ways we restore 'meaning' to the mechanical processes of production and consumption, ensuring that 'usefulness' becomes a criterion of 'marketability'. Such strategies may modify but cannot challenge the market/consumer model. Before we can modify the meaning and use of any commodity, we must first enter the market as consumers to acquire it.

Dominant though the market is, it does not completely exhaust the patterns of leisure production and provision. What the market cannot or will not produce for us as consumers, we look to the state to provide for us as citizens. Thus the role expected of the state is essentially compensatory: to remedy deficiencies in the provision made by the market, leaving its operations otherwise impeded.

The activities of the state represent no attempt to make the market system more accountable. This is not surprising, given that one of its historical roles has been to establish and maintain the conditions in which the market system can operate. It may even protect the market against itself, intervening to protect the long-term interests of the system against short-time abuses of it. The public interest is defined as the legitimation of the 'right' sort of private enterprise.

The state is itself accountable, it can be won to some strategies other than the simple protection of the market system. Capitalism no more 'needs' the provision of free or low-cost leisure facilities through local authorities than it 'needs' a National Health Service. Both are compromises, more or less forced upon the state by the shifting balance of political power and public opinion.

Historically the state's involvement in leisure can be seen as an uneven attempt to extend leisure choices into areas which are not immediately profitable. Public provision can be made compatible with private profit but there is always a tension between the models of leisure each embodies. In leisure as in welfare, the universal public provision of facilities is a direct alternative to the selective private purchase of commodities. The citizen, to whom benefits accrue as of right, stands in contrast to the consumer, who must earn them in the market-place. These contrary influences account for the ambiguities of state intervention, its vacillation between promoting private and public interests, between care for and control of the leisure of its citizens, between the eradication of inequality and the maintenance of social divisions.

That social divisions are maintained by the state is perhaps more evident in its direct regulation of the conditions and rewards of work than in its much more indirect control of leisure. Yet through its control over the social divisions generated by employment, the state helps to ensure that inequalities in and around work will be reproduced outside it. Those with relatively more control over their work tend to have relatively more control over their leisure: class does not end at the factory gate or office door, gender even less so. To play their ascribed role in the reproductive system of family life, women must sacrifice control over their own leisure to the needs and demands of children and husbands. This is the purest form of the social control of women's leisure which begins before, and continues after, the phase of child-rearing. The terms on which women gain access to leisure are controlled, directly and indirectly, physically and psychologically, by dominant male interests. The pattern is consistent, despite the variations wrought by class and age. The social construction of age is itself a form of social control. For the young and the old alike, disparities occur between what they would psychologically like to do, what they are physically able to do and what they are socially permitted to do.

The control of leisure resources (and thus the ability to make choices) is a reward for participation in the productive process. Those who occupy an inferior position within production (the working class), whose priorities are defined as lying outside the productive process (women), who have not yet gained productive roles (the young) or given them up (the old), will find their capacity to choose restricted. That they may often not feel the lack of choice may simply indicate the limited expectations they have come to hold.

Choice is thus both materially and culturally constrained by social divisions. Materially, leisure resources are unequally distributed. Choice is restricted to how we dispose of our *personal* resources. But we exercise little control over the social allocation of those resources. Cultural constraint finds its most powerful expression through legal prohibition, but equally important are the day-to-day, routinised, expectations we hold of each others leisure conduct. And as we internalise these constraints, so we come to make 'realistic' choices which are appropriate to our economic and social conditions. Whether through lack of time and money, or fear of others disapproval, we learn what we cannot 'afford' to choose.

This curtailment of choice through the operation of social divisions is never complete. Political pressure, the economic cycle, and even individual mobility can change our material circumstances. Public opinion does bring alterations in the legal restrictions on specific forms of leisure activity. Cultural expectations change too. We can even choose to use our leisure to campaign to change the conditions which influence it. We can also choose to create something other than that provided by market and state by instituting our own local leisure interest groups.

Thus choice may be exercised in ways which challenge rather

than accept the constraints which stem from social divisions. But the financial and social costs are high, and it is not surprising to find such active choices the prerogative of those best able to bear them. For most people, leisure choice in contemporary Britain operates within what is 'known' to be the most available and appropriate set of activities as defined by our location in the patterns of social division.

The changing balance between 'control' and 'choice' is one of the central issues posed by post-industrial theorists. On the one hand, social change may create the possibility that increased control of the productive process may force us from the necessity of labour, thus altering not merely the scope but the very nature of leisure choice. Rather than living with the externally imposed demands of employment, we may be able to choose our involvement in production, breaking down previously existent barriers between work and leisure. On the other hand, these same social changes may further reduce our power to control, subjecting us to the impersonal forces of technology dominated by corporate and governmental interests. We may become more controlled as consumers and citizens, our lives monitored and recorded, as control of that most precious commodity, information about ourselves, passes to those with the means of obtaining, storing and retrieving it. Our economic, political and cultural preferences known, the potential to channel our subsequent choices is increased. It is the nightmare of science fiction come true: a small body of self-interested élites choosing what we need to know, what we are able to decide, what we ought to consume. The same technological processes which could diversify knowledge and control also have the capacity to increase their centralisation.

One of the successes of modern capitalist ideology has been to persuade us that control and choice of leisure are unrelated. Control can be safely left in the hands of corporations and government whom we hold accountable through consumer demand and electoral opinion respectively. 'Choice' is what they give us: a range of leisure goods and services within which we choose. We are persuaded that all alternatives are totalitarian: other forms of control will diminish 'consumer choice'.

This has become the common-sense of leisure. Our sense of democracy becomes tied up with our rights to pursue our 'own' leisure pursuits without interference. We have come to live the definition of leisure as 'time free to choose'. The choices we can and do make disguise those we can't and don't. These limited choices allow us to feel that we shape our own lives. Rarely do we consider either the narrow range of things represented by that pattern or the interests served by their production and consumption. Economic and political constraints on leisure choice remain hidden, cultural and social constraints taken for granted. External constraints are internalised as the natural order of things, social divisions are turned into a pluralism of differences in taste and interest.

In some ways we understand all too well the way our social system works and our place within it. We know that in reality our choices are restricted, but this makes us value those which we can make all the more. We know that government and commerce seek to control our leisure, so become all the more determined to base ourselves away from their interference, in the 'spontaneous' patterns of friendship and family. We have no illusions save one – that our families and our leisure are our own to control, to mould into our own chosen patterns. By accepting such a diminution of leisure choice, we leave the real decisions to others.

Control involves the power to set the limits of these particular choices. Our collective lack of control leaves us with diminished arenas in which to exercise choice. The separation between the public world of power and control and the private world of choice is more imaginary than real. The two aspects, control and choice, are intimately connected in the structuring of our lives. In studying leisure we can (or ought to be able to) see these interconnections.

We argued in Part I that the development of leisure is dynamic. Both continuity and change are evident in its forms, meanings and the social context in which it is pursued. In Part II we have been tracing change and continuity in the leisure operations of market and state, the structure of leisure opportunities stemming from social divisions and most fundamental of all, in the changing economic shape of British society.

Leisure is more than a footnote in the political economy of post-war Britain. It has become one of the key sectors of the economy. The expansion of the leisure market has enabled corporate diversification, monopolisation and vertical integration. The commercial dominance of a small core of companies over leisure is nothing new: it is essentially the earlier history of the mass media now extended to other leisure commodities. What may represent a change is that such domination is not merely within leisure market, but across other sectors too. As many companies diversify 'out of' leisure as diversity 'into it'. Takeovers and mergers represent more efficient ways of concentrating capital, market research and mass advertising more efficient ways of guaranteeing a market. The domination of leisure by monopoly capital continues trends visible from the turn of the century but which have gained added impetus in the more favourable conditions of the modern British economy.

Not the least of these favourable conditions have been the policies adopted by government. Though anxious to protect the public interest against outright monopolies, they have in practice encouraged the formation of larger and hence more 'efficient' enterprises. Such state policies seemed for a while to be producing a 'corporatist' strategy with government, big business and organised labour working in a balance of interests to plan economic and social development. The return of economic crisis has reasserted the differences of interest between capital and labour. The failure of corporatism to resolve this antagonism has led to political polarisation. The election of a Conservative government committed to monetarist policies signalled a realignment of economic and political interests in favour of the free play of market forces. The change in political life which post-war 'consensus' politics appeared to represent was reversed. Deeper continuities in British politics resurfaced. Neither the policies of monetarism nor the images it presented of British society were new. The control of money supply and the attack on government expenditure have their nineteenth century precessors. Out of the same century came the idealised figure of the thrusting entrepreneur about to be released from the chains of excessive government interference – a fiction no less powerful for its historical and contemporary inaccuracy.

Whatever monetarist theory might say, political pragmatism made it difficult to hive off state leisure provision into private hands. Such provision is in any case often a hidden subsidy to private enterprise (for sports equipment to be sold there must be somewhere to use it). What can be done is to progressively diminish the quality and quantity of 'public' provision. Sports and Arts Councils can be 'encouraged' to seek private funding in the form of sponsorship; local authorities forced to reduce the framework of recreational provision and to sell off valuable resources (e.g. playing fields) to private control. The preference for private provision and consumption of leisure is a 'change' from the view of the state as being responsible for its citizens' welfare. But it also contains a continuity with the 'patronage' of leisure in the nineteenth century, even if the patron is less likely to be his local lordship than your friendly high street bank.

The deterioration in the quality of the social environment which current government policy enthusiastically endorses also serves to sharpen social divisions. Unemployment, by definition a destroyer of leisure, has been distributed unequally between classes and races, sexes and ages. The problem and the reactions to it are defined as 'new'; in fact they are historically consistent. The disequilibrium between the demand for labour and supply of it has always been a feature of industrial capitalism. The admission that it has been deliberately created and that no immediate solution is available may be novel, but the reaction is the same. The unemployed, especially the working class, the young, the black, emerge as a social problem. Once the unemployed drank too much; now they sniff glue and watch video nasties. Social scientists queue up for research funds to investigate how the unemployed live. What society is going to do *about* unemployment is forgotten in the rush to find out what the unemployed are going to do *with* it. Further weighty volumes are added to the annals of investigating the lives of the poor.

If class remains the principal mechanism through which inequality is perpetuated, there are differences in the ways other social divisions are exacerbated by economic recession. The removal of paid work and hence access to leisure is experienced differently between black and white, old and young, male and female. The very complexity of social divisions makes it difficult to see the unemployed as a homogeneous entity. Their victimisation thus appears individual and accidental rather than collective and systematic. The illogicality of its outcomes masks the logic of the system.

Nevertheless, this logic does exist, and does produce social changes. Manufacturing is being exported to the low cost areas of the developing countries. Western manual labourers are displaced by those of the Third World or more efficient automated systems.

Manufacturing industry and blue collar occupations decline as the service sector and white collar occupations increase. Change is evident in the nature and distribution of employment, on which depends our sense of society and the role of leisure within it. The exaggeration of the focus and nature of change in post-industrial theories does not mean that we must respond by denying that any change is taking place. It does, however, mean that proper emphasis is given to the continuities in the structures and forces which underlie change.

No serious analysis of the future should ignore the continued domination of corporate capital. Nor should the social consequences of this – the continuing centrality of the market model and consumer roles – be omitted in the search to discover new life styles. Other central aspects of the organisation of capitalist societies show an equal resistance to change. Social divisions persist, and are even intensified by growing polarisations between skilled élites and the unskilled mass of workers, and by the increasing gulf between those in work and those out of it. The nuclear family continues to be hailed as the model of domestic life and as a central means of satisfying complex human needs. Only now, family life can be enhanced by plugging into the new technology.

These are substantial continuities from the present into the future. But it is in the social effects on attitudes and life styles that 'real' changes are anticipated by post-industrial theories. In particular, the work ethic will become anachronistic with the reduction of compulsory labour and the expansion of free time. 'New values' are required to adjust our lives to the coming of post-industrial society.

We do not have to believe that the work ethic has ever been more than a way of making a virtue out of necessity to see the potentially radical effect of the changed patterns of work and leisure in post-industrial society. The definition of leisure as time left over from work will require alteration if there is relatively little work for time to be left over from. Capitalism has defined leisure as time in relation to the processes of production, reproduction and consumption. Reproduction could expand to fill the vacuum vacated by production: families could become men's as well as women's work, but this would require a revolution in definitions of gender. Such extended family involvement could generate additional consumer demand since there is no natural limit to the economic wants of the family. But this expansionist vision would still require the distribution of resources through which people could take advantage of these new opportunities. The productive system of capitalism is ill-equipped to cope with such a transformation. While the wage is related to paid employment, how can capitalism face a distribution of 'rewards' which is separated from employment? If worklessness is to be the common condition, how will the expanded free time of the population be financed? The 'incentive' system of contemporary capitalism (and its penalisation of the workless) looks ill-adjusted to the creation of a leisured society.

In reality, we would expect the contradictions to be of a different kind. Post-industrialism often assumes a harmonious set of outcomes from these changes – a universal reduction in working time and an equally distributed set of 'rewards' in terms of time, money and opportunity. This optimism seems misplaced. The decline of work will not be equally distributed, and worklessness will continue to be penalised by a loss of income. The 'free time' of the workless will continue to be viewed with suspicion and be subject to scrutiny and control.

The future does not contain a carefully ordered reallocation of work and leisure for all, but the creation of permanent structural unemployment for some. This will be the major route by which capitalism arrives at its 'post-industrial' stage. The cost of policing the inevitable social conflicts will be gladly borne – indeed it is already being paid. For visions of the future we should look not to dual career families, communes of craft workers, or the autonomous leisure seeking professional, but to the streets of the inner cities and the picket lines of our major industrial conflicts.

Leisure, in its conventional sense, will become the preserve of a population just large enough to maintain the legitimacy of political power. Some new employment may be generated by the services demanded by this group – not least in the already visible re-emergence of domestic service. The rest – the growing reserve army of the unemployed – will become permanently dependent on casual work, state benefits and, no doubt, on private philanthropy.

Which of the various post-industrial prophecies will come true depends not on the inevitable progress of technological change, but on the economic and political power which commands the uses to which such technology will be put. The current concentrations of economic and political power press for those changes which will ensure their continuity. Their concern to let market forces run free will guarantee the continuity of capitalism's endemic cycle of depression and expansion, with the fruits of expansion being grudgingly – if at all – shared out.

Industrialisation did not create British capitalism and the present deindustrialisation of Britain will not destroy it. The search for new sources of profitability continues, as does the process of dumping the unprofitable.

It should, we hope, be clear that the two sets of tensions which we have outlined in this chapter are different, but not separate. The process of change cannot be isolated from the issues of power and control. The direction of change – which future possibilities will be realised and which will be jettisoned as 'utopian' – depends on the possession of power. Post-industrial changes may extend some aspects of private choices, but they seem unlikely to disturb the concentrations of power which guarantee control. In some ways, the prospects are bleaker than this. Far from undermining the concentration of power, some of the social changes we are now witnessing seem set to increase and enhance the concentration of power and control.

7
Conclusion

We began this book by explaining the nature of our project (Chapter 1). We suggested that the analysis of leisure needs approaches more internally consistent than those generally available (Chapter 2) and which take proper account of the historical dynamic of leisure (Chapter 3). At the end of Part I we drew out what emerged as common and recurrent themes in our analysis, principally that leisure has been and is socially constructed around the axes of time and space, institutional forms and social identities.

In Part II we attempted to sketch, and it really has been no more than that, the outline of a more adequate approach. We focused especially on the political economy of leisure (Chapter 4), its reproduction of social divisions (Chapter 5) and the role projected for it in the social changes emphasised by theories of post-industrial society (Chapter 6). At the end of the second part we tried to stress the connections between what have come to be used as mutually exclusive terms: control and choice of leisure, continuity and change in leisure and society.

We have, in fact, two conclusions, this one addressed primarily to intellectual issues and an epilogue addressed to political ones. This recognises differences of interest within our potential audience and the genuine difficulty of linking the abstractions of intellectual analyses with the concrete concerns of political action.

There is also another consideration. We accepted, and have done our best to fulfil, the publisher's brief that this work should be accessible to as wide an audience as possible. There is, though, a point beyond which ideas and language have to become genuinely more difficult, in order to grasp the full complexity of leisure. It is a point we have now reached. Rather than try in one short chapter to change gear suddenly, we want to trace the process whereby that transition originally took place within the academic disciplines which inform our perspective. In the Preface we noted how our work belongs in what has come to be known as 'cultural studies'. Its origins lie in literary studies, history and sociology; latterly it has been influenced by Marxist and feminist theory. To trace, explain and evaluate these formative influences would be a book in itself. All we can do here is to present some of the 'moments' (a typical cultural studies word) when intellectual orthodoxy was challenged by theoretical insights with the power to reshape the study of society.

We have chosen the focus on texts which mark these transitional moments. They are C. Wright Mills, *The Sociological Imagination*, Raymond Williams, *The Long Revolution* and Michele Barrett, *Women's Oppression Today*. These are not merely historical documents; their arguments remain pertinent. If the analysis of leisure is to be reformed it will need to use the perspectives these texts have helped to establish.

The sociological imagination

Writing about the state of American sociology in the late 1950s, C. Wright Mills offered an analysis which remains remarkably applicable to the state of the British sociology of leisure in the 1980s. He saw social science as polarised between two equally negative influences. At the one end, was an excessive concern with abstract elaborations of models of the social order which he termed 'Grand Theory'; at the other, an obsession with narrowly defined social problems and the methods of investigating them 'scientifically' which he dubbed 'abstract empiricism'. These interests predominated in an academic context itself inimical to serious intellectual enquiry. Social science research was becoming bureaucratised, supervised by administrators, executed by technicians, accepting the goals of limited social engineering imposed by funding agencies. Consequently the emphasis on freedom and reason, typical of the classical social analysts, had been fragmented into three endencies. First, towards discovering the iron laws of history (subsequently to become known as historicism); secondly towards pseudo-philosophical system building (theoreticism); thirdly towards an exclusive preoccupation with technically efficient means of measurement (empiricism). Even at its best, social science appeared as a species of liberal pluralism, pragmatic in its approach to sociological problems, seeking to further human adjustment to existing society and abdicating as impossible and undesirable any attempt to analyse or even describe society as a totality.

Much of this, if refined in kind and reduced in scale, is true of contemporary British social science. Abstracted empiricism is an accurate portrait of much recreation research. Liberal pluralism is precisely the habitual stance of the consensus in leisure sociology. The mantle of grand theory has distressingly been donned by some revered figures of Marxist thought (and by apparently more grounded theories such as ethnomethodology). It is not, however, the validity of Mills' critique which interests us, as much as his set of prescriptions for recapturing the principles and practices of the sociological imagination.

Before considering these, it is necessary to concede some deficiencies in Mills anlaysis. He is prone to a mass society perspective. The majority of the population are seen as cheerful robots whose salvation will only be achieved by an élite of men endowed with reason. 'Men' there is significant, for in Mills language 'Man' and 'men' become synonymous. Little attention is paid to the experience of women and nearly all his examples come from the male social world. The inferior position of women in and outside work and family receive cursory mention.

These are considerable shortcomings. Despite them, though no doubt others will here part company with us, we see Mills' vision of the sociological imagination as valuable. We would even suggest that its own ultimate logic ought to be able to supersede flaws in his own work.

Mills' position is clearly stated at the outset:

The sociological imagination enables us to grasp history and biography and the relations between the two in society. That is its task and its promise... No social study that does not come back to the problems of biography, of history, and of their intersections within a society, has completed its intellectual journey. (*The Sociological Imagination*, Penguin, 1970, pp.12–13.)

History is not here background but the essence of the social scientist's work:

> We more readily become aware of larger structures when they are changing, and we are likely to become aware of such changes only when we broaden our view to incude a suitable historical span... Awareness of structure, in all the meanings of this central term, as well as adequate statement of the troubles and problems of limited milieux, require that we recognise and that we practise the social sciences as historical disciplines (p. 165).

Just as we need the horizontal axis of history, so we need the vertical axis of the individual and the society. Their interconnection is that between 'the personal troubles of the milieu' and the 'public issues of the social structure'. Understanding how personal troubles come to be experienced as disconnected from public issues, and the individual's milieu from any sense of social structure, is one step in the analysis. The second is to restore a sense of connection, to establish that private troubles are public issues as experienced by individuals, public issues the sum of those private troubles and their location in the social structure. It is this ability, to situate human activity within the social structure without reducing its complexity or denying its meaning, which defines the sociological imagination:

> To be aware of the idea of social structure and to use it with sensibility is to be able to trace linkages among a great variety of milieux. To be able to do that is to possess the sociological imagination (p. 17).

What is at stake in such an enterprise is reason itself and that freedom which its exercise secures:

> Freedom is not merely the chance to do as one pleases; neither is it merely the opportunity to choose between set alternatives. Freedom is, first of all, the chance to formulate the available

choices, to argue over them – and then, the opportunity to choose (p. 193).

Social science needs to establish the present and future possibilities of freedom rather than simply accept the inevitable:

> the social task of reason is to formulate choices, to enlarge the scope of human decisions in the making of history. The future of human affairs is not merely some set of variables to be predicted. The future is what is to be decided – within the limited, to be sure, of historical possibility. But this possibility is not fixed: in our time the limits seem very broad indeed (p. 193).

The relevance of Mills' version of the sociological imagination to our project should now be clear. We have been trying, at a very modest level indeed, to recover the sociological imagination for the analysis of leisure. We have been trying to suggest how the leisure of the individual needs to be understood within the patterns of the whole society and how both require an historical analysis of the dynamics of social structure. We have tried to show how the most private leisure identities are actually publicly generated as definitions of class and race, age and gender. We have argued that the most individual of milieux, especially the family, have to be understood as socially constructed and defined. The leisure of the family has to be related to the location of the family in the social structure and to the location of leisure in the market and State systems. What now passes as leisure choice does not meet Mills' definition of freedom; what poses as futurology denies the capacity to reason. The correspondence between our approach and that of Mills is so close that he is even able to explain the nature and sources of some likely reactions to this book:

> It is of course, intellectually easier (and politically more advisable) to acknowledge one trend at a time keeping them scattered, as it were, than to make the effort to see them all together. To the literary empiricist, writing balanced little essays, first on this and then on that, any attempt to 'see it whole' often seems an 'extremist exaggeration' (p. 170).

There is one important sense in which Mills' work diverges from the concerns in cultural studies. That is in his reservations about its central concept.

> In contrast with social structure, the concept 'culture' is one of the spongiest words in social science, although, perhaps for that reason, in the hands of an expert, enormously useful. In practice, the conception of 'culture' is more often a loose reference to social milieux plus 'tradition' than an adequate idea of social structure (p. 177).

The long revolution

This might almost be a comment on the work of Raymond Williams whose work is a sustained attempt to clarify the meanings and potentialities of the concepts 'culture' and 'community'. Particularly relevant for our purposes is the essay 'Britain in the Sixties' which concludes *The Long Revolution*, first published in 1960. This remains his most accessible statement, though the essays in the recently published *Towards 2000* revise the argument considerably. Culture is Williams organising concern:

> We are seeking to define and consider one central principle: that of the essential relation, the true interaction, between patterns learned and created in the mind and patterns communicated and made active in relationships, conventions and institutions. Culture is our name for this process and its results. (*The Long Revolution*, Penguin, 1965, p. 89.)

In any particular period, culture assumes the form of a set of commonly communicated meanings which Williams calls the 'structure of feeling'. This structure and the economic, political and cultural systems on which it reflects, are not static. The long revolution is the process of the change in these systems and of the 'conceptions of man and society' they generate and sustain. The project therefore is to see change and continuity in culture and the structures of feeling to which it gives impression:

> We have been trying to develop methods of analysis which, over a range from literature to social institutions, can articulate

actual structures of feeling – the meanings and values which are lived in words and relationships – and clarify the processes of historical development through which these structures form and change (p. 319).

In interpreting this long revolution, we are handicapped by prevailing modes of thought, especially those which stem from the idea of the market. It has become the way we define freedom and assess the legitimacy of all other forms of activity:

> The central point... is that the concepts of the organized market and the consumer now determine our economic life, and with it much of the rest of our society, and that challenges to them have been so effectively confused that hardly any principled opposition remains (pp. 331–2).

The consumer image has two major effects. One is that the underlying logic and actual workings of the market are misrepresented. Consumer needs are located as the causes of economic activity when they are in actuality its effects:

> It is then clear why 'consumer' as a description, is so popular, for while a large part of our economic activity is obviously devoted to supplying known needs, a considerable and increasing part of it goes to ensuring that we consume what industry finds it convenient to produce. As this tendency strengthens, it becomes increasingly obvious that society is not controlling its economic life, but is in part being controlled by it. The weakening of purposive social thinking is a direct consequence of this powerful experience, which seeks to reduce human activity to predictable patterns of demand (p. 323).

Secondly, the consumer image legitimises private and personal concerns as against public and communal interests. Commitment to the goal of individual consumption makes us resentful of the intrusion of other objectives, especially if they involve the diversion of resources away from personal spending. Hence we resent paying taxes and rates, failing to connect them to the provision of public services on which our general standard of living depends. Even so, we may occasionally realise that 'most of our cultural institutions are in the hands of speculators' yet can find as the only alternative model the equally despised figure of tbe bureaucrat.

For lack of viable alternatives (as a direct result, Williams believes, of the failure of socialist thought and policies), we come to endorse those real but minimal freedoms which are offered by the operation of the market. Private satisfaction engages us; public provision does not. In this forsaking of the public realm the private world of the family is crucial:

> In this personal revolt, nobody is deceived by what societies say they are doing; whatever this may be, the individual is likely to suffer, and the best he can hope for is to minimize its pressures: by detachment, by apathy and scepticism, by seeing that at least he and his family are all right... ...The personal revolt asserts individuality, in this world of impersonal abstractions, but the assertion, commonly is also a withdrawal from social thinking: I and my family are real; the rest is the system (pp. 129–130).

This makes a limited kind of sense in a society whose contours are not only indistinct but shifting. Older modes of understanding have to narrow a perspective and insufficiently sharp a focus to be adopted as ways of framing the social organisation. The class model, for example, seems no longer to describe how societies work, either for how individuals see themselves within it or for the process of change at an individual or social level.

The essential continuities of class, differentials in the ownership and control of social capital, are actively disguised:

> the growing feeling that class is out of date and doesn't matter is being used to ratify a social system which... is still essentially based on economic classes (p. 362).

The discrediting of alternative models encourages us to confuse the specific historical processes of contemporary capitalism with universal human experience. Work is defined as a kind of moral exchange between relative equals rather than the enforced sale of labour by those who have no other marketable assets. Such dominance of the market model and our moral evaluation of work produce a definition of leisure as simultaneously free from market relations and an extension of them.

The reintegration of work and leisure, the private and the

public, the economic or political and the cultural, will only be achieved by the establishment of 'a real feeling of community – the true knowledge that we are working for ourselves and for each other' (p. 363). It is this 'different version of community, a pattern of new consciousness' (p. 360) which the Labour Party has failed to provide. The long revolution remains uneven and unfinished: the need to create 'new, common institutions' (p. 375) unmet.

The work of Raymond Williams touches on the 'problem of leisure' through a more general concern with the problem of culture. There are losses as well as gains in this approach.

The influence of literary studies is not wholly beneficial. While he is careful not to be dismissive of the status of everyday human activities, his actual working definition of culture is one confined to creative forms of communication: drama and film, books and newspapers, radio and television. Partly as a result there is a total separation of this approach from Marxist thought which Williams' subsequent work has sought to rectify. Most damagingly of all, his understanding of gender relations is weak. His analysis of consumerism and the family makes no mention of the strategic roles inhabited by women nor of the more general structures of sexual inequality on which such roles depend. But, as in the case of Mills, the essence of the project remains valuable.

Like Mills, though using different terminology, Williams is concerned with the individual's place in the social organisation and the dynamics of change in the social system and perceptions of it. His analysis of why and how the market/consumer model has come to predominate over class interpretations is particularly relevant. The 'pluralism' of the leisure consensus, the weakness of validations for public provision and the preference for privatised family life all reflect the domination of the market model. The emphasis on changes in the appearance of inequality yet continuity in the underlying dimensions is close to, though perhaps narrower than, our conception of social divisions.

More subtle than Mills vision of alienated humans, Williams' description of the withdrawal into the familiar certainties of private life sees its logic and strengths while emphasising its damaging consequences. That what is viable for individuals is unviable for society as a whole is the paradox of contemporary leisure we have been trying to establish. Against this is the need to establish a sense of 'community' which we too would wish to endorse in Williams' terms: not romantic ideals about intimate social interaction but a sense of things and relationships held in common. We use a quote from Williams as a preface to our political epilogue since he makes most clearly the connection between cultural analysis and the failure of socialism. There remains, however, the significant absence, as intellectual analysis and political practice, of feminism.

Women's oppression today

In *Women's Oppression Today* Michele Barrett has provided one of the most coherent attempts to establish lines of communication between Marxist and feminist analyses of contemporary society. The difficulties are not glossed over. The Marxist model of a capitalist society in which the primary antagonism is that between capital and labour is not easily compatible with the feminist model of a patriarchal society where the main form of domination is that by men over women. This problem is exacerbated by an imprecise use of the major concepts used by each approach, not only those of reproduction and ideology but also those of patriarchy and sexuality. A central concern of the book is with the clarification of such conceptual issues and their application to specific areas of women's oppression, especially in eduation and more general state policies.

The original argument is much wider and deeper than our rather limited concern with leisure can incorporate. Three aspects of the discussion have some direct purchase for us: the role attributed to culture in the perpetuation of gender inequality, the pervasive nature of the sexual division of labour, and the absolute centrality for gender relations of the modern family household.

Barrett argues that many discussions of ideologies about gender see them as either independent of the way society is organised (what she calls 'idealism') or simply reflecting directly the interests of the dominant group in society, whether that group is seen as capitalist or male ('reductionism'). This arises because such discussions are too abstract, being neither historically specific nor empirically informed. The inequality of women is produced and experienced culturally as well as materially:

the continuance and the entrenched nature of this oppression cannot be understood without a consideration of the cultural processes in which men and women are represented differently – created and recreated as gendered human subjects (*Women's Oppression Today*, Verso, 1980, p. 41).

Literature is used as an example of the representation through culture of ideologies about gender. It is a complex process. Literature is produced and received in a particular social context but it can never simply be reduced to a reflection of it. Not one single model of 'woman' is presented; rather a range of ideas and images within which any model has to operate if it is to be credible:

> What they can offer, I suggest, is an indication of the bounds within which particular meanings are constructed and negotiated in a given social formation; but this would depend upon considering a fairly wide range of such products (p. 107).

Nevertheless, certain tendencies are evident. Gender stereotyping is common, especially in children's literature and advertising. Compensation for the inferior social position of women is present in their elevation to a morally superior plane, as in much Christian imagery. Collusion – 'women's willing consent and their internalisation of oppression' – is shown by their lack of resentment, even acceptance, of their misrepresentation. Finally there is recuperation, the rescuing of dominant images from any potential threat by delegitimising the credentials of their opponents, a prime example being media trivialisation of the women's movement.

The gender divisions to which culture gives validation are rooted in the sexual division of labour:

> women's oppression in capitalism… is inexplicable without an understanding of the connections between the division of labour at work and in the home (p. 153).

The assumption that the woman's major commitment should be to the role of wife and mother has been used to validate systematically unequal employment conditions for women. The timing, nature and rewards of their paid employment are inferior to those of men. Not the least effect has been to imbue the trade union movement with a set of beliefs about the need to protect men's work from female incursions which have been a source of resistance to claims for equal treatment. These tendencies have been exacerbated by capitalism but are not intrinsic to it. The sexual division of labour can and does operate in non-capitalist societies and capitalism might well be able to operate without it.

The same is true of the family, even though historical and contemporary variations are so great that the term itself may be inadequate to encompass them all. In the modern family, cultural stereotypes and a rigid sexual division of labour find powerful expression and confirmation. How the family works (and who works most in it) has to be the fundamental concern of feminist analysis:

> the gender divisions of social production in capitalism cannot be understood without reference to the organisation of the household and the ideology of familialism. This area represents the primary site of relations between men and women, of the construction of gendered individuals, and is closely related to the organisation of social production. The structure and ideology of the family in contemporary capitalism is surely the most salient issue for any Marxist feminist analysis to address (p. 186).

The family is the major agency of gender socialisation, ensuring that both children and adults reproduce in their daily behaviour the 'natural' boundaries of male and female conduct. Like the more general ideology of familialism of which it is an integral part, such gender typing is a systematic distortion of social reality, since most families have come to rely on women's work outside the home for the income to sustain their standard of living. The ideology expresses the reality of the 'bourgeois' family which has been successfully imposed as an ideal on the rest of society. The effect is a profoundly conservative one:

> The tendency of the family-household system is to encourage conservatism and militate against protest, and the close relationship between the economic aspects of household support and the highly intense personal and emotional relationships is an important factor in this (p. 212).

Thus the family can be understood as the social unit most appropriate for a capitalist society, especially as there is a close fit between the economic need for consumption and the psychological predispositions established by the housewife role. The success of the family lies not in the simple imposition of a compulsory way of life on a duped populace but on its capacity to abrogate to itself the most valued human emotions:

> this is not to suggest that needs for intimacy, sexual relations, emotional fulfilment, parenthood and so on are in themselves oppressive. What is oppressive is the assumption that the present form of such needs is the only form and that the manner in which they should be met is through the family as it is today (p. 251).

The liberation of women can only be achieved through a challenge to the family and what it stands for. A redivision of labour, the economic independence of women and the removal of gender ideologies are incompatible with the nuclear family and the capitalist system it tacitly supports.

This argument has more implications for the analysis of leisure than might at first seem apparent. Before explaining how they have emerged in our discussion, two reservations must be noted. We would not dispute the evidence on which Barrett's argument is based nor disagree with the substance of her theoretical elaboration. Our difficulty is with her characteristic mode of interpretation: how she understands other people's understandings of the positions they find themselves in. The first example comes from the discussion of the cultural production of gender relations. It is based very largely on literature, and literature of a quite conventional kind. The explanation offered, that this is where she feels most confident, remains unsatisfactory, especially in view of her own admission that no case has been made for the excessive concentration of feminist analysis on this area. At the very least, there might have been some attention to what the reading public actually consume, especially as the popular fiction market is heavily structured by gender. Alternatively, the role of the media in sustaining gender images might have been given more attention. No one (or, come to that, no pair of writers) can do everything and others are actively exploring these areas. It is perhaps as a reaction against this rather restricted definition of the object of cultural analysis, that feminists have recently begun analysis of the culture of everyday life, of which leisure is one instance.

The second example is more substantial but less easy to pin down. It is that the interpretation of family life becomes one-dimensional. Only the oppressive aspects are noted: there are, in this view of the world, no 'happy families'. That the family may ultimately rest on fundamental inequalities of gender and induce conservative views of society and human possibilities, need not and should not blind us to its attractions and satisfactions. Getting married, making a home, bringing up children, are some of the mainsprings of motivation in contemporary society. This is not specifically denied in Barrett's analysis but nor is it sufficiently acknowledged. It is, as we have said, a question of the quality of understanding how people see themselves. The importance of grasping the power of these motivations, and thus the centrality which the family holds in the organisation of our social identities remains a vital issue in the analysis of contemporary culture.

Taking Barrett's project as a whole, these are relatively minor qualifications. The essential effort, to bring both Marxist and feminist approaches to bear on the analysis of society, is one with which we are in sympathy. We have tried in this book to apply them to the understanding of leisure, with what we recognise to be mixed success. In so doing, we have drawn implicitly on the central aspects of gender inequality identified by Barrett: culture, the division of labour and the family.

We have tried throughout to emphasise that leisure activity is cultural. It expresses meanings and values. Individuals and groups may create unique patterns of culture but they must always draw in part on those meanings existing in the culture around them. Some meanings are so entrenched that leisure cannot but give them expression. Gender we argued to be so powerful a meaning that leisure has come to be one of its principal forms of celebration. At those moments in leisure when people feel and appear most free of social roles, they are in actuality most bound to rigid expectations of gender behaviour. Even some of specific processes Barrett describes – stereotyping, compensation, collusion, recuperation – are evident throughout all of leisure and not just the most obvious instance of the media presentation of gender.

The sexual division of leisure clearly reflects the sexual division of labour. The commonplace observation that the experience of leisure cannot be divorced from the experience of work is as central for domestic work as it is for the more visible case of paid labour. The qualitative and quantitative inferiority of women's leisure sharpens with the entry into the roles of wife and mother. Leisure has to be sacrificed in order to carry out these roles within existing social arrangements. Far from being the way in which women realise their leisure potential, the family curtails their leisure opportunities.

The expanding involvement of the family unit in creating leisure often depends on the hidden labour of the woman. Family leisure is thus based on the same gender assumptions which find expression through it. The roles of wife/mother and husband/father have their differences rather than similiarities emphasised in family home life. Rather than start from the family as a 'given' social institution, we have tried to show how it is as much an effect as a cause of the way society is organised. The conservation of family life and its commitment to individualised consumption are actively encouraged by economic and political interests.

In short, we have taken the analysis of the gender division of leisure to be crucial, in an effort to rescue gender from its ambiguous status in leisure analysis. Typical treatments of it have included ignoring it altogether, noting but failing to explain its statistical significance or assuming that gender equality is in the process of being achieved by new forms of family life. We have tried to make gender a central rather than a marginal factor, to analyse gender inequality in leisure, and to insist that observable changes in the gender roles of the family are in practice quite limited. This would not have been possible, even to the limited extent that we have managed to achieve it, without the kind of argument which Barrett has advanced. Many problems, not least those of terminological inaccuracy and theoretical inconsistency, remain. We may even have fallen foul of the tendency to incorporate the factor of gender inequality without sufficiently revising the theoretical framework. If we have not quite found our way round some of these problems, it has not been for want of guidance.

Leisure, culture and hegemony

The whole of this book has been an attempt to apply to the analysis of leisure an approach derived from cultural studies. We have taken texts by Wright Mills, Williams and Barrett to repre-

much wider range of work, some of which is noted in the
er reading. We began with a critique of existing approaches
and have ended with this attempt to explain the guiding principles
of an alternative. There are perhaps three ways in which our
analysis of leisure differs from established orthodoxies and reflects
the guiding influence of cultural studies. One is an emphasis on the
social and historical construction of leisure, the second a way of
interpreting leisure as culture, the third a theoretical model of
society in which leisure can be inserted.

The social and historical construction of leisure are continuously
apparent in how the spatial, temporal and institutional boundaries
of leisure have come to be defined. Together these also construct
the meaning of leisure. Not only a way of 'doing' leisure has been
instituted but a way of 'seeing' leisure. Thus the word 'leisure' is
inseparable from the social context which originally produced, and
continues to reproduce, its reference points. Recognition of this is
evident in the observation that the problem of leisure necessarily
involves consideration of work. But more needs to be said. What
proper leisure analysis requires is the identification of the processes which compartmentalised social experience into work life,
family life, leisure life. Leisure as a concept is a reflection and not
an explanation of this fragmentation. The definition of leisure is
not, then, a problem to be resolved early on in order that the real
analysis may proceed. Leisure cannot be defined abstractly, but
only through analysing how it has come to be defined in certain
ways, whose definitions have counted and how such definitions are
reproduced as part of the fabric of common-sense. If this is done,
then what would otherwise be taken for granted as the social
context *of* leisure becomes the social context *which defines it*. State
regulation, market domination, the family as a social institution,
the division of labour by class and gender – these are not a
'background' to the study of leisure, they are inextricably embedded in the social organisation of leisure.

It is too easy to interpret leisure as wholly determined by
political, economic and social institutions and interests, as if its
meanings can be simply derived from their workings. Human
conduct is rarely so pliable, least of all where, as in leisure, it
cannot be directly supervised. The meanings expressed through
leisure may be those 'received' from the way society is organised
but they can be constructed into unique patterns, given particular

slants, even on occasion usurped by the activation of meanings other than those which are socially 'approved'. Leisure activities are often mediated through groups – families, friends, clubs – who generated their own sets of meanings, always more than the simple aggregate of individual motivations.

Understanding the nature and derivation of the individual and collective meanings of leisure is no easy task. The framework of cultural studies can be positively helpful, since it delivers a double sense of culture. There is the culture as a whole, connected to economic, political and social arrangements, which leisure invariably mobilises in some way. But there is also the other sense of culture as subsets of meaning actively created by individuals and groups.

This autonomy of meaning creation is relative rather than absolute. There is a cultural mix: new meanings are created within the process of re-creating established ones. Nor is the capacity to create meanings equally distributed. In a society of structured inequality, different kinds of meanings cannot compete on equal terms. Some interests have the ability to make their definitions and meanings prevail over others. They possess cultural power.

Such cultural power is not exercised uniformly or automatically. The activities of the state and commerce do not naturally interlock, the family does not inherently orient itself towards consumption as a major goal. These things must be made to happen. Only in conservative daydreams and radical nightmares do things work so smoothly. The cultures which groups create often threaten to outrun the dominant modes of interpretation which must be continuously extended and adapted to reincorporate them. This process Stuart Hall has called 'ideological work'. Innovations in leisure may test the limits of the dominant ideas about what are acceptable leisure meanings and experiences. Hence there is 'cultural work' to be done, legitimising and incorporating new forms, while marginalising and suppressing others.

From this perspective, leisure is never wholly free nor totally determined activity. It is always potentially an arena for cultural contestation between dominant and subordinate groups. Here cultural studies has evoked the work of Antonio Gramsci which provides a model for analysing culture as creation from below and appropriation from above. In *Marxism and Literature*, Raymond Williams has summarised the concept of 'hegemony' which expresses this relationship:

it sees the relations of domination and subordination, in their forms as practical consciousness, as in effect a saturation of the whole process of living – not only of political and economic activity, nor only of manifest social activity, but of the whole substance of lived identities and relationships, to such a depth that the pressures and limits of what can ultimately be seen as a specific economic, political and cultural system seem to most of us the pressures and limits of simple experience and common sense. Hegemony is not then only the articulate upper level of 'ideology', nor are its forms of control only those ordinarily seen as 'manipulation' or 'indoctrination'. It is a whole body of practices and expectations, over the whole of living: our shaping perceptions of ourselves and our world. (*Marxism and Literature*, Oxford University Press, 1977, p. 110)

Hegemony has become a significant concept for cultural studies because it condenses, or crystallises, a number of major themes about the processes of cultural domination and conflict. First, it emphasises the field of culture – a national culture – as being made up of different cultures and sub-cultures, embodying divergent social perspectives. Secondly, hegemony stresses the work – the cultural struggle – that is needed to unite aspects of these divergent cultures under the 'leadership' of a dominant culture. Thirdly, hegemony identifies cultural conflict as a process which does not just happen at the level of formal political ideologies, but also involves the patterns of everyday thinking and habits of mind – precisely those aspects of social ideologies which we take for granted because they are so 'obvious'. Finally, hegemony contains the idea that cultural domination – the creation of hegemony itself – is always in a state of tension. Hegemony involves the effort to dominate a society in which the divergent interests and perspectives always threaten to outrun the ability of the dominant culture to contain and incorporate them.

Leisure has been, and remains, integral to the struggle for hegemony in British society in two main ways. It is one of the areas of social life in which the cultural conflicts over meanings, views of the world and social habits has been fought. The efforts to repress and exclude 'undesirable' uses of free time and the attempt to replace them with leisure patterns which are civilising and profitable has been a continuous part of the development of leisure in Britain.

The very idea of leisure is itself central to the struggle for hegemony. We have come to 'take for granted' the division of social time into the categories of work and leisure. Equally, we have become habituated to the conventional economic and psychological relationships between these two spheres of life. We know – it has become second nature to us – that leisure has to be 'earned' and that free time is only meaningful when paid for by sacrifices elsewhere. These everyday truths, just like the proverbial wisdom of 'The devil makes work...', have become part of our collective commonsense. In the process, we have lost sight of the economic, political and social conflicts which were required to make them come true. We have lost our own history. These 'knowledges' – the conventional wisdom about leisure in our society – form the hegemonic bedrock on top of which move the more particular cultural conflicts about the uses of free time.

Our discussion of leisure has finally to reach out to these difficult theoretical questions of how cultural domination actually works. Our insistence that leisure is socially and historically constructed leads us to stress the process of definition itself as a form of cultural conflict. The complexity of the meanings of leisure leads us to consider them as an integral part of the more general patterns of meanings we call cultures. Their imposition from above and creation from below and the consequent state of tension, leads us to the concept of hegemony.

We began with leisure and have ended with cultural studies. That has been in part the project we have set ourselves: to test the validity of 'cultural studies' against the more conventional sociological definition of leisure. It represents our involvement in what is or should be the current effort of cultural studies, to apply its distinctive theoretical and methodological perspective beyond the study of 'formal' ideologies and their dissemination to the lived experience of culture. Previous work on youth culture, crime, working-class culture and sport has been in the same vein. Theoretical elegance cannot be the ultimate test of cultural studies. That can only lie in its ability to explain, empirically as well as theoretically, how social experience is commonly interpreted and understood. There is, however, another test of the validity of intellectual perspectives which is how far by interpreting the social world they can also be a means of changing it. This is our final consideration.

Further reading

C. Wright Mills' *The Sociological Imagination* (Penguin, 1970) was first published in 1959. Of his many other writings, *White Collar* (Oxford University Press, 1957) is the most relevant to the study of leisure.

Raymond Williams has been a central influence on the development of cultural studies. Closest to our specific concerns are the conclusion to *Culture and Society, 1750–1950* (Penguin, 1961) and the final part of *The Long Revolution* (Penguin, 1965). His progressive engagement with Marxist analysis is evident in *Marxism and Literature* (Oxford University Press, 1977). Extensions and revisions of some of his earlier positions are presented in *Towards 2000* (Chatto and Windus, 1983).

Michele Barrett followed her *Women's Oppression Today* (Verso, 1980) by collaborating with Mary McIntosh on a study of the family and familial ideology entitled *The Anti-social Family* (Verso, 1982). Of the many critiques of male dominance in sociological studies, we would single out Ann Oakley's introduction to her *The Sociology of Housework* (Martin Robertson, 1974) for its clarity and incisiveness. The development of that critique into cultural studies was one of the projects of the Women's Studies Group of the Centre for Contemporary Cultural Studies in their *Women Take Issue* (Hutchinson, 1978).

The collection of History Workshop Conference papers edited by Ralph Samuel as *People's History and Socialist Theory* (Routledge & Kegan Paul, 1981) deals with some of the problems and arguments involved in linking theoretical analysis with empirical studies.

Stuart Hall has provided complex accounts of the origins and development of cultural studies as represented in the history of the Birmingham Centre. See his essays in S. Hall *et al.* (eds), *Culture, Media and Language* (Hutchinson, 1980) and in T. Bennett *et al.* (eds), *Culture, Ideology and Social Process* (Batsford, 1981), as well as his own *Reproducing Ideologies* (Macmillan, forthcoming).

Our own involvement in previous efforts to develop a cultural studies analysis of specific empirical subjects include contributions to S. Hall and T. Jefferson (eds), *Resistance through Rituals* (Hutchinson, 1976); S. Hall *et al.*, *Policing the Crisis* (Macmillan, 1978) and J. Clarke, C. Critcher and R. Johnson (eds), *Working Class Culture* (Hutchinson, 1979).

Epilogue

It has been the gravest error of socialism, in revolt against class societies, to limit itself, so often, to the terms of its opponents: to propose a political and economic order rather than a human order… the alternative society that is proposed must be in wider terms, if it is to generate the full energies necessary for its creation…

If socialism accepts the distinction of 'work' from 'life' which has to be written off as leisure; if it sees politics as 'government' rather than as the common process of administration; if it continues to see education as training for a system and art as a grace after meals…, if it is limited in these ways, it is simply a late form of capitalist politics, or just the more efficient organization of human beings around a system of industrial production. The moral decline of socialism is in exact relation to its series of compromises with older images of society and to its failure to sustain and clarify the sense of an alternative human order. (Raymond Williams, *The Long Revolution*, Penguin, 1965, pp. 131–3.)

The final editing of this book took place in the summer of 1984. The miners were in the middle of their longest ever strike, the official figure of unemployment stood at four million, the welfare state was being slowly dismantled and opinion polls showed less than 40 per cent of the electorate willing to support the Labour Party. It might seem perverse to choose such a time to argue that socialists ought to concern themselves with the issue of leisure. The very weakness of socialism's efforts to counter these tendencies is, however, not unconnected with its inability to understand and act upon the 'politics of leisure'.

Some connections are direct. The failure to develop and implement a socialist policy for the mass media was evident in the daily

231

vilification of the miners' cause and everything it represented. Others were more subtle; public attention was about to be diverted by the start of Wimbledon... These are merely the most obvious ways in which leisure has come to have political significance. Important though control of dominant leisure institutions and their capacity to shape public consciousness ought to be for practising socialists, a socialist approach to leisure cannot end there. Still less can it rest content with the advocacy of nationalisation as the answer to the leisure problem.

The difficulty lies in finding viable socialist answers to the problems capitalism has created and camouflaged. Our insistence on the political importance of leisure could help to understand why socialism keeps encountering and failing to resolve this problem. But we have to go back to the basics. First, we have to understand why and how leisure has come to be so important in contemporary society. Second, we must analyse why socialism has failed to see leisure as a political issue at all. Third, we need to consider ways in which socialism as a movement might benefit from an active appreciation of leisure.

It's a free country

Leisure is now central to capitalist economic and cultural domination. While this has always been so to some extent, its range and pervasiveness have increased. The leisure market is now a major source of profit, its fluctuations an index of the state of the economy as a whole. The consumption of leisure goods and services has moved from a peripheral to a central role in the modern capitalist economy. The exploitation and management of such demand is no longer a casual matter. The institutions and techniques designed to support that effort have repercussions well outside leisure. The emphasis on marketing strategies which appeal to known consumer preferences, for example, has become the dominant mode of contemporary politics. The ideological implications are wider still. The ability of consumer-orientated capitalism to deliver the leisure goods is used as its political validation. Its effectiveness is contrasted with the economic stagnation of the Eastern bloc and the 'backwardness' of the Third World. Any alternatives to the market model at home or abroad are dismissed because they threaten to diminish 'consumer choice'. This ideological use of leisure equates the public interest with the pursuit of private gain by both seller and buyer. Leisure is the perfect model of the free play of market forces, to which other systems – of health, housing and education – are being made to approximate. The only role for public provision is either as indirect subsidy to commercial activity or as compensation for those too inadequate to compete in the market-place of consumption.

In such ways has the market become the major institutions and ideology of leisure. Far from being the antithesis of freedom, it has been represented as its realisation. Broader questions of freedom and control have been narrowed around the right to consumer choice. Noone seriously interested in understanding *how* capitalism works can afford to underestimate the economic and cultural importance of leisure. It also demonstrates *why* capitalism works. These ideas have gained widespread acceptance because leisure can genuinely be seen as an area of some freedom, where positively evaluated experiences are most keenly felt. It is obvious that most people's daily lives are not motivated by political abstractions but by the concerns which secure and mark out a more intimate framework of home and family, friends and relatives. Impenetrable to the public influences of economic and political change, our private lives inform our sense of who we are.

From such a perspective the appeal of any kind of socialism will be judged against its ability to make this life more viable in its own terms. The problem is that these terms are inimical to socialism, since they are those of an adjustment to capitalism. Basic socialist ideas remain abstract, with no apparent connection to everyday life. And when applied to specific issues they seem to come up with answers which run counter to the immediate interests of ordinary families. As anyone knows who has ever tried to argue against the sale of council houses, the right of the individual to private property is more direct and tangible than abstract and ambiguous arguments about the collective right to public provision.

The mobilisation of the private interests of the consuming individual as paramount is not mere intellectual stupefaction induced by the propaganda of monopoly capital. It is much more reflection of circumstance, assuming that what provides freedom in leisure can be applied across the board, as a working principle of society. Its habitual use demonstrates not susceptibility to capitalist ideology or even a rampant selfishness but a positive valuation of such freedom and control as does exist, however limited and deformed it might be. In the absence of alternatives, it will be adhered to. The questions then arise as to why such alternatives are, or are seen to be, absent and what might be done to make their presence felt.

'Entertaining programmes'

British socialism lacks a 'cultural politics' which might engage with the myths and realities of contemporary leisure. We claim no great originality for attributing this lack to rigid and monolithic ideas about what socialism is or ought to be. Primarily these definitions assume that a more just society can be brought about by commanding the heights of economic and political power. The 'revolution of everyday life' – if there is such an objective – will follow from gradual changes within the economic and political systems. Thus changes which are not gradual or not immediately translatable into piecemeal reforms become defined as romantic irrelevancies. The political means have become the political ends.

The concerns of socialism are so reduced in scale and kind as to make even the most central issues confused. Take the obverse of leisure: work. What possible criticism can there be in an age of mass unemployment to a programme based on 'the right to work'? There are in fact several, which together demonstrate the narrowness of vision on which such an ideal rests. 'Work' here, for instance, is the capitalist definition – the right to paid employment. It does not mean economically useful or socially necessary work, just any kind of work. What is really being claimed here, and it does not compose into a slogan, is the right not to suffer the economic deprivation and social stigma of unemployment.

Converted into a practical policy, the right to work requires the aim of full employment. As argued earlier in Chapter 6, it does not seem to us likely that in the foreseeable future capitalism will want or need full employment. It is therefore an open question whether its restoration can or should be a socialist aim. It would be more socialist to reduce the extent to which we all have to labour, releasing our time and energy to explore other kinds of activity. It is not the total amount of employment, but the distribution of work and its rewards which require remedial action. More genuinely radical would be strategies to undermine the dependence of income on employment. A guaranteed minimum income and a system of job-sharing would be the first steps.

If these are too drastic to consider and socialists are to be in the political business of job creation, let us at least create jobs which are worthwhile. Instead of training people to perform tasks for the profit of someone else at some hypothetical time in the future, let us develop skills in helping others now and convert those into jobs. Any measure of human misery will show that there is still plenty of work to be done in making life bearable for others. Let us have a radical programme to create jobs which have social uses other than just keeping people in employment.

It is, of course, too easy for well-heeled intellectuals to prattle on about our narrow idea of work, the need to liberate everyone from labour, etc. But this is no longer a mere academic argument: it is the reality of 'post-industrial' capitalism. It is a disservice to four million or more unemployed to pretend – for that is what it is – that jobs can be recreated for them. Even worse is the open admission by Labour Party leaders that the best they can hope to do is to reduce the total of unemployed by a million or so. Now is the time to develop a socialist programme for employment based on a socialist conception of work. Otherwise paid employment as an institution and ideology of capitalism will be vindicated (by socialists) at the very moment it is demonstrably failing.

Our criticism of the right to work is not yet exhausted (though our readers may well be). For the right to work generally applies to men, though feminists with some success have endeavoured to argue for its extension to women. Missing in the equation is that work in the home which does not fit the capitalist definition of work as paid employment. A socialist definition of work cannot remain so confined; it must recognise the reality and the problem of domestic work. The sexual division of labour has for long been justified by the organisation of employment and the disorganisation of forms of child care supplementary to that of the family. The practice of family life has remained basically unaltered because there is no viable alternative. If we are interested, as socialists ought to be, in redistributing work and its rewards, in distinguishing that which is useful and ncessary from that which is not, then domestic work must be included in our political calculations. If the existing system has become such that not all men 'have' to go out to work, then there is real potential for change in the way the sexes divide and interrelate their roles. In a perverted way, this is already happening to those couples where the wife can find employment which eludes the husband. Whether the individual adjustment involved can provide a pattern for the diffusion or more flexible sex roles, seems doubtful. Yet in an enforced way, such situations may serve to remind us that changes in the nature of employment reveal the arbitrary and 'unchosen' nature of the social arrangements which normally support it.

The problem of leisure, we have argued, is also the problem of work. The two are divisible only by the curious mental habits of the capitalist mode of life and the limited kinds of socialist thought which reflect what they should be trying to supersede. Socialist thought has not even achieved for leisure the foreshortened perspective which has been adopted for work. Radical attitudes to leisure vary between an enthusiastic endorsement of it as a natural apolitical part of life, frequently with overtones of masculine domination (sport, drinking, the wife and kids at home), and a gloomy and puritanical view of informality and spontaneity as diverting energies away from the real cause. The latter is in part a by-product of the process by which those deeply committed to socialism convert leisure into political interests, so tending to see political interests as an adequate definition of leisure. Underneath it all is a quite genuine fear of totalitarianism. It is all right to come up with programmes for economic and political life but a programme for leisure begins to sound like something out of Stalinist Russia. And so it may, if the programme takes the form of a finished product rather than the design of a process. Capitalism has a programme for leisure; socialism needs one. Its elementary forms are already perceptible in the research and policies of the Greater London Council, often producing some of its most popular measures from 'unexpected' quarters. The general consideration has to be to recover the ideals of choice from the market with which it has so successfully been associated. An emphasis on using public funds to enable groups to follow leisure interests which they cannot themselves resource is a significant start. Challenging the power of leisure conglomerates by taxing and licensing their activities in order to divert funds directly into less profitable sectors would be equally important. Real choice and accountability should be substituted for, and thus become revealing of, the lack of them in the current system.

This will not be an easy task. The definition of current leisure activities as free is deeply ingrained and not without some validity. An alternative version of what lesiure might be requires more than socialist programmes and policies. It also needs some socialist practice.

'Let's have a party'

Socialism has not only failed to understand the significance of leisure in contemporary capitalism or to redefine its vision of the future to encompass a version of leisure as the realisation of some kinds of freedom and inequality. It has also failed as a movement to see that leisure could provide potentially powerful forms of political expression. It has not learned from some of its opponents, such as the Young Conservatives, who understood long ago that social and political activity can reinforce each other, albeit in this case in their mindlessness. It has also not learned from some of its erstwhile supporters. The Campaign for Nuclear Disarmament has shown in both its phases that serious moral concern is not lessened by a sense of festivity. A political demonstration of dissent actually gains if it is simultaneously a cultural celebration of unity. The involvement on equal terms of men and women, young and old, parents and children, can temporarily break down the social divisions which normally inhabit leisure. Egalitarianism need not remain a creed; it can also be a practice.

Even more ignored have been those forms of cultural expression which capitalism has delivered as economic commodities yet are convertible into political messages. The most obvious example is that of pop music. The way in which 'Rock Against Racism' identified the musical medium with the moral message seems to have fallen on deaf socialist ears. This is one important reason why socialism has apparently failed to communicate with its most 'natural' constituency of the young. Socialism speaks to it in a language it does not understand, one more likely to be associated with the schoolroom and with the pulpit than with the street or the dole queue.

More is required than 'socialist' discos, clubs, sports and carnivals. They need to be part of a wider effort to identify socialism with more rather than less fun, freedom not restriction, play as well as work. That is one way to see the difference between a political party of restricted goals and ossified leadership and a genuinely popular movement encouraging spontaneity and full participation. It also helps to break down the division between the dullness of the public world and the brightness of the private which has become the habitual way of contrasting work and leisure.

To reconnect the private to the public is again an effort which has been made outside the mainstream of socialist politics. At the core of the women's movement is the conviction that personal identity can be understood and claimed politically. It involves doing things, some directly political, some not, but always together. Its particular strategies, often initially separatist, may not be generalisable. The insistence that there is not and cannot be any division between the personal and the political should be more widely applied.

There is, for example, the related and difficult question of the family. The principles, images and practices of socialism in relation to the family are extraordinarily weak. The principle too often dissolves into whether we approve or disapprove of the family and should therefore seek to support or abolish it: a series of false and bizarrely unreal oppositions. A real alternative would be to consider ways of living inside and outside families without reproducing the normal inequalities of family life – an extension of genuine choice into the taken-for-granted. Positive images of family life are consequently left in the hands of those who wish only to use them as an effective vehicle for marketing. The shamelessness of all this is counterbalanced by no version of family life as it actually is or might be. Finally, the practice: the things families can do together do not currently include socialist activities, despite the (often literally) manful efforts to provide facilities for childcare at conferences and demonstrations. Indeed, often the commitment to socialism requires the sacrifice of time and effort which might otherwise be used for the benefit of the family. The connection between the private world of the family and the public world of politics has to become a visible part of socialist organisation. Socialism cannot appeal to families 'out there', it must bring them 'in here' to events, networks, physical and social bases which have to be an integral part of that elusive endeavour of 'building a movement'. The very difficulty of trying to describe it shows how far off its realisation we are.

'Time gentlemen, please'

We have argued that leisure has already acquired a political significance, if largely unrecognised by socialist thought or practice. Ultimately, what is at stake is the politics of time. Time is the invisible resource that structures many of the conflicts and inequalities of leisure. It is time which is inequitably distributed between workers and non-workers, young and old, and, especially, between men and women. Our arguments about work, leisure, freedom and control crystallise around the political issue of time.

Where socialism has historically focused on the socialised control of the state and the economy, we believe that socialism must also advocate the socialised control of time. This requires, on the one hand, a wider understanding of the dimensions of inequality in power and resources. Power is personal as well as institutional, resources are psychological as well as material. On the other hand, the process of socialist planning should distinguish between the obligations of collectively organised 'social' time and the freedom of individuals to control time. This distinction between socialised control and personal autonomy should be central to socialism. The clock cannot be stopped or turned back, but its regulation of human affairs need no longer be automatic.

To achieve even that promise requires socialism to 'work' at extending its understanding, its programmes and its activities to encompass what we now call 'leisure'. This is not and cannot be an effort to be left to one side while the work of recruiting members, attracting votes or getting the message across is being completed. Unless the contemporary significance of leisure is understood we shall continue to be confused by the problem of why public attention always seems to be somewhere else. Unless the problem of work and leisure is clearly and radically redefined, we shall remain locked into managing the contradictions of an alien system. Unless socialism becomes a movement of wider appeal and more varied expression, we shall continue to be defined as narrow-minded 'politicos'. Unless the politics of time is confronted we shall find our socialism perpetuating inequality. Leisure and all it implies is not the only or even the principal item for the agenda of contemporary socialism but it can no longer be dealt with under 'any other business'.

Further reading

The Leisure Shock (Eyre Methuen, 1981) by Clive Jenkins and Barrie Sherman presents an argument about how the decline of work and its consequences for non-workers might be socially managed. They argue for trade unions taking greater responsibility for the division of employment, and for social policies which, through financial, educational and leisure provision, can make non-work a more realistic and socially valued part of life. The book, however, does tend to equate work with employment, and the problems of the sexual division of labour do not emerge as central to the relationship between work and leisure.

Andre Gorz's *Farewell to the Working Class* (Pluto Press, 1982) also begins from the decline of employment, but develops this into a critique of orthodox Marxism's view of the working class as the central agent of historical change. Instead, he presents a challenging argument for a socialism which uses the possibilities of post-industrialism to construct a creative tension between individual autonomy and the socialised control of resources (including time) through the state. Here, too, though there are problems about how far the existing sexual division of labour is taken account of in the 'decline of work'.

By contrast, Anne Phillips' *Hidden Hands* (Pluto Press, 1984) presents a powerful critique of the male assumptions built into socialist policies about work and full employment. She sets out the case for including the problems of the sexual division of labour in any socialist attempts to plan 'work', and explores the conflicting interests of male and female workers in any future reorganisation of working time.

Author Index

Bailey, P. 90
Baran, P. and Sweezy, P. 144
Barrett, M. 220–5, 230
Bell, D. 198
Bennett, T. 230
Booth, C. 48
Branson, N. and Heinemann,
    M. 90
Burman. S. 91
Burt, C. 5

Campbell, B. 180
Clarke, J., Critcher, C. and
    Johnson, R. 12
Coates, K. and Silburn, R. 47
Cunningham, H. 90

Delamont, S. 180
Dennis, N. *et al.* 47
Donajgrodski, A. 90
Dumazadier, J. 47
Dunning, E. and Sheard, K. 90
Dyer, R. 144

Finch, J. and Groves, D. 180

Gamarnikow, E. 180
Gorz, A. 198, 240
Gramsci, A. 227

Hall, S. 144, 227, 230
Hammond, J.L. and B. 90
Hargreaves, J. 144
Hobsbawm, E. 90
Hoggart, R. 14, 47
Howkins, A. and Lowerson, J. 90
Hutt, C. 143

Jackson, B. 47
Jenkins, C. and Sherman, B. 240
Johnson, R. 12, 13
Johnson, R. 12

Kaplan, M. 47
King, R. and Raynor, J. 179
Kumar, K. 181, 189, 198

Larrabee, E. and Meyersohn,
    R. 47
Liddington, J. and Norris, J. 91

Malcolmson, R.W. 50
Marwick, A. 91
Mass Observation 91
Massey, D. 198
Mills, C. Wright 46, 212–16, 230
Muncie, J. 180

Neulinger, J. 2, 8
Newman, O. 10, 144

Oakley, A. 230
Open University 180

Parker, S. 14, 16–22, 26, 45, 46–7,
    147, 180, 193
Pearson, G. 12
Phillips, A. 240
Phillipson, C. 180
Prior, J. 6

Rapoport, R. and R. 30–6, 39, 45,
    46–7, 147, 180, 193
Roberts, K. 14, 36–44, 45, 46–7,
    122–3, 138, 180, 182
Rowbotham, S. 91

Samuel, R. 90, 230
Scarman, Lord 4
Scott, J. 180
Steadman-Jones, G. 9, 90
Stevenson, J. 90
Sutherland, W. 8

Talbot, M. 180
Taylor, B. 91
Thompson, E.P. 1, 12, 49, 90
Thompson, P. 90
Toffler, A. 198
Tomlinson, A. 12
Touraine, A. 181
Travis, A. 144

Vicinus, M. 91

Walvin, J. 90
Watts, T. 12
Westergaard, J. and Resler,
    H. 179
Whannel, G. 144
Williams, R. 14, 40, 47, 131, 145,
    216–20, 227–8, 230, 231
Wilson, E. 91

Yeo, E. and S. 90
Young, M. and Willmott,
    P. 22–37, 41, 45, 46–7, 182

Subject Index

adventure playground   134
advertising   78, 81, 103, 105, 106,
   163, 166
age, as social division   35, 146,
   153–9, 174, 176, 203
Arts Council   87, 113, 206

boys   157–8
brewing industry   103–6, 165

children   31, 81–2, 163–73
cinema   71–2, 111
citizenship   139, 202
class
   domination theory   37–8, 40–4,
      122, 179
   as social division   70, 146–53,
      156, 174, 176, 202, 207
   and social structure   10, 24, 41,
      61, 76–7, 147, 187–90, 218
community   149, 216, 219–20
community studies   14, 149
Conservative Party   141–3, 235
consumer
   choice   40, 45, 96–7, 118, 145,
      195, 200–10, 215
   demand   103, 136
   irrationality   120–1, 143
   market model   32, 43, 96, 100–
      1, 142, 146, 177, 200, 217,
      219

resistance   116, 143
sovereignty   96, 116, 143
Co-operative movement   57, 61,
   75, 96
cultural studies   212, 227
culture   14, 33, 41, 148–50, 216–
   20, 224, 226–9

dancing   72, 121
discos   85, 162–3
do-it-yourself   107, 110
domestic labour   21, 159, 169,
   192, 221–5, 235–6
drink   44, 53, 67–8, 75 (see also
   brewing industry)

economic trends
   commercialisation   9, 66, 71–2,
      84, 88, 100–1, 205
   domestic market   61, 72–8, 80–
      1, 101–2, 164–5
   monopolisation   88, 100–6, 110,
      111–12, 143, 185, 201, 205–6
   service sector   101, 185–6
enclosure   54
extension pattern   18

factories   56
fairs   53
family
   centredness   24–5, 28–9, 77, 81–

2, 106–12, 218, 219
  ideology 222–5
  rituals 169
  unit 21, 22–30, 33, 39, 42, 45,
    59, 77, 164–76, 183, 215, 235
  see also sexual division of labour
fashion 83
femininity 44, 161–2
feminism 20, 183, 220–5
functionalism 20, 43

gambling
  bingo 44, 87
  football pools 75, 88
  gaming 44, 88
  greyhounds 74
  horse-racing 74, 88
gender
  as social division 11, 21–2, 25,
    33, 39, 44, 50, 70, 77, 97–8,
    146, 157, 159–64, 165, 174,
    176, 202–3, 209, 213, 219,
    220–5
  relations, 84, 162–3, 175
girls 85, 157
Greater London Council 236

hedonism 171
hegemony 227–9
hire purchase 81
history
  models of 22–3, 28, 48–51
  role of 20, 46, 214
holidays 53, 56, 61, 72, 80, 170–5
home computers 9, 192
hooliganism 120–1
housewives 17, 21

ideology 44, 166, 232–3
industrialisation 23, 28, 48–9, 51,
    55–6, 59
inequality 30, 71, 75, 87, 126,
    138, 146–8, 173–4, 176–8, 219,
    227

job satisfaction 26

Labour Party 140–2, 219, 235
leisure

as compensation 3, 37, 59, 70,
    136–7, 178
  definition of 11, 15, 17, 20–4,
    36, 41
  growth of 36–7, 43, 58–60, 69–
    71, 94–5
  markets 116–20, 145, 165, 200–1
  opportunity 146, 176–9, 194,
    201
  social construction of 42, 52,
    58–9, 69–70, 78, 89, 95–5,
    97, 226–9
  statistics 26–7, 106–7, 111, 159,
    164, 170
life-cycle 30–6
life-skills 6, 129
local authorities
  expenditure 130, 133, 134–7,
    141–2
  history 58, 65, 87
  libraries 65
  parks 65, 125, 133–4
  sports centres 185–8
  swimming baths 65

market model *see under* con-
    sumer
masculinity 81–2, 161–2
mass media
  BBC 72, 79, 83, 112, 103–6,
    138
  commercial television 112, 132
  press 119
  radio 72
  television 44, 88, 149, 237
mass society theory 37, 40, 116,
    213
Mechanics Institutes 58
middle class 76–7, 148–9, 188
music 64–5, 72, 83, 88, 149, 237
music hall 66–8, 72

needs 3, 95, 100–1, 136, 139, 140,
    143
neutrality pattern 18

old age 33–4, 153–5
Open University 130
opposition pattern 18

patronage 53–4, 139, 143, 207
place 160–1, 171
play 172–3
pluralism 38–44, 87, 103, 118, 122, 213, 219
police 65–6, 125–6, 141
post-industrial society 2, 32, 181–98, 208–10, 235
pre-industrial society 32, 51–6
professionalism 7–9, 139, 143
Protestant Ethic 1–6, 88
public house 53, 57, 66, 68, 75, 88, 103–6 (*see also* brewing industry)
public space 52–3, 65–6, 98, 125–6, 133, 152, 195 (*see also* local authority parks; streets)
puritanism 54

race, as social division 85–6, 146, 152–3, 174, 176
railways 57
rambling 69, 72, 133
rational recreation 58, 64–5, 137, 140
recreation research 13, 37, 40
regions 27, 55, 71, 75–6
retirement 153
riots 53, 126, 158
religion 53–5, 126, 158

Saint Monday 52, 61
sexual division of labour 59, 82, 97, 107, 161 (*see also* gender)
shopping 96, 192
smoking 44, 114
social control 9–10, 58–9, 94–5, 138–40, 158, 200–10
socialism 57, 231–40
sponsorship 112–15
sport
  animal 53–7
  athletics 53, 63
  canoeing 135
  cricket 53, 63, 135
  cycling 63, 69, 72
  football 53, 62, 74
  golf 63, 136

rowing 63, 135
rugby 63
squash 135
teams 63
and class 62–3, 149
and gender 62–3, 161–2
and history 53, 62–3, 74–5, 86
Sports Council 7, 11, 87, 135–7, 138, 155, 206
state policy
  culture 130–2
  education 6, 19, 128–9
  legislation 54, 56–7, 58, 61, 68, 74, 82, 88, 123
  licensing 66–8, 142–5
  local *see under* local authorities
  sport 132–7
  welfare 87, 126–8, 132, 136, 154–5, 166
streets 56–7, 66–8, 125–6, 134, 152
Sunday schools 58

technology 3, 19, 181–4, 187, 190–6
time 97, 146, 155, 160, 171, 193, 239–40
trades unions 186, 188

unemployment 2, 34, 71, 158, 194, 207, 209, 234–5
upper class 55, 62–3, 76, 147–8
urbanisation 51, 55, 61, 73

waged work 2, 17–22, 23–5, 39, 45, 185, 191–4, 208–9, 218, 234–6
wakes weeks 53
women and leisure 21, 26, 33, 59, 72, 73, 77, 84–5, 154–5, 159–60 (*see also* gender)
Workers' Educational Association 69, 130
work ethic 208
working men's clubs 68–9, 75

youth 30, 35, 82–88, 117–18, 134, 155–9